CHICKEN SOUP FOR EVERY MOM'S SOUL

CHICKEN SOUP FOR EVERY MOM'S SOUL

New Stories of Love and Inspiration for Moms of All Ages

Jack Canfield
Mark Victor Hansen
Heather McNamara
Marci Shimoff

Health Communications, Inc.
Deerfield Beach, Florida

www.hcibooks.com
www.chickensoup.com

We would like to acknowledge the many publishers and individuals who granted us permission to reprint the cited material. (Note: The stories that are in the public domain or that were written by Jack Canfield, Mark Victor Hansen, Heather McNamara and Marci Shimoff are not included in this listing.)

Saying I Love You. Reprinted by permission of LindaCarol Cherken. ©2004 LindaCarol Cherken.

Behind Blue Eyes. Reprinted by permission of Jennifer Graham. ©2001 Jennifer Graham.

Words to Love By. Reprinted by permission of Ave Maria Press. Excerpted from *Words to Love By* by Mother Teresa. ©1983 by Ave Maria Press, P.O. Box 428 Notre Dame, IN 46556. Used with the permission of the publisher. All rights reserved.

Princess. Reprinted by permission of Kristy Ross. ©1997 Kristy Ross.

An Impromptu Dance at Dusk. Reprinted by permission of Marian Gormley. ©1995 Marian Gormley.

(Continued on page 362)

Library of Congress Cataloging-in-Publication Data

Chicken soup for every mom's soul : new stories of love and inspiration for
  moms of all ages / Jack Canfield...[et al.].
    p. cm.
  ISBN-13: 978-0-7573-0248-0
  ISBN-10: 0-7573-0248-3
    1. Mothers—Anecdotes. 2. Motherhood—Anecdotes. 3. Mother and child—
I. Canfield, Jack, 1944-

HQ759.C523 2005
306.874'3—dc22

2004060705

Publisher: Health Communications, Inc.
        3201 S.W. 15th Street
        Deerfield Beach, FL 33442-8190

Cover design by Andrea Perrine Brower
Inside formatting by Dawn Von Strolley Grove

We dedicate this book to baby Navarrette, who witnessed its creation from coauthor Heather's womb. We welcome you and all new babies with our deepest wishes for a world full of joy, peace and love.

Contents

1. ON LOVE

2. A MOTHER'S COURAGE

3. ON MOTHERHOOD

4. BECOMING A MOTHER

5. INSIGHTS AND LESSONS

6. SPECIAL MOMENTS

7. MOTHERS AND DAUGHTERS

8. LETTING GO

9. A GRANDMOTHER'S LOVE

10. TIES THAT BIND

Acknowledgments

The path to *Chicken Soup for Every Mom's Soul* has been made all the more beautiful by the many great supporters who have been there with us along the way. Our heartfelt gratitude to:

Our families, who have been chicken soup for our souls!

Inga, Travis, Riley, Christopher, Oran and Kyle for all their love and support.

Patty, Elisabeth and Melanie Hansen, for once again sharing and lovingly supporting us in creating yet another book.

Willanne Ackerman, Heather's mom, for taking time out of her busy-filled days to read every story and edit the ones that needed a bit more oomph—all because she would do anything for one of her children. Pete Ackerman, Willanne's husband, for giving Willanne the freedom to do anything for one of her children. Katy and Laura McNamara, readers extraordinaire, who read all the stories out of a backpack while on a trip through Italy with the entire McNamara clan. Heather's brother, Danny, for always being there when needed. Rick Navarrette, who we know is going to be a wonderful father—just like Heather's dad—Jim McNamara.

Sergio Baroni for supporting us and for sharing his

truth, joy and love of life. Thank you for the ever-present song in your heart. Marci's always loving and supportive parents, Marcus and Louise Shimoff, and Lynda, Paul, Susan, Max, Francesca, Silvia, Ivan, Aaron, Jared, Tony and Vickie for being such a great family. Catherine Oxenberg and Bonnie Solow for being cherished soul sisters, and Bill Bauman for his profound gifts of love and wisdom.

Carol Kline for her invaluable contribution to the creation of this book. Your clear insight, sound judgment and extraordinary skill in evaluating and editing stories were a supreme gift. And your friendship is always deeply treasured.

D'ette Corona for amazing us with her near-miraculous abilities and achievements in obtaining permissions, communicating with contributors, and so much more. We thank you deeply for your great dedication, heart and spirit.

Our publisher Peter Vegso, for his vision and commitment to bringing *Chicken Soup for the Soul* to the world.

Patty Aubery and Russ Kamalski for masterfully developing and advancing *Chicken Soup for the Soul* books and projects around the globe. Thank you for continually opening new channels for achievement and success.

Sue Penberthy for her calm, steady presence, her devoted help in obtaining permissions and her never-ending support. Cindy Buck for the precision, brilliance and joy she brings to the process of editing.

Patty Hansen, for her thorough and competent handling of the legal and licensing aspects of the *Chicken Soup for the Soul* books. You are magnificent at the challenge!

Laurie Hartman, for being a precious guardian of the *Chicken Soup* brand.

Veronica Romero, Barbara LoMonaco, Teresa Esparza, Robin Yerian, Jesse, Ianniello, Jamie Chicoine, Jody Emme, Debbie Lefever, Michelle Adams, Dee Dee Romanello, Shanna Vieyra, Lisa Williams, Gina Romanello, Brittany

Shaw, Dena Jacobson, Tanya Jones, Mary McKay and David Coleman, who support Jack's and Mark's businesses with skill and love.

Allison Janse, our main editor at Health Communications, Inc., for her deep devotion to excellence and for always being a joy to work with. Bret Witter, Elisabeth Rinaldi, and Kathy Grant for maintaining high standards of excellence.

Terry Burke, Tom Sand, Lori Golden, Tom Galvin, Sean Geary, Kelly Johnson Maragni, Patricia McConnell, Ariana Dainer, Kim Weiss, Paola Fernandez-Rana and Teri Peluso, the marketing, sales, and PR departments at Health Communications, Inc., for doing such an incredible job supporting our books.

Tom Sand, Claude Choquette, and Luc Jutras, who manage year after year to get our books transferred into thirty-six languages around the world.

The Art Department at Health Communications, Inc., for their talent, creativity and boundless patience in producing book covers and inside designs that capture the essence of Chicken Soup: Larissa Hise Henoch, Lawna Patterson Oldfield, Andrea Perrine Brower, Anthony Clausi and Dawn Von Strolley Grove.

All the *Chicken Soup for the Soul* coauthors, who make it such a joy to be part of this Chicken Soup family. We're especially grateful to Jennifer Read Hawthorne who has worked with us on past books. Thank you for all we gained from sharing the journey with you.

Our glorious panel of readers who helped us makes the final selections and made invaluable suggestions on how to improve the book:

Willanne Ackerman, Joan Acuna, Diane Alabaster, Patty Aubery, Lindsay Baer, Alex Bunshaft, D'ette Corona, Allison Janse, Carol Kline, Eloise Leslie, Barbara LoMonaco, Nicki Lovett, Katy McNamara, Laura

McNamara, Rita Navarrette, Sue Penberthy, Cindy Schwanke and Julie Young.

And, most of all, everyone who submitted their heartfelt stories, poems, quotes and cartoons for possible inclusion in this book. While we were not able to use everything you sent in, we know that each word came from a magical place flourishing within your soul. Thank you.

Because of the size of this project, we may have left out the names of some people who contributed along the way. If so, we are sorry, but please know that we really do appreciate you very much.

We are truly grateful and love you all!

Introduction

Mom. Mother. Mama. Mommy. No matter what name we use, a mom is one of the most significant people in our lives. A mom loves unconditionally. When we are small, she feeds us, clothes us, protects us from harm and guides our lives in every way. As we grow up, she's our cheerleader and our conscience. Even when we are grown, she never stops wanting the very best for us. The mother-child relationship goes beyond time and space.

The experience of motherhood has many facets: the glow of pregnancy; the fatigue of labor; the ecstasy of giving birth, seeing your baby's face for the very first time; the challenge of living with a toddler; the challenge of living with a teenager and the bittersweet pangs of seeing your babies leave the nest. Yet motherhood doesn't end there—grown children still need their moms and as our own mothers age, we find ourselves mothering the invincible woman who gave us life.

This book is filled with stories about all aspects of motherhood, some humorous, some poignant, some inspiring—because motherhood is funny, poignant and inspiring. Whether you are an expectant mother, a new mother, a mother with children at home, a mother of children long grown or even a grandmother—these stories are for you.

They will inspire you, entertain you and remind you of your most important role of all: being a mom.

Some things about being a mom never change, but in today's world, a mom has new and unique challenges. In this book, you will find stories about love, courage and wisdom, as well as stories about the lighter side of mothering—or of being mothered. In the same way that mothers over the ages have sat together and shared their experiences, you will enjoy the stories from mothers and about mothers showcased in this book.

Our goal in writing this book is to honor moms everywhere. We offer these stories in the hope that they will help moms to celebrate their lives. May this book be a gift of inspiration and love.

Share with Us

We would like to invite you to send us stories you would like to see published in future editions of *Chicken Soup for the Soul.*

We would also love to hear your reactions to the stories in this book. Please let us know what your favorite stories are and how they affected you.

Please send submissions to:

Chicken Soup for the Soul
P.O. Box 30880
Santa Barbara, CA 93130
fax: 805-563-2945

You can also visit the *Chicken Soup for the Soul* Web site at:

www.chickensoup.com

We hope you enjoy reading this book as much as we enjoyed compiling, editing and writing it.

1

ON LOVE

Motherhood: All love begins and ends there.

Robert Browning

Saying I Love You

Love is a fruit in season at all times, and within reach of every hand.

Mother Teresa

When I was a new mommy, I invented a quiet little signal, two quick hand squeezes, that grew into our family's secret "I love you."

Long before she could debate the merits of pierced ears or the need to shave her legs, my daughter, Carolyn, would toddle next to me clasping my finger for that much-needed support to keep her from falling down.

Whether we were casually walking in the park or scurrying on our way to playgroup, if Carolyn's tiny hand was in mine, I would tenderly squeeze it twice and whisper, "I love you." Children love secrets, and little Carolyn was no exception. So, this double hand squeeze became our special secret. I didn't do it all the time—just every so often when I wanted to send a quiet message of "I love you" to her from me.

The years flew by, and Carolyn started school. She was

a big girl now, so there was no need for little secret signals anymore . . . or so I thought.

It was the morning of her kindergarten class show. Her class was to perform their skit before the entire Lower School, which would be a daunting experience. The big kids—all the way to sixth grade—would be sitting in the audience. Carolyn was nervous, as were all her little classmates.

As proud family and friends filed into the auditorium to take their seats behind the students, I saw Carolyn sitting nervously with her classmates. I wanted to reassure her, but I knew that anything I said would run the risk of making her feel uncomfortable.

Then I remembered our secret signal. I left my seat and walked over to her. Carolyn's big brown eyes watched each of my steps as I inched closer. I said not a word, but leaned over and took her hand and squeezed it twice. Her eyes met mine, and I immediately knew that she recognized the message. She instantly returned the gesture giving my hand two quick squeezes in reply. We smiled at each other, and I took my seat and watched my confident little girl, and her class, perform beautifully.

Carolyn grew up and our family welcomed two younger brothers, Bryan and Christian. Through the years, I got more experienced at the mothering game, but I never abandoned the secret "I love you" hand squeeze.

Whether the boys were running on the soccer field for a big game or jumping out of the car on the day of a final exam, I always had the secret hand squeeze to send them my message of love and support. I learned that when over-sentimental words from parents are guaranteed to make kids feel ill at ease, this quiet signal was always appreciated and welcomed.

Three years ago, my daughter married a wonderful guy. Before the ceremony, while we were standing at the back of the church waiting to march down the aisle, I could hardly look at my little girl, now all grown up and wearing her grandmother's wedding veil, for fear of crying.

There was so much I wanted to say to her. I wanted to tell her how proud of her I was. I wanted to tell her that I treasured being her mom, and I looked forward to all the future had in store for her. However, most important, I wanted to tell her that I loved her. But I was positive that if I said even one word, Carolyn and I would both dissolve into tears.

Then I remembered it—our secret signal. I left my place and walked back to Carolyn. As the organist began to play, *Ode to Joy*, I took Carolyn's hand and quickly squeezed it twice. Our eyes met, and she returned the signal.

There were no tears, there were no words exchanged, just a secret "I love you" that I created one sunny afternoon, when I was a new mother.

I am no longer a new mother . . . but a new grandmother. Today, I was strolling with my little grandson, Jake. His tiny hand was holding on to my finger, and I couldn't help remembering his mother's hand in mine over thirty years ago. As we walked, I gave his hand two quick squeezes and whispered, "I love you." He looked up and smiled.

LindaCarol Cherken

Behind Blue Eyes

Love cures people—both the ones who give it and the ones who receive it.

Dr. Karl Menninger

Samantha stood in the center of the shabby social services office wearing a threadbare pink sweat suit. The flickery fluorescent lighting illuminated shaggy boy-cut blonde hair, dirty fingernails, a runny nose and huge blue eyes ringed with dark, tired circles. Around the thumb jammed between her teeth, she stared up at me and asked, "Are you my new mom?"

My husband, Dan, and I had gone through all the usual contortions to have a second child. His and hers surgeries, artificial insemination. Nothing happened. I had always envisioned adopting, but my husband was unconvinced. Dan's initial reservation about adoption was understandable given that, at the time, the evening news was filled with terrifying stories of anguished biological and adoptive parents fighting for the rights to be some little one's "real" mom and dad. Still, we decided to move forward.

Our ten-year-old son, Matthew, was also a little slow to jump on the adoption bandwagon. He had been the center of our universe for a long time, and he liked it that way. He was also a typical kid in that he wanted to fit in and not be "different" in any way. We planned to adopt a baby from China, which especially concerned him; he feared that an Asian baby in our Caucasian midst might invite dreaded attention.

As part of the adoption agency screening process, a social worker came to interview Matthew, and we encouraged him to "just be honest." So, with prepubescent eloquence, our son explained to the attentive social worker that he loved being an only child, that he didn't want a sibling from another country, that he didn't like Chinese rice, that people would stare at us if we had a Chinese baby, and that basically a little brother or sister would pretty much ruin his life. He was evangelistic in his passion, Galilean in his logic. Brilliant. When he was through, my husband and I watched the social worker back out of the driveway, wondering if she would even make it back to the office before setting fire to our application.

Miraculously, when the whole screening process was finished (references, fingerprints, credit and criminal checks, etc.) my husband and I were approved. My son remained skeptical, and my husband was still a bit nervous even as we settled down to wait. Then, on a bitter January morning we got the call.

The social worker told us about a little girl, suddenly available—a four-year-old white girl from New York—who had come into this world with cocaine humming in her veins. "How soon can you be here?" the social worker asked.

Our preliminary visit was to last about an hour or so. Taking Samantha's hand in mine, I led her down the steps and out the door. We walked though a winter-bare park with Samantha on my shoulders. She got shy around Dan and wouldn't accept a "pony ride" from him. She had no mittens and her icy little fingers squeezed my hands. Her chatter was nonstop and more than a little desperate. Her blue gaze focused over my shoulder, or off in the distance, but never settled on my face. Her eyes were both blank and wild, like a wary captive.

In the park, we stumbled upon a dry fountain and pitched our pennies in, making silent wishes. I wished for the chance to quell the quiet panic in her eyes.

After the visit, we took Samantha back to the social worker. We were told to think about the adoption and to let them know. There was little discussion in our car on the way home. Our fears were too numerous and too ethereal to put into words, but our commitment was already rock solid. The next morning we brought our daughter home.

From the very first day, Samantha called me "Mom." I had waited years for this moment, anxious to be privileged again with that most singular title. But there was no epiphany when she said it, no fireworks, no choir of angels. I knew that to Samantha, "Mom" was just the lady who was taking care of her at the moment. No more intimate than "Waiter" or "Stewardess." All the meaning had been drained from that word the night her "real mom" took the garbage out and never came back.

After her biological mother left, Samantha lived with a steady succession of mothers. Some were just temporary care for a night or two; others were longer "trial visits." One, Samantha's mother for five months, told Samantha they were going to adopt her into their family soon, that the other children were her "sister" and her "brother." When Samantha came to us, one of her few possessions was a little purple sweatshirt, hand decorated with craft paint spelling out the words "Little Sister." But, one night, when Samantha had said something inappropriate in front of the biological kids, she was abruptly stripped of her title and sent away. A dishonorable discharge for the littlest soldier.

Now at our house, Samantha was somebody else's daughter, somebody else's little sister. Matthew's initial fears about a new sibling thrusting him into the limelight were replaced with relief; his new sister looked remarkably like him and the rest of the family. There would be no undue attention, no compulsory rice.

At first he treated Samantha like a cute new pet. "Want to come in and see my new sister? Look what she can do!" After a few days the novelty wore off, and routine set in.

But Sam remained enthralled with Matthew. She lingered over the many pictures of him that covered the walls of our house: Matthew in a soccer uniform, Matthew at the beach, Matthew with Grandpa. On her third day with us, Samantha found some old catalogues and asked for scissors. Patiently she cut out pictures of two dolls, a boy and a girl. She turned over one of the silver frames and lifted the back. With great care she arranged her boy and girl on the mat and replaced the frame, beaming. "Look, Mom! Look at the picture of me and Matthew!"

For reassurance, or maybe just to remind herself who he was, Samantha had taken to calling our son "Matthewmybrother." When she had been with us about a week, she called to him at bedtime. With her wide blue eyes shining up at him, she said, "Matthewmybrother, I'm glad your room is next to mine so that you can protect me from the monsters." For a boy of ten, not that far removed from believing in monsters himself, this was high praise. He swaggered out of her room like he had just been knighted.

My husband, too, had bonded with Sam. The little blondie who wrapped around his legs was just as tightly wrapped around his heart. He did not need to fear a parental tug-of-war over this child. Her biological parents had neglected and abandoned her, having fallen so deep into their dark, destructive world that there was no hope—or risk—of them climbing out.

We saw glimpses of their lives through Samantha. One day, she deftly took a rubber plastic blood-pressure hose out of a play doctor's set and tied it around her forearm, pulling it tight with her teeth. Then she tapped on her veins as though feeling for "a good one." The father who had shot up in front of Samantha never once came looking for her.

As the weeks passed, Samantha worked hard to learn the names of all of her new relatives. "Is it Uncle Dale and Aunt Kelly, or Uncle Kale and Aunt Delly?" She knew Grandma and Poppa and numerous cousins. And I was Mom.

She called me "Mommy," "Mama," and sometimes, "Mumsy," because Matthewmybrother did too. I knew that if Samantha were to draw a picture of her mom it would be my face she would draw, my stick hand holding her stick hand. But I had been a mother for ten years. I knew the difference between the word and the relationship it represented. Once, when I left Samantha with my parents for an evening, she asked my mother, "If she doesn't come back, are you my new mom?"

Weeks turned into months. We were progressing as quickly as legally possible from foster parents to adoptive parents. Samantha nestled down into family life preferring hand-me-downs from her new cousins to store-bought clothes, getting crushes on the same Montessori teachers as her brother had a few years before. She danced around the living room with my old rhinestone earrings clipped to her ears. She smiled at herself smiling back at herself from the silver frames on the piano . . . and the desk . . . and the walls.

And we were friends, she and I. We baked cookies. We

shopped together—a lot, once I discovered the "pink aisle" at the toy store. She put on my lipstick and gave me elaborate, fanciful hairstyles. And during all this time, she called me "Mom." But it still felt more like "Aunt," or "teacher" or "pal." During all of our mother-daughter moments, Samantha's big blue eyes checked me out, looked me up and down, kept me at a distance.

Once, in the middle of the night, I went into Samantha's room to check on her. She was sitting up in bed. She hadn't called out to us, and she wasn't crying, but when I came close to the bed her eyes registered fear. "I dreamed you were a witch, and you were going to kill me." I held her, whispering that I would never hurt her. She was safe now. That night she told me about violence she had witnessed, about playing with rats, about being locked in the trunk of a car. Other times, only late at night, only in the dark, and only when I wasn't looking at her, she told me of many horrible experiences she had lived through in her four short years.

Therapists had warned me that of all the hurts that Sam had endured in her short little life, the cruelest blow was from her biological mom. I should be patient, they said. She needs to learn to trust again.

When a tiny brain is growing, a circuitry network of neurotransmitters and jumpy dendrites branch out, creating a blueprint for the future. Through experience, children lay down patterns in their brain, designed to keep them safe and help them thrive. Children learn to recoil from big dogs, or scary clowns, or weird Uncle Max with fermenting breath, but they don't usually recoil from mom.

Moms are supposed to be the soft lap, the gentle hands that soothe away the nightmares. They are supposed to be the big warm blanket you wrap up in when the world is too cold and too rainy. But what happens when Mom *is* the stinging rain? When it is Mom who *is* the monster under the bed?

Samantha did not trust me. Nothing I said was accepted as truth. She had to see things with her own eyes. "Don't touch that knife; it's sharp," led to bloody fingers. "Wait on the curb; a car is coming" sent her running into the street to see for herself.

Samantha had come into our home with a "colorful" vocabulary. Once I overheard Barbie and Ken arguing in language that could make a hard-core rapper blush. I explained to my angel-faced daughter that those were not nice words; they make people uncomfortable. That night, at a restaurant with friends, she spewed profanity throughout the dinner, all the while gauging their reaction. Our son was highly entertained. Our friends were not.

Samantha challenged me in a thousand different ways, calculating the results, evaluating the extent of my affection. How far could she go before I'd be gone? She broke treasured heirlooms, defied rules, lied, hoarded, stole. She did not scare us off, but still she refused to depend on me, to believe in me. When I tucked her in at night, and whispered, "I love you," she squirmed. When her runaway mind kept her up at night, restless and anxious, I massaged her hands and feet, but her muscles stayed taut and tense beneath my fingers. I ached to relieve her from her post of hypervigilance, to loosen her grip on her emotions, to hear her genuine laugh, to help her just let go and resume her rightful role as innocent child.

Intellectually, I knew her therapists were right. I would nod my head. Yes, yes, I know. But secretly my gut clenched. I wavered between self-disgust and self-pity. What arrogance had me thinking that my house, my family, my love, could reach this broken little girl? If, in the end, she could not love me back, but she was safe and content, surrounded by health and hope, shouldn't that be enough? Perhaps there would be no sacred bond or whispered trust between us. But if she could live without pain and in relative peace, shouldn't I just be thankful, and let the rest go?

One night, about a year after Samantha arrived, I was awakened by a choked cry. I hurried in and found Samantha sitting up in bed, her white nightgown a mess. She had gotten sick all over herself and her bed linens. Cleaning up throw-up was my domain, so my husband helped Samantha to the bathroom as I began to strip her sheets. I could hear Dan speaking quietly to Sam as he knelt with her in front of the toilet bowl. I was filling up a bucket when suddenly she let out an anguished cry. Her words were loud and distinct, "I WANT MY MOMMY!"

She was hurting and needing help, scared and needing comfort. She was a child who needed her mom. And not her biological mom, or her foster moms, or the social workers. She wanted *me*! What kind of a mother rejoices when her daughter is sick and in distress? I couldn't help it—my heart sang.

I cradled my daughter's head while her little body heaved. It wasn't pretty, but it was real. I knew then that although I wouldn't be Samantha's first mom . . . or her second or third, nothing could keep me from being her last. And that was more than enough.

Jenny Graham

[EDITORS' NOTE: *Today, Sam is a healthy, happy teenager who loves music, horseback riding and her family.*]

Words to Love By

God has sent the family—together as husband and wife and children—to be his love.

I once picked up a child of six or seven in the street and took her to Shishu Bhavin (a children's home) and gave her a bath, some clothes and some nice food. That evening the child ran away.

We took the child a second and a third time, and she ran away.

After the third time I sent a sister to follow her. The sister found the child sitting with her mother and sister under a tree. There was a little dish there and the mother was cooking food she had picked up from the streets.

They were cooling there.

They were eating there.

They were sleeping there.

It was their home.

And then we understood why the child ran away. The mother just loved that child. And the child loved the mother. They were so beautiful to each other.

The child said "bari jabo"—it was her home.

Her mother was her home.

Mother Teresa

Princess

The dress hides far in the back of the closet, behind years of accumulated plastic-sheathed memories. Carefully, I pull it from the dark recesses, past layers of archived prom dresses, granny gowns and jean jackets that mark a fabric trail of my increasingly distant and often troubled youth. As the dress faces the morning light for the first time in many years, tiny sparkles wink at me through the dusty garment bag hiding its loveliness. Removing it from its transparent covering and holding it to my cheek, I smell its fragrance and the musty perfume of the past.

My mother bought the dress more than forty years ago for a cocktail party at the general's house. As the wife of an army captain, she experienced alternating pangs of excitement and worry at the extravagant purchase. The dress hung for many days, weighed down by assorted tags, while she fought a silent battle with herself. The precarious balance between womanly desire and financial practicality shifted in favor of one position, then the other.

Self-absorbed like most ten-year-olds, I didn't understand my mother's budget dilemma. I knew only that something black and wonderful had entered her closet and hung in solitary splendor amidst the flowered house-coats and practical day dresses.

I don't think she actually decided to keep the dress until the day of the party. When I crept into her room late that afternoon, the offending tags finally lay discarded in the trash. My mom hummed happily from behind the closed bathroom door. Eager with anticipation, I slipped back out the door.

After what seemed like hours, my mother's voice beckoned me into her room. What I saw when I bounced through the doorway took my breath away! My sensible mother, who made me eat my vegetables, ironed my father's shirts instead of sending them out, drove me to Brownie meetings, and baked chocolate chip cookies, was transformed into an elegant beauty clad in a soft ebony cloud.

"What do you think?" she asked as she turned slowly in front of the mirror.

I stood mute in wide-eyed wonder and then reverently delivered the highest compliment I could think to give. "You look like a princess."

And she did.

The dress tightly enclosed her slim waist, then flared out in a bell-shaped skirt. The black taffeta underskirt rustled as she twirled, and lamplight bounced off silver and blue confetti-sized sparkles strewn over the black organza overskirt. The dress shimmered like stardust scattered by a fairy godmother. It was a dress fit for a princess, and that night, in my eyes, my mother ruled the kingdom.

Years later when my mother and I found the dress in the back of her closet smothered with layers of her past, she told me that the night of the general's party was one of the most memorable nights of her life. Not because of the dress, but because of the admiration she saw in my ten-year-old eyes and the compliment I had given her. Then she repeated the words I had said more than three decades ago as she had stood regally before her mirror dressed in stardust and midnight.

I wanted to cry. Not tears of joy for the poignancy of the moment, but tears of sadness for the many years lost to us because of the complexities of adolescence. Because that special year, the year I discovered a princess in my mother's lamp-lit bedroom, was the last year of my child-hood when we fit together snugly and comfortably like two interlocking pieces of a puzzle.

In the intervening years between that long ago moment of love and our reminiscing, the bond forged between my mother and me in my early childhood was sorely tested. During my rebellious teens and early twenties, she saw little in my eyes but anger and heard little in my voice but recriminations.

Though as adults my mother and I slowly built a strong relationship, I longed to take back those hurtful years of my youth and replace them with memories of love and kindness. But I couldn't. I couldn't change the past any more than I could iron out the wrinkles etched deep in her face or restore to her the vitality of her youth. I could only stand beside my beautiful seventy-year-old mother and whisper, "I love you, Mom."

And she could only smile and reply, "I've always known that."

As I stand in my bedroom smelling the past from deep within the folds of my mother's dress, I am thankful I have it to remind me of the strength of a mother's love and the power of a moment. But I am most thankful my mother and I still have time to build enduring memories that will sweeten the past with their musty perfume.

Kristy Ross

An Impromptu Dance at Dusk

Each day of our lives we make deposits in the memory banks of our children.

Charles R. Swindoll

Engrossed at the computer, I was typing some very impassioned poetry written by my eighty-two-year-old neighbor, Rosemary. My six-year-old son, Jake, ran up to me. "Mom, let's do something fun together. Now! C'mon!"

Deeply engrossed in the stories of Rosemary's unfulfilled dreams and missed opportunities, I was ready to reply, "Jake, we'll do something in a little bit. I want to work a little longer." Instead, Rosemary's words haunted me, carrying new meaning in my own life. I thought of her sad laments. The wisdom of her years spoke to me, and I decided the poems could wait. My son could not.

"What would you like to do?" I asked, thinking of the new library books we could read together.

"Let's dance," he replied.

"Dance?" I asked.

"Yes, just you and me . . . pleeeeez; I'll be right back,"

he said as he dashed out of the room. He returned a few moments later with his hair a bit wet and combed over to the side, a shy smile and his black, flowing Batman-turned-into-Prince-Jake cape over his shoulders. He pulled me off my chair and led me upstairs.

The blinds were up and the descending sun was casting shadows against the picturesque night sky. Jake led me to the middle of his braided wool rug and then turned on the radio. "There Mom. I found us some rock and roll." He took my hand, and we danced, twisted, turned and twirled. We giggled and laughed and danced some more.

My side aching, I told him I needed a rest. Ever so seriously he responded, "Mom, let me put something romantic on now." He found a beautiful slow song, bowed, and then took my hand as we began to slow dance together. His head was at my waist, but our feet kept rhythmic time.

"Mom," he said a moment later as he looked up at me, "can you get down on your knees and dance with me so we can look at each other's face while we dance?" I almost responded with why I wouldn't be able to comply with his ridiculous request. Instead, captured by the moment, I laughed, dropped down on my knees, and my little man led me in a dance I will always cherish.

Jake looked deep into my eyes and claimed, "You're my darling, Mom. I'll always love you forever and ever." I thought of the few short years I had left before an obvious list of my faults would replace Jake's little-boy idolization. Of course, he would still love me—but his eyes would lose some of the innocence and reverence they now revealed.

"Mommy," he said. "We'll always be together. Even when one of us dies, we'll always be together in our hearts."

"Yes, we will, Jake. We'll always be together no matter what," I whispered as I wiped a silent tear.

Dusk quietly settled in as this Mom and her Little Prince danced together, ever so slowly, cheek to cheek . . . and heart to heart.

Marian Gormley

Billy the Brave

As young Billy Spade lay down in his bed,
His mom sat beside him and happily said,
"Tonight's your big moment, your very own room.
Your brother's at Grandma's, in bed I assume.
When I was a girl, my room was my own.
I know that it's scary to sleep all alone."
"Scary?" said Billy, a smile on his face.
"No way would I ever be scared of this place.
You may have forgotten, I'm brave Billy Spade.
Nothing could scare me, 'cause I'm not afraid.
If a lion came over and knocked on my door,
Then let himself in and started to roar,
Then stood there and growled with claws and teeth bared,
I wouldn't be frightened. I wouldn't be scared.
I'd walk over to him, and grab his big snout,
And look in his eyes, then I'd start to shout.
'Look here Mr. Lion,' I'd say without fear,
'You better stop growling and get out of here!
No sound you might make, and no thing you might do
Could possibly scare me. I'm not scared of you.'
Then the lion, just knowing that he had been beat,

Would turn and start running. He'd make his retreat.
That big, silly lion should never have dared.
I wouldn't be frightened. I wouldn't be scared."
"You're a very brave boy," said Billy Spade's mom.
"But when the room's dark, and silent, and calm,
And you're all alone, why you just may find
That frightening thoughts may enter your mind."
"No way!" said Billy, "not Billy the Brave,
For even if monsters came out of their cave,
And into my bedroom in one of my dreams,
I know that it's not all as bad as it seems.
With big ugly faces, sharp toothed and long-haired . . .
I wouldn't be frightened. I wouldn't be scared.
I'd walk right up to them and yell 'You're not real!
Get out of my room!' and then they'd start to squeal.
'We're sorry! We're sorry!' they'd rant and they'd rave,
As they'd back through the door and they'd carefully
     wave,
And then they'd run screaming on back to their cave,
Just glad to escape from Billy the Brave.
So as you see Mom, I think I have made,
My point very clear, that I'm not afraid.
Even if aliens from a planet called Zed,
Came into my room with six eyes on their head.
Or a ghost floated in, and said to me 'Boo!'
I'd say to them all 'I'm not scared of you!'
You see Mom, it's useless for you to have cared.
I wouldn't be frightened. I wouldn't be scared."
"Okay," said his mother, "I hope you sleep tight.
You're a very brave boy and I love you, good night."
And with that she walked out and closed Billy's door.
So no one was inside his room any more.
And as Billy lay there, he started to think.
And while he was thinking, he slept not a wink.
He thought about lions, with claws and teeth bared.

He thought about monsters, sharp toothed and long-
   haired.
He thought about aliens from a planet called Zed.
He just couldn't rid all these thoughts from his head!
He thought about ghosts coming in saying "Boo!"
Then what do you think that Billy might do?
He jumped out of bed, and he ran to his mom,
Where she lay asleep, all quiet and calm.
Then he jumped into her bed where she calmly lay,
Just in case *she* got frightened, or *she* got afraid.

J. T. Fenn
Submitted by Malinda Young

Cellular Love

My mother called tonight while I was cooking dinner. Again, for the third time today. I knew it was her because the words "Mom's cell" lit up my own cell phone like a marquee on Times Square. I lay down my cutting knife and shook the pieces of onion and red pepper from my hands. Mom with a cell phone; boy, have things changed!

There was a time in my life, B.C. (Before Cell phones), when my mother would become anxious, depressed or even mildly hysterical if she couldn't reach me by phone. No matter that I worked full-time and ran a marathon life shuttling kids, groceries and the dog from one end of town to the other. If she called the house, and I didn't answer, something had to be wrong.

"Where are you? I've tried a hundred times but you don't answer. Is anybody there?" were the plaintive words I'd find on my answering machine after returning home from a long day at work. If my mother got lucky, she'd reach my daughter and tell *her* to leave me a message, which I'd usually find about a week later, written in crayon on the back of the phone bill. "Call Gramma. She wants to know if you still live here."

I move about the kitchen banging pots, the cell phone balanced precariously between my cheek and raised left shoulder. I make a mental note to cancel the chiropractic appointment I made for neck pain and resolve to buy a headset instead.

I toss the salad as my mother shares the events of her day: a doctor's appointment for my father who can't see as well as he thinks but she lets him drive anyway, lunch with a friend whose husband has Alzheimer's disease, and an exercise class for osteoporosis even though she's sure the teacher has shrunk two inches since she began taking the class. It doesn't really matter what we talk about. What matters most is the invisible line of connection we create in spite of the time and distance between us.

A friend is dying of cancer, and my mother wants to know if she should visit her or wait to be asked.

"You should go," I tell her.

What about Eleanor's husband, the one with Alzheimer's. Should she invite them to dinner or would it be too hard?

"For whom?" I ask.

At seventy-eight, my mother now lives in a country whose borders are defined by mountains of fear. Its landscape is restricted by age, illness and the loss of much of what and whom she has cherished and known. The roads she traveled on so easily in her youth have become more treacherous as she loses confidence in her ability to navigate through the world we live in today. Yet she faces these obstacles with a will of iron, determined to fill her life with meaning and purpose. At times, this translates into trying to control a part of mine.

"Did you use that Silver Palate spaghetti sauce recipe I sent you? It has all the essential vitamins and lots of black olives, which are good for your system," she counsels.

"Oh, yeah, it was great!" I fib as I stir a jar of store bought marinara sauce into the pasta. When I was a new wife and mother, this type of domestic micromanaging drove me crazy. Now I'm just grateful that someone is still worried about my vitamin intake and regularity.

"I'm sending you some articles about skin care. I think you should do something about those little brown spots on your face," she says with the authority of a dermatologist.

I look in the mirror and notice a blotch of spaghetti sauce on my chin.

When I left for college, I didn't realize that my departure would trigger an emotional spiral downward that took my mother months to overcome. She began marking her life by the events that occurred in mine: the afternoon I graduated from law school, the evening of my wedding, the morning my son was born. She needed so much more assurance once I was gone, and sharing the everyday events in our lives was the salve that soothed her loneliness. If I was preoccupied or too tired to talk, I would simply listen to her stories while I folded clothes or packed school lunches for the kids.

An outsider listening to our conversations might think them trivial, but in reality, they are the bedrock upon which our deeper and more profound understandings occur. I hear in her words the true concern she has about my father's failing eyesight and her fear that many of her lifelong friends will soon be gone. I know that underlying her recipes and medical advice is the fear that I'm working too hard or not taking care of myself. In discussing the more banal whats, whos and whys of our lives, we open doors to an intimacy we both want from our relationship.

Several years ago, I sent my mother a Mother's Day card that still hangs on her refrigerator door. On the cover, a woman is applying red lipstick in the rearview mirror of her station wagon while driving the kids to school. The caption reads: "Oh my God, I think I've become my mother!" Printed on the inside are the words: "I should only be so lucky."

I hang up just as my husband walks through the door, cell phone falling from my ear like an oversized clip-on earring. He picks it up off the floor as I acknowledge, "My mother just called." Whatever the cost, whenever the time, she has my number. It's called cellular love.

Amy Hirshberg Lederman

Mini Massage Therapists

Little deeds of kindness,
Little words of love,
Help to make earth happy
Like the heaven above.

Julia Fletcher Carney

It had been a long and exhausting day. My husband was out of town for the third night in a row, the house was a mess, the phone kept ringing, laundry and papers were everywhere, my six-year-old twins were screaming, and my head was pounding. It was a reality-based type of day with no dreamy visions of being the perfect mother with a beautiful, spotless home, laundry all neatly folded in drawers and children playing angelically side by side.

My pleas of "Stop fighting, you two!" "Please stop running in the house!" and "Please play quietly!" went unheeded.

"Mom, Jake came in my room!"

"I did not!"

"Yes, you did . . . Mom—he's not listening!"

"You're not the boss of me!"

"But it's my room!"

"So what! Who do you think you are, Princess Tara or something?"

"Mom, Jake is calling me Princess Tara again! Mom!"

I screamed, "Stop it, you two!" Rather than quiet them, my loud reprimand caused their voices to escalate.

"BUT MOM, I TOLD HIM TO GET OUT OF MY ROOM!"

"BUT MOM, SHE COMES IN MY ROOM SOMETIMES WHEN I TELL HER NOT TO. . . ."

I asked my children to work it out between themselves and decided to find a quiet room for a few moments. Within a minute they burst in.

"Mom, she won't share her Disney characters even though she's not playing with them."

"That's because you didn't share your markers with me the last time I asked you."

"Well, you shouldn't have lost your markers. It's your own fault if you didn't take care of them, right, Mom?"

"Mom?"

"Mom?"

I gathered my children and whispered, "Jake and Tara, let's go hug each other quietly for a few moments. I don't feel very well. I'm also feeling sad right now. I love you both so much, and I would love a very special hug from each of you."

Their response was quite different than when I had shouted at them to quiet down. With rather serious looks on their faces, they asked, "But why are you sad, Mom?"

"I don't really know," I replied. "I just know I need some quiet time and some extra special love from both of you right now."

"Okay, Mommy," they whispered. They each took one of my hands, led me to my bed, fluffed up my pillows and told me to lie down. With a big hug and some "I love you's," they said, "Okay, Mommy, you just relax here a few minutes." As they walked away, I heard a lot of excited, conspiratorial whispers.

A few minutes later they were back. Jake brought me a glass of water. Tara brought me my favorite flannel pajamas. I smiled at both of them, took a drink of the water and put my pajamas on. They turned the lights down low, told me to relax on my bed, and started to give me a back scratch. I thought about nothing and simply enjoyed the feel of their four little hands.

Next, they massaged me—first my back, then my legs and arms. My body was sinking into the bed, and I felt totally at peace. They slowly massaged my feet and neck. I felt truly pampered. They then rubbed my temples with their thumbs and massaged my forehead. All the anxiety of the day dissipated. The messy house and to-do lists became inconsequential.

"You are the most special mom in the world," Tara whispered as she worked.

"This is what you do for us every night, Mommy. Tonight's your turn," Jake said affectionately.

Were those really the same children I had spent the day with?

Just when I thought my special treatment was over, they took turns brushing my hair. I was in heaven. I relished every moment and smiled to myself, thinking, *Who really needs a spotless house and folded laundry?*

Tara and Jake whispered to each other, ran into the bathroom, returned with my favorite lotion and slowly massaged my feet again as the peach-scented aroma filled the room.

What did I do to deserve this? I felt more relaxed than I had in a long time. As I thought it over, I realized that rather than scream for quiet or holler that I expected better behavior, I had simply taken a moment to share my need with my children. I had asked for some special nurturing, and thankfully, they were loving enough to give it.

Marian Gormley

The Gravy Boat Rescue

Not long ago my wife and I had a dinner party for some good friends. To add a touch of elegance to the evening I brought out the good stuff—my white Royal Crown Derby china with the fine gold and blue border. When we were seated, one of the guests noticed the beat-up gravy boat I always use. "Is it an heirloom?" she asked tactfully.

I admit the piece is conspicuous; it is very old and it matches nothing else. Worst of all, it is scarred by a V-shaped notch in the lip. But that little gravy boat is much more than an heirloom to me—it is the one thing in this world I will never part with.

Our history together began over fifty years ago when I was seven years old and we lived across the street from the river in New Richmond, Ohio. In anticipation of high water, the ground floor of the house had been built seven feet above grade.

That December, the river started to overflow west of town. When the water began to rise in a serious way, my parents made plans in case the river should invade our house. My mother decided that she would pack our books and her fine china in a small den off the master bedroom.

Each piece of the china had a gold rim and then a band of roses. It was not nearly as good as it was old, but the service had been her mother's and was precious to her.

As she packed the china with great care, she told me, "You must treasure the things people you love have cherished. It keeps you in touch with them."

I didn't really understand her concern. I'd never owned anything I cared all that much about. Still, planning for disaster held considerable fascination for me.

The plan was to move upstairs when the river reached the seventh of the steps that led to the front porch. We would keep a rowboat in the downstairs so that we could get from room to room. The one thing we would not do was leave the house. My father, the town's only doctor, felt he had to be where sick people could find him.

The muddy water rose higher and higher until at last the critical mark was reached. We worked for days carrying things upstairs, until late one afternoon the water edged over the threshold and poured into our house. I watched it from the safety of the stairs, amazed at how rapidly it rose.

Every day I sat on the landing and watched the river rise. My mother turned a spare bedroom into a makeshift kitchen and cooked simple meals there. My father came and went in a fishing boat that was powered by a small outboard motor.

Before long, the Red Cross began to pitch tents on high ground north of town. "We are staying in our house," my father said.

One night very late I was awakened by a tearing noise, like timbers creaking. Then I heard the rumbling sound of heavy things falling. I jumped out of bed and ran into the hallway. My parents were standing in the doorway to the den. The floor of the den had fallen through and all the treasures, including my mother's china, that we had attempted to save, were now on the first floor beneath the steadily rising river.

My mother had been courageous it seemed to me, through the ordeal of the flood. But the loss of the things she loved broke her resolve. That night she sat on the top of the stairs with her head on her crossed arms and cried. My father comforted her as best he could, but she was inconsolable.

My father finally told me to go to bed, and I watched him help my mother to their room. In a few minutes he came to see me, to tell me everything would be all right and that my mother would be fine after a good night's sleep.

I wasn't sure about that at all. There was a sound in her weeping that I had never heard before, and it troubled me. I wanted to help her feel better, but I couldn't think of what I could possibly do.

The next morning she made me breakfast, and I could tell how bad she still felt just by how cheerful she pretended to be.

After breakfast, my mother said I could go downstairs and play in the rowboat. I rowed the boat once around the downstairs, staring into the dark water, but could see nothing. It was right then that I thought of trying to fish for my mother's china.

I carefully put a hook I cut from a wire coat hanger onto a weighted line. Then I let it sink until I felt it hit bottom. I began to slowly drag it back and forth. I spent the next hour or so moving the boat back and forth, dragging my line, hoping against hope to find one of my mother's treasures. But time after time I pulled the line up empty.

As the water rose day after day, I continued to try to recover something, anything, of my mother's lost treasure. Soon, however, the water inside had risen to the stairway landing. On the day the water covered the rain gutters, my father decided we would have to seek shelter in the tents on the hill. A powerboat was to pick us up that afternoon.

I spent the morning hurriedly securing things in my room as best I could. Then I got into my rowboat for the last time. I dragged my line through the water and just as I made the last turn to go back to the stairway, I snagged something.

Holding my breath, I raised my catch to the surface. As the dark water drained from it, I could see it was the gravy boat from my mother's china service. The bright roses and gold leaf seemed dazzling to me.

Then I saw what had helped my line catch: There was a V-shaped chip missing from the lip of the boat. I stowed the treasure inside my jacket and rowed as fast as I could to the stair landing. My mother had called me for the second time, and I knew better than to risk a third.

We left from the porch roof and the boat headed to higher ground. It began to rain, and for the first time I was really afraid. The water might rise forever, might cover the whole valley, the trees, even the hills. The thought made me cold, and I did not look out at the flood again until we landed at the shelter.

By the time we were settled in a Red Cross tent, we were worn out. My father had gone off to help with the sick people, and my mother sat on my cot with her arm around my shoulder. I reached under my pillow and took out the gravy boat.

She looked at it, then at me. Then she took it in her hands and held it a long time. She was very quiet, just sitting, gazing at the gravy boat. She seemed both very close to me and far away at the same time, as though she were remembering. I don't know what she was thinking, but she pulled me into her arms and held me very close.

We lived in the tent for almost two weeks, waiting for the flood to end. When the water eventually receded, we did not move back to our old house, but to a house in a suburb of Cincinnati, far from the river.

By Easter, we were settled in and my mother made a special kind of celebration on that sacred Sunday. My mother asked me to say grace, and then my father carved the lamb. My mother went into the kitchen and returned with the gravy boat. Smiling at me, she placed it on the table beside her. I said to myself right then that nothing would ever happen to that gravy boat as long as I lived.

And nothing ever has. Now whenever I use it, guests almost always ask about it and sometimes I tell the whole story—at least most of it. But there really is no way to tell—beyond the events of the flood—how deeply that small treasure connects me to the people and places of my past. It is not only the object but also the connection I cherish. That little porcelain boat, old and chipped, ties me to my mother—just as she said—keeping me in touch with her life, her joy and her love.

W. W. Meade

Mom's Favorite Child

For weeks, both our mother and our brother had been near death with cancer. Mom and her dying son were inseparable, whether at home or as patients in the same hospital. None of us siblings resented that she turned to him so much during those final days. On a cold day in November, her four remaining sons carried her to his funeral, certain that they were fulfilling her last wish.

The long night that followed was both a horror and a blessing. My oldest sister, Marie, and I stayed with Mom in our childhood home. No matter what we did, Mom wept with grief and writhed with pain. Her cries mingled with the sounds of the icy rain blown against the windows of the old farmhouse, first in gusts, then in brief intermissions of heavy calm. Finally, around three o'clock in the morning, after telling us repeatedly that she would not see another dawn, she closed her eyes. An eerie silence settled over the house, as if death were very close to us again.

When Marie and I saw that she was not dead but was resting peacefully, we knew we should rest too. But we couldn't sleep and started to talk.

Marie was the second child; I was the ninth and last. The two of us had never even lived in the same house, as she already had her own home when I was born. We looked and acted like members of the same clan, but we had never talked real "soul talk." In the dim light of the room adjoining Mom's, she and I whispered stories about our family.

Seeing my mother near death, I felt like a little girl again. I told Marie how I remembered so often the special solace of Mom's lap. That was my retreat when I sought comfort for aching ears, or refuge from warring siblings, or just the closeness of her hug. To me she was always wonderfully soft and warm.

Marie knew the feeling. The shadows danced on the wall, a background to our animated whispers about child-hood—the family struggles, the strict discipline and hard work, the inevitable fights with our siblings.

Then she made a shocking statement.

"It wasn't really so hard for me, though, because I was always Mom's favorite."

I was astounded that she said the word out loud! Mom didn't have favorites! Yet as I let myself think about it, I had to reply, "I can't believe you said that . . . I guess I always thought I was her favorite."

Marie and I both chuckled, each believing that the other had certainly placed second. Then the truth began to unfold, as we continued to swap stories about the calm and loving woman asleep in the next room.

"I have an idea," I told her. "When the boys get here in the morning, let's ask them who was her favorite."

Two of our brothers awakened us at dawn, anxious to see if Mom had made it through the night. She had, and was still dozing. Over coffee at the big family table, I asked them the unspeakable question.

"Marie and I were talking last night, and couldn't agree

on something, so we thought we'd ask you. Who do you think was Mom's favorite child?"

Coffee mugs stalled in midair. The two men's eyebrows arched, and their mouths fell open. They squirmed in their chairs and looked out the window as intently as if counting the raindrops. Marie and I waited.

Finally, one brother spoke. "Well, you know Mom never played favorites. . . ." Then, making uneasy eye contact again, he said, "But if I were honest about it, I guess I'd have to say I always thought *I* was her favorite."

The second brother, grinning with relief that he didn't have to say it out loud first, confessed that he thought he was her favorite.

For the first time in months, we all laughed, as only childhood friends can laugh when finding a hidden treasure and sharing the secret.

How did she manage to make each of us feel like the favored child? She never told us we were. She showered none of us with gifts or special privileges. She was not very physically affectionate with us, and "I love you" was not part of daily conversation. But in her quiet way, she had a gift of presence more powerful than words. My husband (knowing secretly that he was her favorite son-in-law) summed it up: "When she was with you, she was all yours, as if you were the most important person in the world. Then she would go on to the next person, all his for a while."

In those days just before her death, my brothers and sisters and I discovered together what each of us had felt all along. Mom's love had no limits—each child was her favorite.

Sue Thomas Hegyvary

Letter to Josh

In 1989, several days before my oldest son, Josh's, eighteenth birthday, I wrote the following piece and sent it to our local paper asking them to print it. They agreed, and it appeared the next day. It read:

> *My oldest son is celebrating his eighteenth birthday, and I am proud to announce that his father and I are going to survive. Now for all those who have never raised children this might not seem like a big deal, but believe me from my experience this is truly an amazing and wondrous feat.*

Dear Josh,

On your thirteenth birthday we watched as you took those first giant rebellious steps toward adulthood. You no longer accepted, unquestioningly, our answers to why you had to be in bed early and why you could not play outside after dark. We began to see small hints of skepticism and humor in eyes that once held only adoration and respect for all we said and did.

And . . . your father and I began to discuss, in depth, the

feasibility of sending you to military school until you were eighteen.

On your fourteenth birthday you were no longer content to remain in the neighborhood. You wanted to claim the whole world as your domain, and your ever-widening circle of friends now contained names we did not know. We reluctantly accepted your mad dashes to answer the phone (acknowledging that most of the phone calls were now for you anyway) and on the few occasions when we did answer, it seemed strange to hear girls' voices asking for you.

And . . . your father and I began to consider in earnest calling several well-established adoption agencies (including the local humane society) to see if they would accept you for the next four years.

When you turned fifteen we learned of all-night skating and midnight bowling, that no one goes to the early movies and everyone lives at the mall. Our conversations with you became minimal and usually turned into heated debates. Pros and cons rang through the house. Your sentences began with "All my friends are doing it" and ended with "Wait till I'm eighteen."

And . . . your father and I began to seriously contemplate running away.

It was on your sixteenth birthday that a very real panic began to set in as you proudly announced to all who would listen that you were going to get your driver's license. I stood there in shock, numbly thinking, *This kid wants my car keys,* and remembering all the Band-Aids, every tube of first-aid cream and the numerous trips to the emergency room as you gradually worked your way from the stroller to tricycles, from big-wheels to bicycles, to roller skates and ice skates, skateboards and snow sleds.

And . . . your father and I decided that, when we did run away, we were taking both of the cars with us.

Your seventeenth birthday brought more changes. It seemed the only time we saw you was when you were hungry or needed to use the car. The refrigerator hated to see you coming and we hated to see you go. Our conversations now centered around college versus the armed forces, and we felt a little lost when we took our first family vacation without you.

But, Josh, we are truly proud of the man you have become, of your many accomplishments, the awards and trophies you have received over the years and your involvement in so many wonderful organizations.

And now . . . your father and I watch with equal measures of pride and apprehension as you walk out into that world you wanted to claim as your domain so long ago.

Happy birthday, Josh.

Love,

Mom and Dad

Initially we intended to give Josh a mild ribbing—he was a kid who loved to instigate and loved a good laugh, even when the joke was on him. But it became a way of letting him know that I believed in him and supported him in the hard decisions coming up as he entered the adult world with all its complexities and challenges.

Now I regard it as a loving reminder of a time that passed all too quickly.

My daring toddler, my lovable little boy, my wonderful rambunctious teenager, Joshua, died when he was twenty-one.

Linda Masters

My Mother's Blue Bowl

Visitors to my house are often served food—soup, pota-toes, rice—in a large blue stoneware bowl, noticeably chipped at the rim. It is perhaps the most precious thing I own. My mother gave it to me in her last healthy days. The days before a massive stroke laid her low and left her almost speechless.

For much of her life my mother longed, passionately, for a decent house. One with a yard that did not have to be cleared with an ax. One with a roof that kept out the rain. One with floors that you could not fall through. She longed for a beautiful house of wood or stone. Or of red brick, like the houses her many sisters and their husbands had. When I was thirteen, she found such a house. Green shuttered, white walled. Breezy. With a lawn and hedge and giant pecan trees. A porch swing. There her gardens flourished in spite of the shade, as did her youngest daughter, for whom she sacrificed her life doing hard labor in someone else's house in order to afford peace and pret-tiness for her child, to whose grateful embrace she returned each night.

But, curiously, the minute I left home, at seventeen, to

attend college, she abandoned the dream house and moved into the projects. Into a small, tight apartment of few breezes, in which I was never to feel comfortable, but that she declared suited her "to a T." I took solace in the fact that it was at least hugged by a spacious lawn on one side, and by forest out the back door, and that its isolated position at the end of the street meant she would have a measure of privacy.

Her move into the projects—the best housing poor black people in the South ever had, she would occasionally declare, even as my father struggled to adjust to the cramped rooms and hard, unforgiving qualities of brick— was, I now understand, a step in the direction of lightening her load, permitting her worldly possessions to dwindle in significance and roll away from her, well before she herself would turn to spirit.

She owned little, in fact. A dresser, some chairs. A set of living-room furniture. A set of kitchen furniture. A bed and wardrobe (given to her years before, when I was a teenager, by one of her more prosperous sisters). Her flowers: everywhere, inside the house and outside. Planted in anything she managed to get her green hands on, including old suitcases and abandoned shoes. She recycled everything, effortlessly. And gradually she had only a small amount of stuff—mostly stuff her children gave her: nightgowns, perfumes, a microwave—to recycle or to use.

Each time I visited her, I marveled at the modesty of her desires. She appeared to have barely any, beyond a thirst for a Pepsi-Cola or a hunger for a piece of fried chicken or fish. On every visit I noticed that more and more of what I remembered of her possessions seemed to be missing. One day I commented on this.

Taking a deep breath, sighing, and following both with a beaming big smile, which lit up her face, the room and

my heart, she said, "Yes, it's all going. I don't need it anymore. If there's anything you want, take it when you
leave; it might not be here when you come back." But
there was nothing there for me to want.

One day, however, looking for a jar in which to pour
leftover iced tea, I found myself probing deep into the
wilderness of the overstuffed, airless pantry. Into the land
of the old-fashioned, the outmoded, the outdated. The
humble and the obsolete. There was a smoothing iron, a
churn. A butter press. And two large bowls.

One was cream and rose with a blue stripe. The other
was a deep, vivid blue.

"May I have this bowl, Mama?" I asked, looking at her
and at the blue bowl with delight.

"You can have both of them," she said, barely acknowledging them, and continuing to put leftover food away.

In giving me these gifts, my mother had done a number
of astonishing things in her typically offhand way. She
had taught me a lesson about letting go of possessions—
easily, without emphasis or regret—and she had given me
a symbol of what she herself represented in my life.

For the blue bowl especially was a cauldron of memories. Of cold, harsh wintry days, when my brothers and
sister and I trudged home from school burdened down by
the silence and frigidity of our long trek from the main
road, down the hill to our shabby-looking house.

Slogging through sleet and wind to the sagging front
door, thankful our house was too far from the road to be
seen clearly from the school bus, I always felt a wave of
embarrassment and misery. But then I would open the
door. And there inside would be my mother's winter
flowers: a glowing fire in the fireplace, colorful hand-
made quilts on all our beds, paintings and drawings of
flowers and fruits and, most of all, there in the center
of the rough-hewn table, stood the big blue bowl, full of

whatever was the most tasty thing on earth.

There was my mother herself. Glowing. Her teeth sparkling. Her eyes twinkling. As if she lived in a castle and her favorite princes and princesses had just dropped by to visit.

A blue bowl stood there, seemingly full forever, no matter how deeply or rapaciously we dipped, as if it had no bottom. And she dipped up soup. Dipped up lima beans. Dipped up stew. Forked out potatoes. Spooned out rice and peas and corn. And in the light and warmth that was her, we dined.

Alice Walker

Always Believe in Miracles

Where there is great love there are always miracles.

Willa Cather

The year was 1924, and it was a few days before Christmas. Outside, a blinding snowstorm raged around the typical city row house into which my family had moved from the country only two months earlier. We hadn't yet become acquainted with any of our new neighbors.

I didn't see the snowflakes making frosty designs on my window, nor was I aware of my mother's lonely vigil by my bedside. I was a little girl of five, deep in a feverish coma, and had the only case of the dreaded diphtheria in Philadelphia.

Two weeks earlier, my illness had been diagnosed by the neighborhood's family doctor, whose office was a well-worn room in the basement of his home at the corner of the block. Immediately, my father and older sister had been given shots of antitoxin and shipped off to relatives until the danger passed. My mother, refusing to trust her child to a strange hospital, in a strange city, stayed behind to nurse me at home.

The city posted yellow warning signs on our front and back doors announcing a contagious disease. To make doubly sure no one other than the doctor approached, a policeman stood guard, twenty-four hours a day, outside each door. It was also their duty to see that my mother remained inside. Mail was laid on the doorstep, and the officer would tap on the door, then move back some distance to see that my mother opened the door only a crack and quickly took the mail inside.

In those days, Christmas shopping didn't begin in October, nor were toys given in the abundance popular today. A week or so before was time enough to prepare, and the tree was to be decorated by Santa Claus when he came on Christmas Eve. This year, in my family, it was different. With the sudden onset of diphtheria, no thought had been given to Christmas. My getting well was all that mattered.

Late in the afternoon of December twenty-third, the policeman tapped on the door. There was a letter on the stoop from my mother's sister. She was Catholic, and she'd enclosed a small bag of medals with her letter. "I can't be with you," she wrote, "but I want to help. My priest has blessed these medals. The bag is never to be opened, just pin it on your little girl's nightgown and believe."

My mother, willing to try anything, pinned the medals to my gown, but with little hope, as she looked down at my drawn cheeks and proceeded to apply cool compresses to my forehead. My eyes remained closed. During his visit, the doctor's face was grave, and he only shook his head sadly before taking his leave.

Late the next afternoon, my mother heard a faint call. Rushing into my room, she burst into tears of joy. The fever had broken and my eyes were open! Uncomprehending but overcome with gratitude, she fell to her knees and hugged me, but her relief was suddenly shattered when my first words were, "Mama, it's

Christmas Eve. What is Santa going to bring me?"

"No, no!" she cried. "Honey, you've been sick a long time, but it isn't Christmas Eve yet." But try as she might, she could not persuade me to think otherwise, and I fell asleep that night with sugarplums dancing in my head.

Downstairs, my mother was frantic. She told me years later how she even considered putting on some of my father's clothing and trying to sneak out to the corner store to get me a few toys, but of course she didn't. Come morning, all she could do was hope to convince me that Christmas was yet to arrive.

Christmas morning came, and I awoke with the usual childish anticipation. My mother, exhausted with heartache, was still half-asleep when the policeman gave his familiar tap on the door. Wearily, my mother opened it, and then gasped in surprise. On the doorstep was a large country basket filled with a Christmas dinner for two and an assortment of toys for a five-year-old girl. My mother's eyes silently questioned the policeman, but he only smiled and shrugged his shoulders. There was no answer there. Where had this spirit of Christmas come from? Would she ever know?

I recovered fully, unaware that two miracles had occurred that Christmas. My father and sister returned, and we settled into life in the city. As the years passed, my mother made a lasting friendship with one neighbor in particular, a friendly Irish woman and busy mother of six. Although they were close friends for years, it was only much later that my mother finally discovered the secret of the second Christmas miracle. Her friend with the thick, Irish brogue and smiling eyes—at the time a complete stranger—was the one who had understood, as a mother, the awful predicament my mother faced and cared enough to leave that wonderful Christmas basket on our doorstep. Thanks to her, I *still* believe in Santa Claus! You just have to know where to look for him.

Gerrie Edwards

Love on Trial

A story is told about Fiorello LaGuardia, who, when he was mayor of New York City during the worst days of the Great Depression and all of World War II, was called by adoring New Yorkers the "Little Flower" because he was only five foot four and always wore a carnation in his lapel. He was a colorful character who used to ride the New York City fire trucks, raid speakeasies with the police department, take entire orphanages to baseball games, and whenever the New York newspapers were on strike, he would go on the radio and read the Sunday funnies to the kids.

One bitterly cold night in January of 1935, the mayor turned up at a night court that served the poorest ward of the city. LaGuardia dismissed the judge for the evening and took over the bench himself. Within a few minutes, a tattered old woman was brought before him, charged with stealing a loaf of bread. She told LaGuardia that her daughter's husband had deserted her, her daughter was sick, and her two grandchildren were starving. But the shopkeeper, from whom the bread was stolen, refused to drop the charges.

"It's a real bad neighborhood, Your Honor," the man told the mayor. "She's got to be punished to teach other people around here a lesson."

LaGuardia sighed. He turned to the woman and said, "I've got to punish you. The law makes no exceptions— ten dollars or ten days in jail." But even as he pronounced sentence, the mayor was already reaching into his pocket. He extracted a bill and tossed it into his famous sombrero, saying: "Here is the ten-dollar fine, which I now remit; and furthermore, I am going to fine everyone in this courtroom fifty cents for living in a town where a person has to steal bread so that her grandchildren can eat. Mr. Bailiff, collect the fines and give them to the defendant."

So the following day the New York City newspapers reported that $47.50 was turned over to a bewildered old lady who had stolen a loaf of bread to feed her starving grandchildren, fifty cents of that amount being contributed by the red-faced grocery-store owner, while some seventy petty criminals, people with traffic violations and New York City policemen, each of whom had just paid fifty cents for the privilege of doing so, gave the mayor a standing ovation.

James N. McCutcheon

2

A MOTHER'S COURAGE

A mother's love perceives no impossibilities.

Paddock

My Mother's Strength

The doctors told me I would never walk again. My mother told me I would. I believed my mother.

Wilma Rudolph

When I was just fourteen, I watched my mother age ten years in a sickly green hospital room. It was cancer, and I knew it was bad because although I had seen my mother bear many crosses in her life, I had never seen her face look so drawn, tired and hopeless.

For my mother, though, this cancer was more than another cross to bear. She believed she was watching me, her youngest daughter, die.

Through the glass walls of my hospital room I could see the doctor and my mother. As the young resident started talking, my mother's head fell back, and tears started streaming down her face. Her arms flailed in despair.

When she walked into my hospital room with the doctor, she looked like she had just been dealt the knockout blow of her life. Her eyes stared pleadingly at the doctor.

She wanted me to know—I had that right—but she just couldn't be the one to tell me.

And when the doctor sat on the side of the bed and put his cold, clammy hand on my arm, I knew I was really, really sick. But it was when I looked over at my mother's face—which had gone from a youthful, smiling one with dancing eyes to the haggard, lackluster one before me— that I knew I was dying.

It was Hodgkin's disease. My fourteen-year-old body was riddled with cancerous tumors. The doctor sugar-coated nothing. He told me of the incredible pain I would endure. He told me of the weight I would lose and all the hair that would fall out. The doctors would try to shrink the existing tumors with chemotherapy and radiation therapy, but that was no guarantee. There was the very good chance that I would never turn fifteen.

My head fell back on the pillow, and I closed my eyes. I wanted to shut it all out and run away. When the doctor left the room, I wanted to believe that all the ugliness was walking out the door with him. *Maybe,* I thought, *when I opened my eyes, my mother's face would look young again, and we could go home and bake one of my infamous lopsided cakes.*

Instead, when I opened my eyes, my mother, sitting beside me, took my hand, pursed her lips and said deter-minedly, "We'll get through this."

During my stay at the hospital, my mother arrived in my room every morning and stayed there until the last seconds of the last visiting hour at night. For most of the day no words passed between us except for the occa-sional, "Pat, you should eat something." I spent my days staring out of the window while my mother sat and read or watched television. There was absolutely no pressure to talk about the situation. It wasn't profound words of support and love that entwined our souls. It was simply my mother letting me be.

Three weeks later, on the morning I was to be released from the hospital, my mother brought me my favorite bell-bottom jeans, tie-dyed blouse and earth shoes. Seeing them perked me up like no medication in that entire hospital could. I couldn't wait to wear them.

My mother drew the curtains, and I, like any other clothes-crazy teenager, dressed with great glee. When I pulled up the jeans and buttoned them, I could tell right away that they were not mine. They couldn't be, because they fell off the once rounded hips they used to hug so nicely. I was incredulous. In the hospital gown I hadn't noticed the ravages of illness.

I yelled at my mother as though it was her fault. "You brought the wrong jeans! These are too big!" I screamed.

My mother just walked out of the room and went out to the nurse's station, returning immediately with two safety pins. "Look," she said, "it will be all right. All we have to do is pin them up here in the back. Your top will cover them."

"No, I don't want to pin them. I want them to fit right," I sulked, and folding my arms, sat on the bed and cried to the wall.

When I finally looked over at my mother, her eyes boring into mine, I realized that I had to pin my pants. Without saying a word, she was telling me: No matter how much you pout, cry and stomp like a mule, these pants are not going to fit right without these pins. You are sick. Your body is not the same. You have to accept this.

It was then that I learned to compromise with my mother, and with a force larger than myself—a force I could not see, or hear, or touch, but a force that nonetheless had taken control of my life.

Though I left the hospital knowing the doctors believed that I would only return to die, none of it ever felt completely real. My body was disintegrating, I could barely walk and I couldn't keep food down, but death felt as far away from me as grandmotherhood. I don't know why I had this feeling. Maybe it was because my fourteen-year-old mind couldn't grasp the concept of mortality, or perhaps I felt something telling me that this wasn't going to be the end.

I quickly slipped into the normalness of everyday life at home, surrounded by my mother and my sisters. And my mother and I, in the face of my illness, discovered a special way of being together.

We knew what was destroying my body, but we never said the words *cancer* or *death*. Still, on a day when I was too weak even to feed myself, I looked up at my mother as she was feeding me some mashed food, and something in me felt that one, if not both, of those words needed to be spoken.

"Mommy," I finally said after about the third swallow, "am I really going to die?"

My mother dropped the bowl of food, spilling it all over me and broke into uncontrollable tears that would not stop, no matter how hard I pleaded with her.

I was frozen with fear. I couldn't take back what I had said. Besides, I really wanted to know. If my mother would just confirm it one way or another, whatever she said would be what was real.

Finally, she looked up at me and said, "My baby is not going to die. Do you hear me? I don't ever want to hear you say that again. Do you hear me?"

I heard her. I never said it again. I simply went about the business of fighting for my life.

Yet as my body withered to eighty-two pounds and my hair fell out, I could see how helpless my mother felt. Her hair grew grayer. She even matched me, pound for pound, with the weight she lost. And yet, it was her strength that jump-started my will to make my frail body walk instead of ride in a wheelchair. It was her strength that helped me walk into school wearing a wig amidst stares and whispers from pretty, healthy-bodied girls. And it was her strength that made me see that in the larger picture, those stares and whispers didn't mean a thing.

More than a year went by before I finally went into remission. When the doctor called my mother and me into his office after the last chemotherapy treatment, we didn't know what to expect. Somehow, though, we knew we didn't need to expect the worst. He went through a long-winded dissertation about shrunken tumors and good cell counts before he told us, essentially, that I was in remission.

My mother and I didn't cry tears of joy. We didn't get swept up in a whirl of happiness and giddiness, hugging the stuffing out of each other. We just smiled and squeezed each other's hands. The doctor was really only telling us something that we already knew: that I was not going to die.

Patricia Jones

Learning to Say Hello

*Each handicap is like a hurdle in a steeple-
chase, and when you ride up to it, if you throw
your heart over, the horse will go along too.*

Lawrence Bixby

It was December 1986. As I looked out the window of
Chicago's O'Hare International terminal, the sunlight
seemed unusually bright and warm. This helped to soothe
me and remove some of my anxiety. The precious passengers on Northwest Airlines Flight 517, Korean babies who
had been adopted by American couples, had just begun to
deplane. I watched with awe and anticipation as, one by
one, blanketed bundles with little black tufts of hair peeking out were carried closer and closer to the door. I knew
that one of those little bundles was mine—my daughter,
Sarah Elizabeth Hee-Jin. Sarah had spent ten of her eleven
months of life in an orphanage. When I heard my name
called, I panicked. *What right do I have to mother this little girl?
What can I, a blonde-haired, blue-eyed Caucasian, offer this
orphaned Asian child? Dear God, what was I thinking when I*

decided to adopt Sarah? I wanted to hide, but people were crowding around me. And then I saw her. She was pathetically thin, dehydrated and obviously frightened and confused, but there was something about her that was beautiful. I fell in love with her as she laid her tiny head against my breast, closed her black eyes and fell asleep in my arms.

A full year passed, during which time I poured my entire being into this little girl's emaciated body and neglected soul. I adored each of my other children, yet my love for this little one was a new experience, far beyond anything I had felt before. It was inexplicable. But my love was not blind. I could see something was not right. She was not developing: Her eyes did not connect with people or with things in her environment, her motor skills were minimal for a two-year-old, and she wasn't babbling or making any attempt to speak.

We took trips to doctors' offices. There were referrals to new doctors, which led to further referrals to still more doctors with strange titles who lived far away. One day, as we sat in one of those doctor's offices, our hearts pounding, a tired Sarah fussing and crying, the doctor explained to us in a patronizing tone and in words of twenty syllables, that Sarah was retarded, "microcephalic."

"Micro—what?" We made the five-hour trip home in stunned silence, but in my head, the roar of "NO!" echoed over and over again.

Every day for the next week, I went to the library and read all that I could find on microcephalia. Something about this diagnosis was not right. What they described was not my Sarah. After so much study, it was I who discovered what was really wrong with my heart-child. I told the doctors that Sarah was not microcephalic, but had a chromosome disorder. They didn't believe me. They said grief did terrible things to a mother's mind. But I had found a new courage inside, and I finally persuaded a doctor, a woman doctor who was also a mother, to do the simple test to find out. We took blood and we counted the chromosomes. Sarah had one too many.

But being right brought no reward, only a new kind of nothingness. My child might never walk, might never talk. I was told, with compassion, just to love her and enjoy her as much as possible.

For the following week or two, I was numb. I ate, I slept, I packed lunches for my school-aged children. I went to work, leaving Sarah with a sitter. I drove to a nearby lake and stared at its vastness. I tried to feel grief, or anger, or anything at all. I looked around me hoping to see something black or white or even gray, but there was no color in my life, only a gaping abyss into which my soul had fallen. I wanted my friends and family to take all of their well-intentioned words and hang them on the pieces of someone else's broken heart.

Even in my shattered condition, I knew I was a good mother—but was I the kind of mother this little girl needed? I didn't know how to be a retarded girl's mother. But I loved Sarah; I loved her in a way that was beyond my understanding and I wanted to keep loving her for as long as she lived. So I decided that I would love her and love her well. It was then that my courage surfaced again, and I found a new word to define it. *Yes!* I told myself. *Yes, she will walk. Yes, she will talk. Yes, she will, she will, she will.*

That spring Sarah and I went to the library every day to learn together. I worked her muscles and taught her limbs to move correctly. We licked spoonfuls of peanut butter to make her tongue move more accurately. We played with a flashlight in a dark room to make her eyes focus properly. Minor achievements became major miracles. My courage was contagious: Daddy did the physical therapy; big brother liked to eat peanut butter; big sister dug out her old Dr. Seuss books and read aloud to Sarah. I claimed "dark-room duty." It was my place of refuge. It was my place of prayer. Sarah stared at the flashlight in silence, and there was peace in the silence.

See Sarah. See Sarah run. Run, Sarah, run!

Hear Sarah laugh and sing the ABC song. Sing, Sarah, sing!

Listen, Sarah, listen. Your teacher is calling your name.

She is saying, "Welcome to kindergarten, Sarah."

It was the first day of school, and as I stood at the door of the classroom, I heard Sarah's small voice say, "Don't cry, Mama. Sarah 'yub' you." She thought my tears were saying, "No." She couldn't know how much they were saying, "Yes!"

Yes to new dreams and hopes, to new possibilities and simple pleasures. She didn't know that as she hugged me and said good-bye, I said hello.

Kathi Rose

Pennies from Heaven

I met a man who picks up pennies he finds on the ground because he says they're government property.

I pick them up because I see them as signs from angels to let us know they're around.

Carmen Rutlen

Years ago, when our finances were less than ideal, I took a job vacuuming the halls and carpeted stairwells of our run-down condominium building. Work is work and, I told myself, it was honest work. But it wasn't what I'd imagined myself doing for employment and it dented my pride.

It was certainly difficult work; the portable vacuum weighed twenty pounds and the condominium hallways were mostly stairs, twelve staircases in all, three flights up each. Six staircases a day was all I could manage. Stirred up dirt and dust clung to my skin, sweaty from hauling the vacuum up and down the airless staircases, and there were days when self-pity and wounded pride made the vacuum weigh even more.

On a day that had been particularly hard, when my pride tweaked with every cigarette butt and piece of trash I picked up, I hauled my portable vacuum up the stairs and asked God, in a tone more rueful than meditative, to give me something, *anything*, to perk up my sagging spirit.

On the third floor, nearly hidden in the crevice where the frayed carpet met the wall, glinted a shiny penny. "This?" I asked God. "This is what you give me?" I sighed, but I pocketed the penny and didn't give it much thought beyond that.

Curiously, pennies began to turn up each time I vacuumed the halls. They hadn't been there in the months before as I'd vacuumed up dried-up leaves and crumpled gum wrappers. But now, each time, there was a penny. One penny only. It became a game to me, wondering where and when the lone penny would turn up. Always, before the job was completed, there would be that one coin, as if it were waiting for me. I started to say a thank-you to God each time I retrieved the penny and pocketed it, and began to think of these small, found treasures as my pennies from heaven.

I didn't tell anyone. There are pennies everywhere, right? Considered outdated, what is a penny but a useless coin that doesn't buy anything in this expensive age? The condo-cleaning job was the least of the hardships visited upon me in the last few years, and pennies weighed against family misfortunes and ill luck seemed small change, indeed.

Still, it gave me a jolt of renewed hope each time I spotted one—and more often than not, that hope alone was enough for me.

Finances improved and we moved, and my two children blossomed in their new neighborhood. Life uninterrupted by adversity was welcome, if surprising. Occasionally I picked up a penny when I found it, thanking God in what had now become a knee-jerk response.

When I found myself pregnant with twins, I viewed it as the motherlode of rewards for having survived the previous years so well. When the ultrasound revealed them to be healthy baby girls, I named them Anne and Grace. I grew so huge over the next eight months, there was no more bending down to pick up anything, much less a mere penny.

When I was in early labor, the final ultrasound revealed their perfect feet, the sweet curve of their rumps, and the delicate rope of their spines. And then the flat silent discs that proved to be their unbeating hearts. They had died the night before. In the following hours before they were delivered I knew that my thinking of them as a reward had been only a cosmic joke of some sort, or more likely the imagination of a childish heart.

For months afterwards, the only prayers I offered up were enraged shouts at the kitchen ceiling, and finally even those ceased. What good is yelling at a God who doesn't care, doesn't hear, or more likely, doesn't exist.

The numbness that replaced the anger made it nearly impossible to navigate my daily life. I forgot whatever it was I had once cared for and even tried to make lists of what I loved. I'd loved my other children, hadn't I? Only now their demands and need for comfort seemed overwhelmingly large. I tried smaller lists. Hadn't I liked old books, flea markets, stolen moments with my husband? Didn't I once enjoy lunches out with friends? My funny little dog? It didn't help, and I forgot the lists, forgot my own name once when it was asked, and forgot as well any reason to continue living.

One day, while waiting for my son's karate class to end, I heard a mother call to her daughter. "Annie," she said, and a chubby blonde toddler came tumbling into her arms. I fled for the hallway, and as I tried to gain control of myself, I happened to glance down. There on the carpet was a penny. I just stared at it. A penny?

I picked it up.

After that, pennies began to turn up everywhere. Almost every day but always just one. In odd places. In the rooms of my house where I had just walked before, a penny would suddenly be shining up from the middle of the room. In the waiting room of a doctor's office, outside my mailbox, in the school parking lot as I stepped out of my car. I began to pocket them again, slowly, numbly, and I began again to thank God each time.

My small frequent thanks to God made me question what I was thanking him for—my nine-year-old son slipping his hand into mine, a funny note from my daughter, evening walks with my husband, soup from a friend, even a kind smile from a grocery clerk. I looked up one morning and noticed the blue of the springtime sky. I noticed the rich taste of my morning cup of coffee. I began to be grateful just to be alive.

It occurred to me that maybe God doesn't always choose to speak in dramatic ways; maybe a burning bush isn't his calling card to everyone.

Just maybe, for some, a single penny gleaming in an unexpected place is his touch of grace, his gift of hope. And sometimes that hope is just enough.

Susan Clarkson Moorhead

Shoulder to Shoulder

A faint light poked its nose under the family-room door in the hallway of the mission home. Was it Sara? Was she still awake?

Tugging the lightweight blanket from the bed and wrapping it around my shoulders, I tiptoed from my room. Sara huddled beneath a pilled blue blanket on the couch, staring vacantly at pictures flashing on the silent television screen. A scattering of unopened magazines cluttered the floor beneath the dimmed lamp. I sighed.

Great. Just what I needed at a time like this. Another child to see to, another child to parent. Well, I'd been at it for years. At least it was a role I was accustomed to.

"Sara, we've had a big day. You really should try to get some sleep," I urged in a whisper across the room.

She sat up and rearranged her covers. "I know I should. But I can't."

Sara, long and lean, was beginning to show the week's strain. Eyes darkened to indigo, puffy from crying. Translucent skin stretched taut across flawless cheekbones.

Too thin! Too thin! My mind screeched the warning. I'd

tried to coax her to eat. She had no appetite. But then, neither did I.

We had shared a long week, bedside in the trauma unit. My son Kyle, engaged to Sara, only recently moved to California to serve a temporary stint as a missionary. Instead, he was in critical condition and comatose, the result of a hit-and-run accident.

Taking a seat at the other end of the long couch, I curled icy toes and tucked my cold feet between the cushions before layering my blanket over hers. A companionable silence settled between us. I marveled at how deeply I had come to know this beautiful young lady over the past week.

What would I do without her? How would I manage when she flew back to Colorado in the morning?

On the other hand, I also recognized that, at twenty-two, she was definitely a member of the McDonald's generation—expecting life to be neatly packaged in a Happy Meal. Made to order. Served on a platter. "Immediately, if not sooner," as my daddy would have quipped.

Nothing about Kyle's situation appeared to be that simple. This was not a quick fix, jiffy meal. Did Sara truly understand the gravity of all this? Whether Kyle lived or died, things would never be the same again—for any of us.

I worried that Sara was simply too naive, too young, too inexperienced to recognize the far-reaching ramifications of Kyle's situation. What was best for her? For Kyle? Was this the time to shatter her confidence, destroy her illusions, slap her with reality? A part of me felt that my own fragile faith depended upon the unwavering strength of hers.

Yet, at forty-seven, my jaded rung was higher on the ladder. I had dealt with loss—up close and personal. I had buried numerous friends, aunts, uncles, cousins, four sets of grandparents and, most recently, my own daddy. I was on a first-name basis with death.

And things worse than death. I had witnessed life with the wrappings torn away and knew there wasn't always a prize inside. Glancing over at Kyle's fiancée, I saw fresh tears pooling.

"Sara?"

"Oh, Carol, I don't want to leave tomorrow."

"I know, Sweetie. But the doctor said Kyle is stable. And this could go on for a long time yet. You need to finish your last semester of college. You and Kyle have a master plan, remember?"

"Y-yes."

"The best thing you can do right now is carry it out. For yourself and for Kyle. For you and Kyle as a couple."

"But it's so hard to leave." Sara pulled a tissue from the box on the side table.

"I know."

"I finally found the only person that I love enough to marry. He's my best friend. We talk about everything. I can't lose him now. I just can't!" Her shoulders shook beneath the thin blanket. "I love him so much."

"Yes, I know you do." I gathered her in my arms. "And he loves you, too."

"It would be so much easier if he were aware. If he could know and remember that I was here."

"Somehow, deep inside, I believe he does, Sara. I—well—I feel linked to him," I revealed. "I send thought messages, and I think he receives them. Does that sound crazy to you?"

Sara listened intently with her seeing heart while I confided the sweet, sacred communion I had been sharing with Kyle. "We communicate, Sara. We really do."

"I believe you." She dabbed at her eyes. "It's your own personal miracle. And I'm not surprised. I've always known that you and Kyle share something special." She smiled.

"You should hear him talk about you, Carol. 'My mom' this, and 'my mom' that. He loves and admires you a lot. That's one of the things that attracted me to Kyle. His open respect for you and his dad." Sara leaned her head on my shoulder.

And I held her, a fragile-strong woman-child. The one that Kyle had chosen above all others. Now I was seeing—under the worst circumstances—what he could have only glimpsed under the best. She had eased her way into my heart. I was beginning to love her, too.

No matter what the future held, she would always be part mine. No matter what.

Breathing in the flowered scent of her freshly shampooed hair, I smiled. There would never be mother-in-law problems between us. After weathering this, anything else would be trivial in comparison, even petty.

Look at us now. We were facing the unthinkable together. Shoulder to shoulder. Arm in arm. Hand in hand. I kissed the top of her head, drew her closer, sighed and smiled.

Just what I needed. Another child to love.

Carol McAdoo Rehme

Bound by Love

When my son was only five months old, he had to have major surgery on his head. My husband, Chris, and I were shocked and devastated. Cole's skull had fused together prematurely; he had no "soft spot." No one knows why this happens to some babies. The only remedy is surgery.

How could this have happened to my baby? What did I do wrong? I had been so careful during my pregnancy, eating well and refusing caffeine. No matter how many doctors explained to me that the condition was not my fault, I felt responsible.

The surgery and the ensuing five days at the hospital were the scariest, darkest, most exhausting days of our lives. Cole lay in his tiny hospital bed, IVs poking from his perfect little body. My faith faltered with his every breath. If not for the kindness and sensitivity of people—family, friends and hospital staff—I do not know how we could have made it through.

Even Cole tried to help. When Cole's head swelled so badly that his eyes fused shut and his eyelashes disappeared, I sang to him, my eyes never leaving his face. I was amazed to see him force a weak smile for me. To this day,

I'm convinced he was trying to make me feel better.

After Cole's surgery, his head was swollen and bruised, and he had a dramatic zigzag scar from one ear to the other. I was hesitant to go out in public with my sweet boy. I felt defensive and protective, as if I might snap if anyone asked me what was wrong with my baby.

A few days after coming home from the hospital, Cole and I ventured out to buy some groceries. Still on pain medication, Cole was unhappy and cranky. On the way home, I noticed the gas tank indicator was flashing red for empty, so I stopped for some gas. Cole whined as I tried to get the keys out of the ignition. I needed the keys to open the gas tank, and for some reason I could not manage this simple maneuver. For some minutes, I tried pulling and tugging, until finally I feared I might break the key. Trying to compose myself, I reached for Cole and headed for the pay phone. Chris was not home. My heart raced. Cole began crying, and tears welled up in my own eyes.

I found my AAA card and called for help. This, after all, qualified as an emergency. Minutes later, the AAA truck pulled up, and a burly man stepped down and walked toward our car. His eyes immediately focused on Cole's head, the scar fresh and frightening. "You poor fellow," he said, "what have you been through?"

His kind words directed toward Cole opened a flood of tears in me. I began to sob. The stranger, whose name tag read Ron, simply placed a hand on my shoulder until I calmed down. Then he said to me, "As parents we go through some very hard things. There's nothing worse than seeing your child in pain. I have two kids of my own, and I know all about it. Even an earache can seem like the end of the world. The thing is—we simply get through it." He reached for his wallet and pulled out numerous pictures of his son and daughter.

Cole and I sat with Ron as he talked about each picture.

By the time he finished, Cole was sitting contently on my lap, and I felt a smile, the first in weeks, spontaneously come to my lips.

Although it took Ron less than one minute to get the keys from my ignition, this kind stranger spent over an hour with us, taking the concept of Roadside Assistance to a whole new level.

It's been five years since Cole's head surgery. Sometimes, Cole's red hair parts so that I can see the thick scar that crisscrosses his head; otherwise there are no visual reminders of his surgery.

Yet there are things unseen. The way I feel toward Cole is difficult to describe—it's as though our hearts had been bound together during that surgery.

Recently at the park, a Guatemalan woman asked me about the scar. She said, "The angels came into him while his head was open." I don't know if I believe that, but the thought makes me feel better.

My younger son, Ry, fell from his bed one night when he was two years old and had to have stitches on his chin. I was with him as the nurses at the emergency room held him down while the doctor stitched. He clutched my hand and screamed, and it reminded me of Cole's surgery.

The room started to spin, and I was having trouble breathing. One of the nurses yelled, "Mom going down! Mom going down!" The next thing I knew, there was a wet towel on the back of my neck, and I was being instructed to put my head between my legs.

Going through these difficult things with my children doesn't end—whether it's watching them get stitches or seeing them be teased by other children. My heart is constantly being ripped in unexpected ways, despite both children, ultimately, doing fine. The hard times usually end up bringing us closer together.

Now four years old, Ry likes his scar. He points to it all

the time. The other day, Cole complained that he didn't have a scar to show off like Ry.

"Yes, you do honey, I said, "Remember, you have that big zigzag scar that goes from ear to ear?"

"Oh, yeah," he said. "I guess I forgot."

I'm glad that he's forgotten about the scar, and I hope all the trauma behind it—as long as he remembers the love we forged going through it together.

Victoria Patterson

A Misfortune—Not a Tragedy

Alone we can do so little; together we can do so much.

Helen Keller

I was an ecstatically happy thirteen-year-old riding home for dinner on my new birthday present—a Fleet bicycle made by Schwinn, and it was a dandy. It even had a spring knee-action suspension in front. Better yet, it was the only one of its kind in the neighborhood.

I polished its blue and white frame and fenders to a shiny brightness that could be seen for blocks away. I had been on cloud nine ever since I received it as a gift a few days before. One's first bike is a milestone in any child's life. Like any thirteen-year-old boy there was only one thing on my mind as I pedaled home around four-thirty that afternoon—dinner.

I skidded my bike up to the front porch in a spectacular wheelie and bounded up the steps. As I ran through the hallway toward the kitchen I began to wonder. I didn't smell any tantalizing aroma coming from Mom's spic-and-span kitchen. *Oh well,* I thought, smiling to myself, *maybe we are having cold cuts with pork and beans*—my summer favorite.

I opened the swinging doors to the kitchen expecting to hear, "Jimmy, wash your hands and help me set the table." Instead, my young eyes focused on my mother, ghostly white, lying in a crumpled heap on the kitchen floor—blood oozing from a deep wound on her forehead. I tried to rouse her but to no avail. All I got were moans. Beginning to cry, I knelt beside her quiet form on the floor and asked soberly, "Mom, are you okay?" She answered in an almost unintelligible whisper, "Please help me, Jimmy."

Realizing we were alone, like most children would do, I ran to the phone. This was 1944 and there was no such thing as 911, only the operator's friendly voice asking, "Number please." I blurted out my grandmother's phone number between sobs and said, "It's an emergency, operator, please hurry."

I called Grandma because Dad was still at work, and I couldn't remember his office number. The first words out of Grandma's mouth were, "Jimmy why are you crying?" I could hardly speak through the tears by this time. Between sobs I explained to Grandma about Mom on the floor needing help. All she said was, "I'll call the fire department, and I'll be right there. Hang on."

Grandma didn't own a car but lived nearby. True to her word, her running feet hit the porch at the same time the firemen arrived from the neighborhood station. We all converged on the kitchen to help Mom. She was still lying on the floor, not moving or making a sound. As the firemen worked over her in a huddled mass I heard one of the firemen say, "Get a gurney. She has to go to the hospital *now.*"

Once more I began to cry. Grandma immediately swept me into her massive, comforting grandma arms and said soothingly, "Hush child. Your mother is in good hands;

she'll be okay. God and the firemen are with her." Grandma always knew just what to say.

Little did we know as we watched the firemen wheel Mom out of the house, our family's life would never be the same. We found out later Mom had slipped on the slick kitchen floor she was mopping. As she fell she hit her head on the sharp edge of the kitchen table, causing severe brain damage—resulting in paralysis to the left side of her body. This misfortune, not a tragedy, changed our lives and lifestyle in a matter of seconds.

After weeks of convalescence in the hospital and extensive therapy she was still unable to use her left arm or left leg normally. She never would again, and she was only in her late thirties.

I never will forget the day Mom came home. Dad got her settled in a makeshift bedroom downstairs in our two-story house. He then asked all of us children to gather in the living room. Dad, his usual strong voice filled with emotion, said, "Your Mother will never be the same. The fall damaged the right side of her brain. It is like a lightbulb that shatters and cannot be put back together—this caused the paralysis. She will never again be like the mom you have known. But she will still be your mom—don't ever forget that." We all nodded our heads in agreement.

There were four of us children, myself, thirteen years old; an older sister, fifteen; a younger brother, eight; and a baby sister, three years old. Struggling with Dad's words we all reached out and grasped each other's hands as we gathered around him in prayer. We knew then that our family would not be the same, but it would survive—we were all very confident of that fact—Mom and God were still with us.

After more physical therapy Mom soon was able to shuffle about and once again commence her household duties. She only had the use of her right hand and arm.

Her left arm hung limply to her side. Her partially paralyzed left leg only allowed her to walk stiff legged.

All of us children, and of course Dad, had increased work to do at home, but none of us really minded. After all, Mom was still with us, along with her happy, perky personality. In spite of this life-changing experience our family unit soon knitted. If anything, it was stronger than before. Yes, life was good once more for our family.

Dad never faltered in his role as father, husband and part-time mom. They remained together as Mom and Dad, husband and wife for their forty-six remaining years until Mom—who was in a wheelchair by this time—passed away. We children in the family actually benefited immensely from this misfortune—I won't say tragedy—in many ways for the rest of our lives.

We learned compassion and how to look out for each other. We became a bonded team, working together for the good of the family and, most of all, we learned how to love one another.

At seventy years old I can attest to this fact: No matter how bleak your future can look to you as a child when faced with a family misfortune—I still won't say tragedy—life does get better. Our family found out quickly that even a shattered lightbulb can bring brightness to the end of a long, dark tunnel—all we had to do was reach out together, along with God, and turn it on.

James A. Nelson

My Son, the Street Person

If you don't like something, change it. If you can't change it, change your attitude.

Maya Angelou

Let me start right off by confessing: my son lives on the streets. Of course, in response to casual inquiry about him, I usually say, "He's doing great." If pressed further I say, "He's traveling." No one can fault that. After all, many restless young men spend a year roaming before they settle down and go to college. Get it out of their systems, sow their wild oats, find themselves . . . you know. But questioners may remember that this is his second year out of high school. How many wild oats has he got?

Most of the interrogators let it drop. They are too busy with their own lives, and perhaps they sense some great darkness lurking behind my answers. But some people are tenacious. "Where is he?" they want to know. A tale of fictional intrigue is on the tip of my tongue, but for some reason I am compelled to tell the truth, so I answer, "New York City." I hear the wheels turning—how long can you be traveling in New York City? There are a lot of sights, a few good day trips, but hey, two weeks ought to do it. A writhing can of worms gapes open: "What's he doing? Where's he living?

"My son is a street person," I must respond.

I glimpse the shocked response before it is politely stuffed away. "She's a failure as a parent," they're thinking.

The sociological data on street kids says that they come from divorced, alcoholic, abusive, unloving and often uneducated families. While that's the classic profile, it's no portrait of my son.

My husband, Lee, and I have, amazingly enough, been married for twenty-one years. Despite attempts to cultivate the pleasure of a glass of wine now and then, I must admit the stuff puts me to sleep. We did scold our son and send him to his room on occasion, even grounded him once or twice. But he was an easy child and, in our family, yelling is something you do on the sidelines of a hockey game. We tend to talk things out.

Unloved? This child has been adored, admired and cherished since he was conceived. To this day, he lights up a room when he walks in. There is an energy, a zest for life that can't be missed. So, please, don't say it's lack of love. I did not do everything right. But love him? Yes, that I did.

This kid's so smart his high school teachers still talk about him. Education runs on both sides of the family. Our family tree is practically sprouting with doctors, lawyers and MBAs.

Having eliminated all the usual criteria of homelessness, "mentally unbalanced" is the only one left. He must be crazy, right? Wrong. He's the most rational, practical person you could hope to meet.

My son has lived on the streets for almost a year now. He is not homeless or living out of a cardboard box. He is a squatter, living with a group of people in an abandoned building that is city-owned. There are many cities where street people take up residency, begin repairs and avoid authorities. Others link in, and soon there is a community of sorts, with rules, guidelines for joining and extended support.

In the beginning, I actually imagined that he was planning to write a book, make a documentary or organize assistance for the homeless. I had it all worked out. My son the social activist, the do-gooder. But it turns out that he did not go to New York City to *help* those "poor people." He claims that would be a form of manipulation, taking advantage of street people, standing apart and observing. This is his life. Though he comes home for occasional visits, he does not ask us for any money or help.

My son has *chosen* this life. He is not a failure. It is not a last resort, a desperate attempt to survive or a dead end. He wants to be exactly where he is. Nor did he do this out of a romanticized notion of what it would be like. He knows the hunger, the fear, the violence, the disease.

Day after day, I ask myself, *why? Why did he end up in this place?* I am not able to fully understand or accept it. I cannot change it, or approve it, or even explain it. Yet it doesn't go away. That is my child out there. I have talked to many of my son's friends. After overcoming my initial reaction to body piercing, multiple tattoos, ripped clothes, and dyed hair, I find them to be kind, intelligent, thoughtful people. They are searching for something.

After my initial horror, I began to comprehend some of the appeal of the life he has chosen. It is a day-to-day existence in which there is no worry about career goals, or what the neighbors will think, or making your mark in the world. My son and his friends focus on the basics of survival. How are you going to eat today? Where will you sleep? Will you keep warm? Where will you relieve yourself? These are questions that inspire considerable passion and take up a major portion of each day. Then you are free to pursue your own daydreams. There is, in fact, a freedom in the squats. The price is danger, discomfort, bugs and ill health; the street beats you up and ages you quickly. But the freedom is there. It is not pretty or pastel or romantic, but beneath the dirt and desperation, I can sometimes see freedom shining through my son's eyes.

A strong sense of community exists among his friends. There are a few subgroups: the down-and-out families; the drug dealers and users; the desperate runaways; and the cases, like my son, who are there by choice. Some are old timers, others are new to the life. The group my son is part of has organized their places of shelter into a network of communication that could be a model for any revolutionary group. There is an excitement and purpose in their rejection of a world order they consider decadent and off-target. They are not abusing the earth or taking advantage of people or accumulating wealth. They may be more sure of what they do not want than what they do, but their intention is to do no harm.

They live in the buildings abandoned by society, eat the vast quantities of food society throws out, and scrounge for clothing and comforts of life from the discarded piles on the curbstone. Books on revolution and philosophy are passed around and discussed late into the night. They offer each other protection and help, often giving their only dollar to one whose need is greater. They are proud of their ability to survive. Sometimes I think they are telling us something about the dysfunction of our nation of unhappy, out-of-control consumers.

I know the dangers of his life. On those long nights when fear grabs hold of me and will not let go, the fears parade beneath my closed eyes. I imagine all the guns in New York City. I see berserk crackheads pursuing my son. I picture him caught in crossfire, or poking his head in the wrong Dumpster, or simply ticking off some hothead. I see him cold and shivering, dirty and lice covered, his immune system weakened, disease ready to ambush him. I see him falling in love and wanting to settle down but unprepared for a "normal" life. I see these things, and for all my attempts at understanding, I am simply a frightened mother.

All this pensive philosophy falls away and is replaced by excited anticipation when he returns for a visit. The one form of assistance that he accepts other than spare building supplies, is a round-trip bus ticket home. We cook a big meal, stock up on a supply of his favorite foods, and expect a late night filled with descriptions of the people in his life: the local hotdog vendor, the Puerto Rican brothers who own the corner bodega, the hovering drug dealer, the young squatter couple from Ohio, the artist with AIDS, the old communist who has been living like this for twenty-five years, the guy who taught him plumbing. There are so many stories.

In the daylight, I surreptitiously examine his skin sores, listen to his cough, and check out his cuts and bruises. He plays with his little brother, rests, showers and takes his sisters out for coffee. Soon the local grapevine carries word of his arrival in town. By the second evening a jam session is underway in the back room, the pulsating bass notes lull me into a contented sleep.

What is the price he will pay for this lifestyle? I don't know; I can try to guess. I know that he is young, and he will change. I know that the college graduate we once imagined is a dream deferred. I am much more clear about my cost: the endless days of worry, the incessant wondering about what we could have done differently, the hesitant greeting I give him while I look at the sores on his face with a growing dread. Yet, is this so different from any parent? Maybe my case is more dramatic and extreme than many, but in the end, we mothers all worry and pray for our children whatever their age or whereabouts. Our inability to insure safety and happiness never changes the longing.

Yes, I feel embarrassed when I am questioned, and sometimes I believe I am the failed parent others perceive me to be. Yet I am also proud. This handsome, vibrant young man to whom I gave birth has courage. He is on a quest, even if his goal is not the Holy Grail. He is learning, seeking and questioning everything. What will be his future? In the old days he might have gone west or searched for a river's source; today the cities have become our wilderness. Perhaps he, more than I in my frenetic, practical life, has found what it is all about. Who can say for sure?

So now you will better understand my request. If you pass a strange, grungy kid on the street, wherever you may be, don't look away or grimace in disgust. Look him in the eyes, talk to him, at least give him a greeting—he might be my son, or he could be yours.

Eva Nagel

Postscript: My son is now a trained professional, married and a father himself. He met his wife in New York city. The only sign of their former life is a framed collage of the squat that hangs on their bedroom wall.

3

ON MOTHERHOOD

Nothing else will ever make you as happy or as sad, as proud or as tired, as motherhood.

Elia Parsons

"It's a new workout video. It shows a mother chasing around three little children all day."

Motherhood: A Transformation

Cleaning your house while your kids are still growing is like shoveling the walk before it stops snowing.

Phyllis Diller

Once upon a time I was a nurse, a writer and a wife. Then one day, I had a child. I became a mother.

Added to the list of things I previously was, I became: a chauffeur, a cook, a dresser, a wiper of dirty faces, a cleaner of soiled diapers, a retriever of thrown socks, a finder of lost shoes, a doer of homework, an insomniac. I was a referee in toy wars, a slayer of nighttime dragons, a soother of nervous school jitters. I was a room mother, a den mother, a leader of Girl Scouts, and one day, mother of the bride. I calmed tantrums and bolstered fragile egos.

With each passing day my talents grew: I became a baker of cookies, a sewer of Halloween costumes extraordinaire. I could braid hair in the time most people wash their faces. And I could smile even when I didn't want to.

Where once my body had been my own to do with as I

pleased, it now belonged to someone else. It became: a breast to nourish at, a shoulder to cry on, a lap to sit and cuddle upon. My lips became the kissers of boo-boos, my hips the transporters of small, squirmy bundles. My feet were now used to walk the floor at all hours of the night, my arms became a cradle. I grew eyes in the back of my head, and my hearing became supersonic.

Once upon a time my name was Peggy. Then I became a mother and had as many aliases as a con man. I became— at various times—Mm, Ma-ma, Ma, Mommie, Mom, Mother, MOTHER! And for a brief period of mental vexa- tion, "Peg."

My mind, which used to flourish with egocentric thoughts, now became filled with irrational ideations: *What if she falls out of the crib? What if he chokes on his food? What if I do or say the wrong thing? How will I know I'm a good parent? How will I know I'm a bad one?*

My house, once so orderly and tidy became a disorderly jumble of toys and stuffed animals, dried peas and empty, strewn formula bottles; a carpet of clutter and chaos; a dwelling of disarray.

My heart, once only given to another, was now taken from me and filled to the brim, bursting with devotion and love.

I was a Mother. I was an icon. I'd done something no man had ever done, accomplished a feat so death defying and magical that many wouldn't even attempt it. I became a Mother. And in so doing, I became all that I was, all that I ever wished to be.

Peggy Jaeger

Sibling Rivalry

When my wife, Deeptee, came home from the hospital with our second baby, she hired Meena, a live-in nurse, to come along and help out for the first few weeks. Having read up on sibling rivalry, my wife watched our eighteen-month-old daughter, Chinmya, for signs of jealousy or insecurity. But Chinmya adored her little brother from the start. She loved to help Meena feed and bathe the baby. She even offered to share her toys.

Several weeks passed and the mother of my two children, convinced that Chinmya was suffering no ill effects, decided she could manage without a nurse. As she watched Meena walk out to her car that last day, she heard an unmistakable cry of distress.

"Meena!" yelled Chinmya, running after her. "You forgot your baby!"

Deeptee and Vikrum Seth

Loving Her Best

I hold my breath as the bailiff calls out, "Hear ye, hear ye. The case of Jessica and Sarah Shouse versus their mother, Deborah, for alleged favoritism and discriminatory parenting practices."

Behind me, the audience of mothers stirs and whispers. Across the aisle at the plaintiff's table, Jessica and Sarah are squabbling over who gets to drink first from the single glass.

"Jessica Shouse, come forward," the bailiff commands.

As Jessica stands, I see Sarah's look of outrage. I know what she's thinking: The oldest always gets to go first.

Jessica approaches the witness stand, carrying her notebook, glitter pen and a Sweet Valley High book.

"Tell us about the charges against your mother," the judge says, her voice patient and sweet.

Jessica tactfully removes a wad of pink gum, which she places on the edge of her book.

"On January 10, she gave HER (she points at Sarah with an accusatory finger), two cookies, and I got only one. On February 2, Sarah hit me first, and I got in trouble when I hit her back. In March, Sarah sat in the front seat 118 times, while I got the front only 112 and a half times."

"One hundred twelve and a half?" the judge asks.

"Sarah had a friend over, so she had to sit in the back-seat with her. That only counts for half." Jessica's voice grows louder. "SHE went to summer camp while I stayed home. SHE got special watercolors, and I had to use broken crayons."

"But you didn't want to go to camp! You don't even like art." The words pour out of me. "Jessica would rather read," I tell the judge. I turn to the audience. "I got her books instead of paints."

Empathetic murmuring arises from the women in the courtroom, punctuated by "Shhhh," and "Stop pinching." The judge bangs her gavel. "Please, Ms. Shouse, restrain yourself." Then she looks at my younger daughter.

"Sarah Shouse, will you now take the stand?"

Sarah clambers into the witness chair. The bailiff produces two phone books for her to sit on.

"What do you have to say, Sarah?" the judge asks.

"Jessica always gets to go first. She gets better clothes and more books and even though her room is messier than mine, she never, ever gets in trouble."

I bite my lip, trying hard to contain myself. I glance behind me. "Hang in there," one mom mouths. My hands are damp as I finally take the stand. All the mothers lean forward, straining to hear my every word.

"I have tried to be a good and fair mom. I blended my own organic baby food and bought only developmentally appropriate educational toys. I have offered my daughters coloring books, with and without lines. I have listened to them, played with them. I really did the best I could. I plead not guilty to the charges of Loving Her Best."

The courtroom buzzes.

"Now, for my expert witnesses," I say, my knees weak as I relinquish my seat.

My friend Jackie, a professor of literature at a local university, comes forward. "In grade school, my perfect sister made straight As while I made Cs." She fingers her Phi Beta Kappa necklace. "If I hadn't been so jealous of my sister, I never would have studied in high school and figured out how smart I am."

Next, Linda, a martial arts instructor, tells how her bully of a big sister caused her to take karate. She thought she was getting even, but she ended up getting a career.

Carol, gorgeous in a flowing designer frock, describes how her sister got all the clothes. "That inspired me to open up a chain of boutiques," Carol says.

The judge calls me over. "Are you implying that sibling rivalry has its up side?"

I nod.

"That's a relief," says the judge in a low tone. "My children are five and seven. Running this courtroom is a cinch compared to keeping things equal at home. . . ."

She bangs her gavel.

"Case dismissed."

"You started it!" Jessica's voice bangs into me, startling me out of my courtroom fantasy.

"Mom, she hit me. Plus, she's hogging the slide."

I open my eyes. Sarah sniffles back righteous tears as she snuggles next to me on the park bench. Only minutes ago, Jessica had patiently instructed Sarah on the art of pumping the swing. What happened?

"Let's go home girls, " I say wearily.

"It's my turn to sit in the front!" Sarah proclaims.

"No, it's mine."

"Girls," I make my voice stern, "come here right now."

For a moment, they are both still. Then Jessica reaches out and takes Sarah's hand. The sight of them, standing united, ready to stick together, fills me with a deep love. I watch them walk toward me, Sarah trying to match her sister's stride. As they get close, I hold out my arms. There is plenty of room for both inside.

Deborah Shouse

Motherhood 101

At a recent neighborhood get-together, I was easily the oldest female there. Every other woman had young kids who were racing around, playing, laughing, occasionally generating shrill sounds that made their mothers cringe with embarrassment. One mom ordered her son to settle down, then quickly apologized. I assured her that he was just being a normal kid and that I was actually enjoying all the commotion. She didn't buy it. I said that children grow up way too fast, and suddenly they are gone. I explained that my husband and I had an empty nest: Our "baby" is twenty-seven, our oldest is thirty-one.

She asked, and I told her a little about my job and a lot about my four children. I shared that all four of our fledglings had tested their wings and moved to other parts of the country, that it was really hard to have them so far away, but that it made us feel good to know they were happily living in places that they had chosen for school, career or other unique opportunities. Fortunately, we manage to see all of them, plus our granddaughters, about three times a year.

I asked my neighbor how she spends her days. Almost

apologetically, she stated that before she had children, she had an exciting professional career that kept her traveling all over North America, but that she was now a full-time homemaker, a "domestic engineer." She acknowledged that some days were tiring and monotonous, but stressed that it was mostly challenging and fun. She "couldn't imagine" not being home with her kids every day. I told her that I couldn't think of anything more important than raising a family. She seemed relieved that I didn't judge her negatively for being a stay-at-home mom. The truth is that I envied her immensely.

I had to fight off guilt over having had "latch-key kids." In fact, I felt like crying. Sometimes I miss our children terribly, and I'd give anything to recapture those wasted hours I spent working late in the office or those hours I spent in class instead of being at home with them.

That night I phoned "my baby." My voice cracked the second I heard him say hello. "Mom! What's the matter?" he asked.

"Nothing, honey," I lied. "I just miss you, I guess."

"I miss you, too, Mom," David answered, "but something else is going on. What's the matter?"

"I'm being silly," I confessed. "It's just that I saw all these young kids next door, and I wanted to tell you how sorry I am that I wasn't there when you got home from school every day. I'm sorry that I was gone at night sometimes too, when I had classes. I'd give anything to do it all over again and spend more time with you guys."

"Darn it, Mom. We *never* felt neglected! *Quality* of time is what counts. Some of my best memories are stuff we did together, even just sitting around talking. I can't think of any better mom I could have had, working or not! Never feel guilty! You did exactly what you needed to do."

Dave certainly let me have it. How glad I am that my kids feel comfortable enough to chew me out when I deserve it! I felt a million times better after we hung up. Dave's scolding would have been enough, but he obviously called his sister. Three days later, I received a priceless gift from Alyson in the mail. It was a typed paper that read:

Just a few of the wonderful things my mom taught me . . .

Support your kids' dreams, even if that means they move away
Rescue baby birds and squirrels
Love hearts, Ziggy, and teddy bears
Sing aloud, dance for joy, laugh with delight, smile big
Write
Learn to play music
Value fairness, kindness, honesty, and equality
Keep things in perspective
Surprise your kids with notes in their lunch boxes
Appreciate the simple things and know what really matters
Believe in yourself
You can achieve anything, no matter what the barriers
Help others less fortunate
Make pancakes in funny shapes
Grow and learn
Take family walks in the moonlight
Be sentimental
Drop everything to race outside and see a sunset
Be strong and independent
Look for the good in people and circumstances
Never feel guilty
Teach by example

Work to make a difference
Root for the underdog
Forgive
Siblings can be your best friends
Be loyal
Be silly
Take care of yourself
Be healthy
Treasure friends
Don't give up easily on commitments you make
Stay up late at night to talk with your kids even if
    you are tired
Feel lucky buying groceries
Stop to watch flocks
Cherish life—it is precious
Thank God for everything you have
Count and recount your blessings
Hug and say I love you a lot to the people you love
Put your family first

WOW! Did I teach my kids all *that*?

Karen L. Waldman with Alyson Powers

What I Want Most for You, My Child

My son,

You sit before me at the kitchen table laboring over your ABCs. Your five-year-old brow is puckered in concentration, your pink tongue peeks out of your mouth. As usual you are fully immersed in the moment.

Yesterday you followed a gaily colored butterfly as it flitted from bush to bush. The day before that you were beside yourself in excitement as you romped in a mud puddle.

For you, who have changed your father's and my life in ways you couldn't imagine, what do I want most, my child?

There are days when I want you to reach great heights and conquer the world. Cure a disease, my son, I whisper to myself; write an immortal book; cross some new frontier for humankind. *Ah, but you are being pushy and selfish,* says a little voice within me.

And then there are days when I merely want you to be wealthy and successful. I want you to live in mansions, drive luxury cars and have exotic vacations. *But that won't mean he'll be happy,* says that chiding voice again.

So when I sit down and think in earnest, I realize my dreams for you have little to do with fame or money or worldly success. As I write down my thoughts, prayers and wishes for you, I am in danger of getting as mushy as the last of the cereal in the bowl that you say "ugh" to. But I will go ahead anyway.

May you always have the joy in living, the sheer enjoyment in things humble and inconsequential, that you— like most small children—have now. As we grow older our shoulders sag, our eyes glaze over and we busy ourselves in things mundane and wretched. May your spirit never get jaded so that the beauty around you escapes you, that the ability to wonder, to marvel leaves you.

I wish for you the greatest gifts any person can have: good health and the love of family and friends. May the scourge of loneliness never be upon you. Find a good wife, set up house and family, and find solace there from the world and its troubles.

We live in a time beset by the winds of change: some of it exciting, some of it strange and bewildering. In this fast, ever-changing, sometimes surreal world of technology, I hope you find within yourself a sense of balance, a sense of who you are separate from the machines around you.

We like to think that the happy man is one who has everything. But maybe, my son, the truly happy person is someone who is liberated from that feeling of "want, want, want," which gnaws at one's soul. I know this is a tall order, but I hope you won't end up basing your happiness upon owning every gizmo and bauble on the market.

I am confident that you will find your place in this world. As you grow older, I hope that you will discover that there are things more precious than riches: to be able to laugh with a carefree heart, to sleep with an untroubled conscience, to have the thrill of achievement coursing through your veins. Hold onto these things greedily; never let them go. May you always stand tall and true and triumphant. No one else needs to know; no one else needs to applaud.

Most of all, may your world always be the iridescent bubble it is for you now.

You came into this world, and I thought I could mold you, shape you, teach you. Little did I know that I would be taught some important lessons about life as well. You jump out of bed every morning, my angel, and the day seems to stretch out before you with magical possibilities. You have no time to ponder over yesterday's tearful tantrum, or fret about tomorrow's dental appointment. Isn't there a lesson in this for me, I wonder, to celebrate the here-and-now, instead of constantly looking over my shoulder at yesterday's follies, or craning my neck toward tomorrow's troubles?

I have knelt down beside you and tried to look out at the world through your shiny, ever-curious eyes. And I have learned that life is not a nonstop treadmill to be crammed with productive activities every minute of the day, but a colorful carousel to be savored and enjoyed with all the senses. Sometimes the laundry, the to-do list, the e-mail can wait. I've realized it is all right to waste a little time, to lie on your back on the grass on a spring day and look up at the white cotton-candy clouds wafting in the blue sky. It's all right to lie on your stomach side by side with your child and look down an air vent in your kitchen and imagine the weird monsters lurking down below.

You are and will always be my most precious treasure, my biggest achievement and my proudest legacy.

Saritha Prabhu

And What Do You Do?

Being a full-time mother is one of the highest salaried jobs . . . since the payment is pure love.

Mildred B. Vermont

To me, *housewife* is as appealing a title as *septic-tank cleaner*. Mention either at a cocktail party, and suddenly no one wants to stand near you. *Housewife* might satisfy the IRS because it explains in one word your negative cash flow. But it doesn't describe what I do every day, seven days a week with no sick days, holidays and at times no bathroom breaks.

In previous years, my accountant had listed my occupation on my tax return as *writer*. But between last year's preterm labor (five weeks on the couch) and colic (four months wishing I could put my wailing baby down and sit on the couch), I barely had the time and energy to write a grocery list, let alone something salable. So, I gave up writing to stay home and care for my two young sons. I didn't choose the title for the job.

I could call myself a domestic engineer, like my

sister-in-law did. But if I knew anything about engineering, I'd be able to open and close the playpen without stifling more four-letter words than you hear in an episode of "The Sopranos."

Domestic engineer is far too supercilious a title. Mention it at your husband's office holiday party, and people might ask where you got your degree. After a few eggnogs, you might reply, Episiotomy U. or Postpartum State. The next day at your "office," your responses won't seem as clever—except to your mother, who holds master's degrees from those institutions.

Stay-at-home mom sounds benign enough until you've spent three straight rainy days trapped inside with a two-year-old who thinks Nancy Reagan coined "Just Say No" for him, and a one-year-old who chews on shoes—including the pair you're wearing. Then you'd realize that *stay-at-home mom* is an oxymoron.

A stay-at-home mom stays home only when Dad drags the kids to the Home Depot (thank God) or when the governor declares a state of emergency. Otherwise, she's at a Moms-and-Tots meeting, the supermarket or the mall, dropping quarter after quarter into the Batmobile ride.

Full-time mom is another misnomer, because it implies that working mothers are part-time mothers, and that's just not true. Anyone whose Day-Timer reads "Marketing report due," "Pediatrician appointment" and "Make eighteen cupcakes for preschool party" on the same page is not only working full-time at motherhood, she's working overtime.

Besides, "full-time" doesn't even begin to cover how much time I spend at my job. Most full-time workers put in forty to fifty hours a week. I put that in by Wednesday. In my job, I'm on call around the clock. Add family vacations, where I bring my work with me on a very, very long car ride, and full-time becomes all-the-time.

Homemaker is a quaint title, but inappropriate. I haven't made any homes, though I've seen enough construction videos (thanks to my sons) that I probably could build a decent cabin—or at least a nice shed where I could hide. But really, I'm not making a house so much as I'm trying to keep my toddlers from tearing ours down.

In some ways, *homemaker* sounds worse than *housewife*. To me, a homemaker does all the same things as a housewife, but with a warm smile and a meatloaf she whipped up between craft projects and Christmas carols. She certainly doesn't have a toddler throwing a tantrum on the kitchen floor because she won't let him have animal crackers for dinner. A homemaker? By five o'clock, I'm too exhausted to make dinner, let alone a home.

I wish I could think of a better title for the toughest job I've ever had. But no matter what I come up with, my accountant will likely just put *housewife* on my tax returns anyway. And the Social Security Administration will keep sending me reports with zeros on it. Perhaps that's just how society values what I do.

But the next time someone asks, "And what do you do?" I'll just say that I do what my mother did, and her mother did. I'll say it's such a hard job, my husband wouldn't want to do it, and my father wouldn't know how. I'll say my kids are very proud of what I do. And they should know, because they come to work with me every day. And then I'll go chat with the septic-tank cleaner.

Jennifer Singer

The Littlest Girl Scout

I admit it. I'm not cut out to be a soccer mom.

I'm not class mom material, either.

I don't bake homemade chocolate chip cookies. I don't even boil water. In fact, when my daughter, Alexa, was in kindergarten, as part of a "Why I Love My Mommy" Mother's Day project, her teacher asked her to name her "favorite dish" that Mom cooks.

"I don't have one," she said.

"Oh sweetheart, there must be something your mother cooks that you love. A special dinner? Your favorite dessert?"

"My mommy doesn't cook."

"She must make *something*," her increasingly desperate teacher insisted. "Jell-O?"

After lengthy consideration, my daughter listed "cereal."

So it was with much trepidation that I recently learned Alexa wanted to be a Brownie.

I am a mom who is great at making up stories, singing off-key songs at bedtime and remembering the names of every Pokemon. But with three kids, a dog, a rabbit, a parrot and a veritable aviary of finches, life in our household is disorganized at best. Dinner is a haphazard affair, clothes always need ironing and shirts missing buttons are given safety pins in their stead. I flunked home economics in high school. Clearly, I did not have the makings of a Brownie-badge-earning mom.

"Are you sure?" I asked, trying to mask my dread. Her delighted "yes" sealed my fate.

I made it through the camping trip, even through crafts—though our potholders were decidedly ragged-looking. Then came the year's highlight: the cookie sale. Mentally, I counted my immediate family. I figured they were good for about ten boxes. I'd buy a few as well. That brought Alexa to a total of fifteen boxes or so—not too shabby.

Her dad picked her up after the cookie sale meeting. Horrified, I watched as they struggled through the door with six CASES of cookies. *Cases!*

After coming to, I managed to sputter, "What's all this?"

"Her cookies," my husband answered. "Each girl is assigned six cases to sell."

"But what if we can't sell all these?"

"We bring them back," he said. "No big deal."

"Oh no, Mommy!" Alexa cried out. "We have to sell them all. We just have to! The troop will make fun of me if I don't. One of the other Brownies told me that last year, not one girl brought back any cookies."

Apparently, we were going to be hitting up Grandma for a lot more than the four boxes I had mentally sold to her.

After ten days of ferocious selling, we had managed to sell a case and a half. Cookies were stacked in my home office from floor to ceiling—or at least that's how I remember it. I dreamed at night of Thin Mints chasing me down dark alleys.

After four more days of selling, we still had four cases of cookies.

Then came one of those days that happen to moms like me—moms whose kids never have matching socks and whose kids' toothbrushes end up being chewed by the dog or falling into the toilet.

On that particular day, the dog jumped in the lake after a duck. The duck escaped, but my dog resembled the Creature from the Black Lagoon. One dog bath, one muddy mom and thirteen towels later, the dog was clean. But my two-year-old son had been suspiciously quiet during the whole ordeal. In fact, all the hairs on the back of my neck were standing on end. Even more than kitchen pot-banging, TV blaring and loud bickering, all moms dread "the silence."

You know ... *that* silence.

"Alexa," I said, emerging from the bathroom, mud clinging to my hair, "where's your brother?"

"I dunno."

I went tearing through the house. Was he coloring on my bedroom walls again? No.

I raced to the kitchen. Spilling cereal on the floor? No.

He must be in his room. Was he climbing on top of his dresser pretending to be Superman again? Not there.

"Nicholas!" I called out. Then, fearing my computer keyboard was being covered in apple juice, I ran to my office.

There sat Nicholas.

Surrounded by sixty-one opened boxes of Girl Scout cookies.

In fact, he had the cellophane for the next pack in his teeth, attempting to bust open another box. Thin Mints, Peanut Butter Buddies and Shortbread Dreams, or whatever the heck they're called, were splayed from one end of the room to the other. Cookies were crushed beneath his chubby little feet, and crumbs covered his rosy cheeks.

"Cookies!" he squealed.

As I wrote out a check for over $250 dollars worth of Girl Scout cookies, I came to the realization that I am most definitely *not* a Brownie mom.

But my *son*? He's the hero of Troop 408.

Erica Orloff

Lost and Found

This is how it begins: One night in early September, while watching TV, you decide to make some popcorn. So you go into your kitchen to dig out the old popcorn machine, but it's nowhere to be found.

Then, a week or so later, you feel a chill in the air and decide it's time to get out the portable space heater. But after an hour or two of searching you turn up nothing. Nada. Zilch. Zero.

The pace begins to quicken.

Over the next fortnight, you search for, and fail to find, such items as your hair dryer, Mr. Coffee machine, tea kettle, kitchen shears, assorted luggage, extra-large bath towels, hair mousse, Chinese wok, sewing kit, desk lamp, portable phone, electric blanket, transistor radio and electric blender.

As the mystery deepens—and the list of missing items grows—all kinds of scenarios run through your head. A cat burglar. Early senility. A friend who borrowed your luggage. A blanket deposited at the cleaners. The phone left at the beach house.

Then, before you know it, it's the middle of October—the

time when parents of college freshmen traditionally visit their kids on campus—and suddenly the Mystery of the Missing Household Items is solved: They are all residing in a room on a distant college campus—the one occupied by your college-age son or daughter.

Why is it, I wonder, that nobody warns parents that when your kids go away to college, so do all your small appliances?

And why is it that none of the child experts—not even Dr. T. Berry Brazelton—sees fit to include this developmental phase in their books on raising children: "At approximately the age of eighteen, the average, college-bound teenager goes through a period of relocating household appliances. A general rule of thumb is that after each visit home, the student takes at least four additional appliances and/or household items back to college."

My own first encounter with this developmental phenomenon occurred while walking across a campus on freshmen parents' weekend. From a distance, I spotted my son. I recognized him, in fact, by the sweater he was wearing—an intricately patterned ski sweater I purchased for him in Norway.

However, upon closer inspection, I confirmed that while it was, indeed, the aforementioned sweater, it was not my son.

"He lent it to me," said the young man who was not my son. He then directed me to my son's dormitory.

And what a pleasant surprise it was, upon arriving at the entry to my son's room, to be greeted by an old familiar friend—the "Welcome" mat that had disappeared from my very own front door just a month before.

Inside, I was made to feel equally at home. There, reclining among the batik-covered pillows from my den, I sipped a pineapple frappe from my blender and marveled at how many wonderful patterns could be formed just by stacking up assorted pieces of my luggage in an interesting way.

And the climate control in the room was excellent. My space heater going full blast in the bathroom produced, I thought, just the right temperature, even on a day when it was eighty-five degrees outside. Another plus about the bathroom was that I got to use my own towels again—the monogrammed ones that had been given to me as a wedding gift.

I also enjoyed seeing my white, pearlized wastebasket and matching soap dish again. I'd forgotten how attractive they were.

To my surprise, I felt equally at home in the room across the hall. Invited there by my son's friend, I noted how attractive my desk lamp looked sitting next to my portable phone. And what good reception my radio got, even up here in the hills of the Berkshires.

From there, it was a movable feast over to a room occupied by another of my son's friends. The popcorn made in my popper never tasted better, and I must say that my old patchwork quilt looked mighty good thrown across the back of his friend's futon.

In fact, I was so impressed with this recycling of household goods that at Thanksgiving I scarcely minded when the sleds disappeared from the garage, or after Christmas break the disappearance of an Edward Hopper poster, a small side table and a bedside reading lamp.

At spring break I minded even less when a number of sheets, pillowcases and pillows—along with a small desk chair—vanished. Actually, the house was beginning to look more spacious, less cluttered, somehow.

What I did mind, however, was that awful day at the end of the school year when the son arrived home with a U-Haul trailer. I think you know what was inside.

Alice Steinbach

"Sorry. I thought you were ready
to be kicked out of the nest."

A Long Day at the Track

Time is never more relative than when stretched across the full span of childhood. When my sons were toddlers, sticky and close, omnipresent and ever needy, my days were measured out in two-hour intervals between meals and naps and baths and stories. As our lives moved forward in these minute increments, I did not think it possible they would one day be leaving home "before you know it," as innumerable friends told me. After serving them some twenty thousand meals, lowering the toilet seat thousands of times, issuing countless reminders that cars need oil to run, how could a mother so centrally engaged in their growth not know they were growing up?

Can a woman really forget cooking two and a half tons of macaroni and cheese? Can she forget playing solitaire until dawn on snowy nights, waiting for the sound of tires crunching into the driveway? Can a mother really not notice that her former baby's life has changed completely when he receives, among his high-school graduation gifts, a pair of purple silk boxer shorts and a scented card written in a dainty script? No, I think a mother always knows these small incidents are adding up to Something Big. We just understand, like the fans who come faithfully to the Indy 500 every year, that it's going to be a long day.

Lurching and stalling through the early years, time moved slowly as the rookie drivers tested their limits, learned to take the curves and conferred with their pit crews. I got used to the whining noises and oily fumes, paying only half-attention through each repetitive cycle until a warning flag or frightening accident snapped my mind back on track. Then, in the riveting final laps, time suddenly accelerated. Fixed solely on the finish line, convinced they knew all they needed to know, my sons put the pedal to the metal and ignored any further signals from the pit. They barely stopped home long enough to refuel with a favorite pot roast.

While they forged ahead with a speed that bordered on recklessness, I found myself falling back in time, seized with a ferocious desire to remember everything about this long day at the track. As twenty years of effort compressed in those final laps, I felt the stirring excitement and lumpy throat I often get in movie theaters. Living with two jocks has undoubtedly had a profound influence on my imagination, because the musical score that kept playing in my head as I watched them fling themselves into the world was not Mozart's Clarinet Concerto or Pachelbel's Canon, but the theme song from *Rocky*. I know I should be far beyond the moist, sentimental lumpiness of motherhood by now. But as it turns out, I'm not.

In those months before Ryan and Darren left home, a familiar gesture or facial expression would trigger a sudden onslaught of memories, I would see the faces and hear the voices of all the children in the family album, all the little guys who used to pepper my life but who have now disappeared. Whenever I caught a certain provocative smile, a long-suffering frown, I would be suddenly infused with a peculiar clairvoyance. I would travel back and forth in time, remembering the first time that look appeared, knowing how often it would return to delight or haunt me. I was swamped by one of these mind floods in a shoe store last August, as Darren tried on a pair of loafers in a size that could have comfortably fit both of my feet in one shoe. I remembered the first time I saw those astonishing appendages eighteen years earlier then attached to the smallest, most fragile human legs imaginable. Once more, I was standing woozily next to his crib in the preemie intensive-care nursery, leaning against his incubator for support as I watched his labored breathing. This impatient son, who had crashed into being two months before his due date—very nearly killing us both—lay unconscious amidst his tangle of wires and tubes while I tried to suppress fears about underdeveloped lungs and heart muscles.

He was tininess itself, his delicate pink form stretched nakedly under sunlamps to cure his jaundice, his skinny limbs covered with dark, prenatal fuzz—cilia hair for the amniotic sea he was still supposed to be in. I watched him take a wet gulp of air and then, suddenly, stop breathing entirely. My own throat seized as the line on his heart monitor flattened. The nurse jumped up when she heard the alarm and rushed to his incubator, flicking his tiny heel a few times until the rhythmic beeps of his heart returned again.

"Apnea," she said, sighing with relief. "They get so tired they forget to breathe." She then went back to her paperwork at the nursing station, little Darren Oliver went back to sleep, and I worried about brain damage for the next five years.

Darren's traumatic birth was my first encounter with the reality that motherhood was not, and would never be, entirely under my control.

The young rookies eventually morphed into grown men, putting thousands of laps behind us. The repetitious and monotonous routines of our past *do* accrue into Something Big, with time and patience and a whole lot of luck.

Mary Kay Blakely

The Kiddie Garden

It was a major event, moving into our first house, a cracker-box rambler in the suburbs south of Minneapolis. What an adventure to look out our very own living room window at our very own driveway, our very own front yard with lush green grass—a heady experience for a young married couple expecting their first child. What a change from the apartment living we were used to.

The back yard had not yet been sodded, but I assumed the builder would be coming soon to finish the landscaping. Wrong. So excited about moving into my new house, I neglected to read the fine print where the builder contracted to sod only the front, leaving the back yard full of weeds and clumps of dirt.

In late October, we moved in, one month before our first son made his appearance during a Thanksgiving Day snowstorm. The backyard dirt disappeared under a foot of snow, and the frozen chunks looked like puffy marshmallows in a fairytale landscape.

When spring came, the snow melted, and little by little, as the budget permitted, we bought rolls of sod and covered the back yard area that had become a mud hole when it rained and a dust bowl when it didn't. The money ran out before the yard did, and we never did finish the last ten foot strip running across the back of the lot.

No matter. It would be a perfect place for my very own garden, a place to get on my knees and commune with God while I planted stunning arrays of beautiful flowers—a far cry from the pathetic little pansy plots in our apartment window box.

Alas, being a city kid with a mother whose garden belonged to her alone, I knew nothing about growing flowers like those pictured in seed catalogs. I couldn't even tell the flowers from the weeds. Finally, I decided if it looked healthy, prosperous and happy to be there, it must be a weed.

In time, having a back yard full of weeds and just a few struggling petunias seemed not so important as enthusiasm slipped away and one son was joined by another. Two little boys, growing too fast out of babyhood into toddler-hood, then into noisy, tumbleweed boyhood.

My garden turned into a playground—for all the kids in the neighborhood; Timmy from up the street, Eddie and Debbie from across the back yard, Mark, Carol and Gary from the house on the corner, plus others who just wandered in. We dubbed it the "Kiddie Garden," the only place, it seemed, where kids could dig holes, build play houses and make noise—a place to fool around, get dirty and just be kids.

When I looked out the kitchen window at my "garden" I never did see the panorama of flowers I envisioned when we first moved in. I saw instead, perpetual motion from dirt streaked faces peering out over the tops of T Shirts, pre-school engineers building roads and bridges for their toy trucks. I saw mounded dirt pile forts, and pint-sized warriors waging noisy battles back and forth, trying to capture enemy flags, (sticks in the ground with rags tied at

the top.) There were only two rules in the kiddie garden—
all holes had to be filled back up by the end of the day, and
no fighting. Anyone who couldn't get along had to go
home.

In the winter, the "garden" was flooded and those same
warriors and hole diggers in pillow-puff snowsuits, tried
out their single-runner skates in the safety of the small ice
patch before they attempted to handle the crowded public rinks.

In time, we outgrew the small house on Oakland
Avenue and life moved on. The neighborhood kids grew
up and became adults, making their own way in the world
with their own kids. Today, I see yesterday's children
scurrying non-stop to keep up with the programs
designed to give them "quality time" with *their* children,
and I often wonder if they look back on the days we
laughingly said we were growing the best crops in the
neighborhood—sticky faces, dirty knees and laughing
kids—all playing and thriving in the place we called the
"Kiddie Garden."

Jacklyn Lee Lindstrom

Anniversary Celebration

Every year, a few weeks before our anniversary, I begin looking at my husband and feeling hopelessly nostalgic. I can't help but miss the people we once were—passionate, carefree, romantic—people who couldn't keep their hands off each other. We used to stay up all night just to see the sunrise. We had midnight picnics in the park, and I would wear sexy lingerie on a regular basis.

But that was before three children (ages ten, seven and two). It was before school-board meetings and budget planning, not to mention diaper disasters. Now, a few weeks before our anniversary, I'm feeling the need to rekindle the passion of days gone by (at least for one night). I plan a romantic anniversary dinner with candles, wine, music, grown-up food and no children. I really wanted to give the evening a special touch, but staying up to see the sunrise won't work when you'll be spending the next twelve to fourteen hours chasing a two-year-old. A midnight picnic sounds too dangerous, considering creeps now overrun the park after dark. I opt instead to cap our evening off with lingerie.

After securing a babysitter I'm encouraged and head to

my long-abandoned lingerie drawer. Looking at the ensembles that practically scream sex, I am sure any of these hot little numbers will more than rekindle passion, and I wonder why I ever abandoned them in the first place. I can hardly wait to try them on, and in this spirit I decide my daughter could use an early nap today, leaving me two hours free to contrive an outfit before my boys arrive home from school.

Forty-five minutes and several stories later, my daughter is asleep, and I all but run to the lingerie drawer. My first choice is an emerald and black Wonderbra. I hook the hook and pull the straps over my shoulders, almost giddy with anticipation. Then I look in the mirror and to my utter horror, the full effects of breastfeeding Baby No. 3 are realized as this wonder creation pushes my cleavage to the center of my chest, giving me the appearance of a Cyclops, if you get my drift. The only real wonder is that I can breathe with everything all squeezed together.

Feeling disappointed but not defeated, I remove the Wonderbra and reach for stockings and garters, only to be disappointed again—this time because of a weird rubber-band-around-a-sausage effect I won't even bother to explain.

My little lingerie adventure continues for about thirty minutes, when I realize that lack of oxygen and circulation isn't going to rekindle anything. I slowly close the lingerie drawer and resolve to find another way to zap some wild passion into our marriage.

Over the next few days, I watch my husband closely, trying to determine the best way to top off our anniversary celebration. I see him with our children, reading stories to our two-year-old, helping with homework, coaching a basketball team of six- and seven-year-olds, and the million other daily parental duties that don't exactly scream romance. But then I look closer, and I see us sharing good morning hugs, holding hands at a ball game and always sharing good-bye kisses before work, and I realize that although it's not wild with reckless abandon, we still can't keep our hands off each other. In our own quiet, comfortable way, we are passionate, but now we know passion is more a state of mind than a state of undress.

So this year on our anniversary, as I sit across the candlelit dinner from my husband, I'll know it's okay to feel a little loss for the people we once were, as long as we remember to celebrate the people we've become.

Renee Mayhew

Near Misses and Good-Night Kisses

The art of being happy lies in the power of extracting happiness from common things.

Henry Ward Beecher

It had been one of those mornings—the kind that prompts mothers to think about their lives prior to motherhood.

My six-year-old son had mixed pancake batter in the blender—without the lid—leaving dribbles of Aunt Jemima trickling down cupboards, curtains, walls and stove. As I watched the goo quickly harden into a cement-like substance, I learned that our hamster, Houdini, had once again escaped from his cage.

"Bye, Mom," my boy called as he dashed out the door en route to the school bus. "And, oh, Mom, you're supposed to bring three dozen brownies to Scouts after school tonight."

I thought more desperately about my life before motherhood. At first the memory was so foggy, I nearly concluded that parenthood had mercifully numbed that part of the brain responsible for recalling one's past, carefree life. But then slowly, it began to come back. I recalled sleeping in on Saturday mornings, spontaneous trips to the mall and dining at the kinds of restaurants where soft drinks don't have plastic lids. I dimly remembered a quiet, orderly house and a sparkling kitchen with nary a trace of pancake batter anywhere.

My husband broke my reverie on his way to the garage. He must have been reading my addled mind, for he whispered, "Just think what you would have missed."

"Missed?" I scoffed, refocusing on my kitchen walls. "Hah!"

Yet once alone in the house, I reluctantly pondered what I might have missed, but for the pitter-patter of little sneakers. Cynically, I grumbled that I would have—and gladly—missed a number of sleepless nights and dirty diapers and chicken pox.

Then I smiled in spite of myself, remembering a plump, dozing baby curled in my arms. The memory made me think anew.

I realized I would have missed that sweet, toothless grin and the tiny dimpled fingers clenched earnestly around my own. I would have missed the first, halting "Mama" and the "Mommies" and "Moms" that have followed a thousand times over.

I might never have applauded a successful encounter with the potty, nor decorated my refrigerator with fledgling works of art, nor become a marathon swing pusher.

I certainly would have missed meeting Mr. Rogers, Bert and Ernie, and Kermit and the gang—all good, true friends. I might never have roasted marshmallows in the fireplace to the tune of irrepressible giggles, or felt a small body pressed next to mine during a thunderstorm.

I would have missed countless bedtime stories, good-night hugs and kisses and the nightly litany of "God blesses" that included the crickets under the front porch.

I never would have mourned a fish named Harold, nor housed a birds' nest collection, nor spent a near lifetime assembling a super-galactic command center.

The birthday parties, the trips to the zoo, the sand pies, the dashes through the sprinkler and the walks around the block—I would have missed them all.

I never would have known my parents as grandparents. I would have missed my dad baiting a fishhook with a "Willy Worm," as wondrous brown eyes widened to saucers. I would have missed my mom rocking her "sugar-plum" and singing his favorite country-western tune. There's a deeper love and appreciation for my own parents that I might never have felt had I not been a parent myself.

I would have missed knowing my husband as a father. I would never have witnessed that serene, reflective man transformed into a bucking bronco or riding the Tilt-a-Whirl for the sixth straight time with a curly head tucked securely in the crook of his arm. I might not have learned what it means to truly look up to another—to see a little boy who unknowingly adores his father so much that he walks like him and talks like him and even cocks his head in just the same way.

I wouldn't have shared my child's fears and apprehensions and felt them more poignantly than my own, nor regaled in his joys and successes, nor prayed for his health. I would have dearly missed experiencing the unconditional love a mother has for a child.

And, if the truth be known, I would have missed reliving the magic moments of childhood through my own child's eyes: the visits to Santa and hunting for Easter eggs, trick-or-treating, lighting sparklers and summertime stops for a double-dip cone.

I would have especially missed the laughter—the fresh,

young child's laughter that bounces off the walls and rolls down the stairs, filling a house with life and warmth. It's an infectious kind of laughter, perhaps the glue that keeps a family close.

Suddenly, I laughed out loud myself as the truant Houdini waddled out from under a chair and wiggled his nose at me. I laughed until tears dampened my cheeks, thankful that I hadn't missed a single moment of motherhood.

Sally Nalbor

READER/CUSTOMER CARE SURVEY

We care about your opinions! Please take a moment to fill out our online Reader Survey at **http://survey.hcibooks.com**.
As a **"THANK YOU"** you will receive a **VALUABLE INSTANT COUPON** towards future book purchases
as well as a **SPECIAL GIFT** available only online! Or, you may mail this card back to us.

(PLEASE PRINT IN ALL CAPS)

First Name _____ MI. _____ Last Name _____

Address _____

State _____ Zip _____ Email _____ City _____

1. Gender
□ Female □ Male

2. Age
□ 8 or younger
□ 9-12   □ 13-16
□ 17-20   □ 21-30
□ 31+

3. Did you receive this book as a gift?
□ Yes   □ No

4. Annual Household Income
□ under $25,000
□ $25,000 - $34,999
□ $35,000 - $49,999
□ $50,000 - $74,999
□ over $75,000

5. What are the ages of the children living in your house?
□ 0 - 14   □ 15+

6. Marital Status
□ Single
□ Married
□ Divorced
□ Widowed

7. How did you find out about the book?
(please choose one)
□ Recommendation
□ Store Display
□ Online
□ Catalog/Mailing
□ Interview/Review

8. Where do you usually buy books?
(please choose one)
□ Bookstore
□ Online
□ Book Club/Mail Order
□ Price Club (Sam's Club, Costco's, etc.)
□ Retail Store (Target, Wal-Mart, etc.)

9. What subject do you enjoy reading about the most?
(please choose one)
□ Parenting/Family
□ Relationships
□ Recovery/Addictions
□ Health/Nutrition
□ Christianity
□ Spirituality/Inspiration
□ Business Self-help
□ Women's Issues
□ Sports

10. What attracts you most to a book?
(please choose one)
□ Title
□ Cover Design
□ Author
□ Content

FOLD HERE

Do you have your own Chicken Soup story
that you would like to send us?
Please submit at: **www.chickensoup.com**

Comments

4

BECOMING
A MOTHER

The moment a child is born, the mother is also born. She never existed before. The woman existed, but the mother, never. A mother is something absolutely new.

Rajneesh

Replicas

A mother understands what a child does not say.

Jewish Proverb

After one last agonizing push, my baby is here. All I can see are bright red, squirming legs and feet as one doctor passes her to the next, and she disappears amongst the teal green clothing of the medical personnel.

I try to see what is happening over on that table under the light, but it is impossible from my angle. But my mother is here.

"Oh, she's beautiful!" she tells me, and grabs my hand.

I believe my husband is in shock. He stands behind the nurses and doctor staring in disbelief at our little creation.

Seconds later, a bundled up little person is placed in my arms. And now, for the first time, I look into the face of my daughter, a perfect, innocent human being who has never been exposed to hate, sorrow or cruelty. To my surprise, she isn't crying, but is making a sound somewhere between a hum and a coo. Whatever it is, it sounds beautiful to me. Her eyes are dark and round—she has my eyes!

As my eyes meet the tiny replicas of my own, "Oh my gosh" are the only words I can mutter before I begin to cry.

She looks like an angel. A tear drops from the tip of my nose and lands on her bright pink cheek. She blinks.

"Sorry," I whisper as I wipe my tear from her cheek.

Her skin is so soft; it feels like velvet. Her hair is tinged with blood and looks dark from the wetness.

Caught up in this serene moment, I have forgotten my husband and mother at my side. They both have tears in their eyes.

I look at my husband and say, "This is our baby."

He kisses my forehead.

My attention is once again directed solely to this miracle in my arms and the rest of the world disappears again. Her eyes are looking about now, and her tiny lips are slightly moving as if she is trying to tell me a secret. Her little nose is covered with tiny white bumps that look as if God carefully placed them there. A little hand emerges from the white blanket. It is a bit purple and oh so tiny. With my index finger, I stroke her palm. She grasps my finger and holds on tight. My heart melts. She looks at me again.

"Hi," I say, with a big smile.

"Honey, we've got to run a few tests and give her a bath. I'll bring her right back," a nurse says out of nowhere.

"Okay," I say with a sigh.

I look back down at my daughter and say, "I love you, Summer."

The nurse carefully takes her out of my arms. As she is leaving the room, I watch the blanket move from the wiggling of my baby's feet.

Minutes later, my mother and I are alone in the room. She

hugs me all at once, and I notice she has tears in her eyes.

"There is no love like the love you have for your child," she says, looking into my eyes, replicas of her own.

"I know," I say, and smile.

Melissa Arnold Hill

Pink and Blue Makes . . . Green?

It's come to my attention that there are two types of pregnant people in this world: those who find out the gender of their child as soon as they can and go around calling their stomach "Tommy" or "Jennifer" for the next nine months; and those who refuse to find out the gender of their child one nanosecond before the actual birth, no matter what.

Let me just stop right here a minute and say that I, in no way, advocate one choice over the other. I firmly believe it's a personal choice that should be left to the parents.

But, that said, what I don't understand is why the very same people who refuse to look at the sonogram screen in the doctor's office, are perfectly fine with relying on old wives' tales to predict their baby's gender.

Take, for instance, my friend Linda, who tried to find out what she was having by twirling a needle on a string over her stomach. "It's a girl," she announced gleefully over the phone. "The needle spun in circles."

She was so sure, in fact, that she painted the nursery pink and stenciled ballerina bunnies on the walls. But, as luck would have it, when she tried it again two months later, the needle moved in a straight line, mostly between the refrigerator and television set. And everyone knows what *that* means.

But that's not all. Once, when my friend Julie was pregnant with her second child, she heard she could tell what she was having if there was a white line above her top lip. "Can you come over," she said frantically over the phone, "I think I have a lip line. But I can't tell if it's really a line-line or a pale wrinkle or a milk mustache left over from the bowl of cereal I ate for breakfast."

The big drawback to this method was that, once we determined that it was, indeed, a bona fide line-line, we had absolutely no idea if that meant she was having a girl or a boy.

And, oh all right, then there was the time I tried the Chinese lunar calendar method. But just for the record I want you to know it's a highly respected system based on a complicated numerical combination of the father's birth year, lucky elements, planetary rotation and the number of his favorite local take-out place. (But I could be wrong about this last one.)

But what I didn't see coming was that to get an accurate result you need to be fairly good at math. So, after spending hours adding and subtracting cycle scores and percentages and all that, I came out with a bizarre triple negative number that's only been seen on university entrance exams and certain Wall Street corporate earning reports.

But, that's just the kind of answer I usually get whenever I try to walk on the mystical side of life.

The other day my friend Linda, who's now six months pregnant, said to me over coffee, "I've tried everything. According to the needle test I'm having a boy, the lunar calendar says I'm having a girl, the heartbeat test falls somewhere between a boy and a girl, and the Drano test doesn't say anything at all, but it smells really, really bad," she sighed. "I don't know what to believe anymore."

"Then why don't you save yourself the trouble and just ask the doctor?" I asked.

"What?" she said. "And spoil the mystery? Every parent knows that the gender of your child is the one greatest mystery in the world. Why would I want to go and ruin it?"

Granted I could've mentioned that she was a person who had just mixed urine with Drano to see if it would make green.

But instead, I said simply, "You're right."

With pregnant women, sometimes that's the best way.

Debbie Farmer

Outpouring of Love

It was 8 P.M. and cold. The rain, undecided whether to turn to snow, came down in sheets. It didn't matter to us. Three cars filled with family found their way to the Denver airport to meet the plane that was bringing the most precious of all cargoes—a ten-month-old baby boy.

My daughter Katy and her husband, Don, were adopting this boy, who was coming almost ten thousand miles from his home in the little country of Latvia. The infant had lived every day of his young life on his back in a crib in an orphanage along with 199 other children. He had never even been outside.

The entire family stood at the end of the ramp leading from the plane to the airport, expectant, awed and barely breathing—waiting for a first glance of this child. As passengers began coming off the plane, a small crowd gathered around us. No one in the waiting group spoke. Every eye was damp. The emotion was almost visible. One of the flight attendants handed us a congratulatory bottle of wine. Even passersby, feeling the electricity, stopped, asked and then stayed to watch.

When finally (they were actually the last ones off the

plane) the woman carrying our baby turned the corner and started up the ramp to us, Katy could not contain herself another instant. She started running toward them crying openly, her arms outstretched, aching to hold her baby boy for the first time. Cradling him, she started back up the ramp. Don, with their other adopted child, a two-year-old girl, started running to meet them; he too crying. And when the four of them stepped inside the airport where all of us were standing; it was as if they had stepped into a warm and soft cocoon filled and overflowing with emotion and love. Everyone was hugging them, and then each other. Overwhelmed by the power of the scene, no longer was anyone a stranger, but then, love is like that.

I stood slightly to one side of the hubbub, so I could really "see" it. This poor little boy, so far from home, was hearing no familiar words. Even his name had been changed. He saw no familiar faces. He had been traveling for over twenty-four hours straight and seemed completely dazed. He was being passed from person to person, each one needing to touch him to believe he was real.

I looked closely at him. He had skin the color of chalk, his every rib was showing, and his nose was running. I reached over and found his forehead was warm to the touch. Clearly, he was ill.

I also noticed he couldn't hold his head up by himself or even sit alone, signs that his development was way behind. Plus, he did not respond to noise. Could he be deaf?

At that moment I knew we probably had saved his life. I also realized with a rush of feeling that I would guard him, nurture him and love him with every fiber of my being. Katy was a wonderful mother, and I would be right behind her all the way.

As we finally left the airport for home, I crawled into the backseat of the car and sat between the two car seats full of miracles. Now there were two lives dependent on this family for all things. All the way home I had one hand on him and the other hand on her. I think I was praying.

The next morning we took the baby, who had been named Zachary, to the doctor. She found that Zachary had serious infections in both ears, which had apparently never been treated. She told us that our baby would hear once the infections cleared. The doctor went on to talk about solid foods (Zachary had never had any) and his need for exercise. Sending us home with medicines to help him, she assured us he would "catch up," with care.

And he did, as we watched in amazement! In one short week this child held his head erect, sat alone, then flipped over and crawled on hands and knees. A few weeks later, he reached the stairs, climbed up two of them, then grabbed the rail and, pulling himself to a standing position, just stood there looking at his new mom in triumph!

As the doctor predicted, Zachary's hearing returned and rosy apple cheeks replaced his chalky color. But the most important change of all was that our Zachary began to laugh and cry.

This little boy had never cried. When crying hadn't worked to draw the attention he so desperately needed, he quit early on. As for laughter, I doubt there was too much to laugh about.

Now when Zachary laughs, it is no infant giggle but rather a hearty guffaw right from his toes. When he laughs like that, anyone with him has to laugh too.

Once again, I have seen the tremendous power of love. No one can thrive without it. And with it, all things are possible.

Jean Brody

Love Can Build a Bridge

It's the tiniest thing I ever decided to put my whole life into.

Terri Guillemets

Christina Claire Ciminella entered this world screaming on key and searching for harmony. She was thrust into the eye of the Judd family hurricane on May 30, 1964, attended by the same nurse who had overseen my own birth in the very same room, only eighteen years before. Christina arrived at King's Daughters Hospital, a block from our house, in sleepy Ashland, Kentucky, just as I had when my own eighteen-year-old mother had me. It was a quiet moment of personal joy for humble parents hardly prepared for the greatest job on earth. At Christina's birth, I crossed the threshold to adulthood, ready or not, and took the first baby step on a giant adventure.

Christina and I plunged headlong into an epic, lifelong search for harmony that would alternately unite and divide us a thousand times. A journey that would see us grow up together, scale impossible heights as partners, and embrace the elusive rhythms of a unique mother-daughter relationship. Some say we helped to reshape the history of country music in the process, but for us the experience was deeply intimate and richly private—even though we lived it in the public eye. It's been quite a modern fairy tale, what this infant brought into my life and the lives of millions of other people, but in 1964 there were other, more pressing matters on my mind.

All I knew right then was that I had given birth to a healthy, beautiful little girl. I had somehow known my child would be a girl; I had had a powerfully instinctive feeling months before and had already picked her name. She would be called Christina Claire, and it would fit her perfectly. Much later, of course, she would become "Wynonna," and that too would fit her perfectly. We are not born with our destinies stamped on our foreheads.

When the nurse brought my baby in, I looked into her face and saw myself—her eyes, her skin, her expressions, her spirit. She looked up at me and smiled her first hello. A broad and mischievous grin lit up her face, a sign that told me in no uncertain terms that this was a child to be reckoned with, a child who would be worthy of great things. From that moment on my heart was all hers. I was terrified, elated, proud, and complete . . . all at once. We began our lifelong search for harmony with slow and halting steps, a teenage mother and an unplanned child on a journey that would lead to magic and milestones that neither of us dreamed possible. Wynonna and I were instantly one, a partnership, a team—just the two of us against a frightening and unknown world. On that spring day in 1964, we began our wonderful duet, a blend of heart, mind and soul that continues to this day.

Naomi Judd

Calling Mr. Clean

Maybe it was nesting on steroids. Possibly it was my less-than-neat twin toddlers. Or perhaps it was a compulsive desire to maintain the illusion of order in my life. Whatever the reason, during my last pregnancy I just could not stop thinking about cleaning things. I just couldn't get enough of All Things Immaculate.

So when I saw the sponge, yellow, five inches thick and really squishy looking, I had to have it. Had to have it in a way only a pregnant woman has to have something. It's bizarre, but I actually salivated when I saw it. Had I ever seen anything more useful, more amazing? And for a mere ninety-nine cents! Who could pass up such a bargain? Certainly not pregnant old Pavlovian me.

Myriad cleaning endeavors starring the sponge and myself tap-danced glitzily around in my head. I would try it out first as my own personal bath implement. Unfortunately, it made a squeaky noise as I pulled it across my skin, so I had to nix that idea. I used it to clean the bathtub instead. After that, I couldn't stop thinking about it. I'd giddily daydream, planning our next encounter. Maybe tonight it would be the bathtub again. Or the kitchen floor. Or maybe even the car.

And it didn't stop with the sponge. Other cleaning implements, things that I hadn't glanced at in years, let alone used, became tantalizingly attractive to me. The white scouring brush under the sink. Brillo pads. Bottled cleaning products. I couldn't keep my hands off them.

At the supermarket, instead of standing pondering ice cream bars in the frozen foods aisle as usual, I stood transfixed by Ajax, Soft Scrub and Pine Sol. Mr. Clean winked seductively at me, and I fantasized about just how sparklingly clean I could get my bathroom faucet if only I brought the burly fellow home with me.

I scoured the finish off the linoleum in the kitchen one night. I washed the car every day for a week. Masked and gloved, I obsessively sprayed, spritzed, rubbed, wiped, waxed and polished my way through my last trimester.

And then I had my baby boy, and the romance was over. Whatever hormone it was that caused my sponge fetish thankfully exited my body with my son, leaving me once again a comfortable slob, unconcerned about suds and sparkling appliances. The scrub brush got tossed back under the sink with a shrug; the brigade of impulse-purchased cleaning supplies was relegated to the back of the linen closet. I stopped returning Mr. Clean's calls. The wonder-sponge sulkily disappeared into the basement. I wondered, perplexed, just what I'd seen in the thing when I stumbled upon it about a year later. I held it in my hand and tried to rekindle the old flame. Nothing doing.

And then a couple of days ago, we were at Sam's Club, and there it was. Another sponge. A big, meaty, make-everything-sparkling-clean yellow sponge. My heart skipped a beat. I could practically taste the bone-tingling satisfaction of a cleaning job done right. I started to drool.

And that's when I knew.

That sponge and I were going to be very busy for the next nine months.

Karen C. Driscoll

I Am a Mother

I was in Portsmouth, New Hampshire, getting my hair cut when my husband called. He didn't even talk to me, but the message he gave to the receptionist was simple, "Stop home on your way to the dentist." It was a beautiful day in July. I had ended work a few days before and had lined up appointments for all those things one puts off when one is working full-time.

Just the week before, we had finished our home study with the adoption agency, and we were told we probably had at least a couple of months before we would be matched up with a baby. My husband, Joe, and I had gone through eight years of medical intervention for infertility, and for much of that time I believed I could not be a mother. After much soul-searching, Joe and I realized that our goal was to become parents and that adoption was just as wonderful a way of building a family as giving birth. Our adoption counselor told me I would be a mother, but was it really true?

As I was driving down the highway after the haircut, I thought about my husband's request to stop home. Did he have some time from work to have lunch at home with me? Then I became curious: Joe has no idea where I get my hair cut, so he must have gone to great lengths to track down the phone number. Now, why would he go through all that trouble to find me and just leave a message to stop home? Could it be we got "the call"? Was I a mother already? My heart began to race with excitement, and then I checked myself as I had a dozen times before when we were trying to get pregnant—no, it couldn't be that.

As I pulled into the driveway, the large quilted heart flag that I had made years before as a Valentine's present for Joe was hanging over the driveway. Where had he dug that up, and why was it hanging? As he walked out of the house with a champagne bottle in his hand, I knew.

"Joan, you're the mother of a baby boy!" he told me. Our adoption counselor had called him at work to give him the wonderful news. He filled me in on the details and told me we could pick up our new son the next afternoon.

What should we do first? We weren't expecting a baby for at least a few months; like a couple that is pregnant, we thought we would have time to plan and get ready. We called our parents first. "Mom, Dad, we have a baby boy!" I told my parents. "Oh, Joan, we're so happy that you're a mother," they said. I didn't feel any different than I had the day before. *When will I know I am a mother?* I wondered.

The next twenty-four hours went by quickly, yet I remember every moment in great detail. First, we had to talk with the adoption agency to receive more information and directions. They gave us the phone number of the foster mother who was taking care of our son until we picked him up the next day. We dialed the phone and waited what seemed like eternity for an answer. Mary answered. "Hello," I said, "this is Joan and Joe. Do you have our baby?" "Oh, yes," she said, "he's sitting right here on my lap. Do you hear him?" We listened, and heard his voice for the first time, making his baby sounds.

The next fifteen hours were a rush to complete paperwork, get to the bank for payment to the adoption agency,
and get to the mall before it closed to pick up a few basics.
Although we knew an adoption would happen in the near
future, up until that day I could not allow myself to buy or
borrow any baby things. For years, each time I would see
the grocery aisle that carries diapers and baby food, I
would pass by quickly. I believed that aisle was off-limits
to me; I was not a mother. It's not a very rational feeling,
but one that many infertile women experience, even when
they are told a baby is coming for them through adoption.

At the department store, we ran into an old acquain-
tance. "Hello, what's new?" she asked.

"Oh, nothing," I said out of habit.

"Oh, everything!" Joe said out of excitement.

We rushed on, leaving the poor woman quite puzzled. I
picked out receiving blankets, diapers, bottles, formula
and socks (are baby feet really that tiny?). While I was
stocking up on the practical things, Joe ran off and found
our son's first stuffed animal—Winnie the Pooh.

Around 1:00 in the morning, while we were trying to
figure out how to sterilize bottles, we began to pick a
name for the baby. Previously, it was too hard to look at
books with baby names; what if our baby never came?
Once we picked the name, we tried to get some sleep.
Impossible. We had heard his voice, we had given him a
name, but was he real? What did he look like? Was he
truly going to be ours?

Later that morning, we went to the adoption agency for
last-minute paperwork and to meet the birth mother of
our son. She had made a careful adoption plan for him and
had chosen us to be his parents. It was a very good and
touching meeting. She was his birth mother, the one who
had given him life, but I was his mother too, the one who
would love and care for him every day.

We followed the directions to the foster-care home, and as we pulled up to the house my heart was racing. I don't remember how I got to the front door. Mary opened the door, and as we walked in, she placed in my arms the most beautiful baby I had ever seen. He looked up at me, and said without words, "You are my mother." I will never forget that moment, for that was when all my questions ended.

Looking into his eyes, I knew for certain that I had become a mother.

Joan Sedita

I'll Do It

Life is a journey . . . taken one step at a time.

Anonymous

Finally, I thought as I tallied up the grade on the last test paper. I jotted the score in my grade book, and was just about to leave my office at the college where I taught math when the telephone rang. It was a social service caseworker from New Jersey, and though I'd been half-expecting her call it still took me by surprise.

"Your sister's condition is getting worse," the woman told me. "You said I should let you know. . . ."

"Thank you," I said, and my heart ached for my big sister, Pam, who had battled schizophrenia for years—and even more for her three-year-old daughter, Scarlett, whom I'd never even met. "How can I help?" I asked, and when the caseworker answered I knew there was no way I could agree to her request . . . and no way I could refuse.

Growing up Pam and I shared a bedroom and played on the same community league softball team. But after high school I went to college to get my engineering degree. I got married, moved to Florida and looked forward to start-ing a family. "I can't imagine a life without children to raise," I told my husband. But things didn't work out—the kids, or the marriage.

Newly divorced, I enrolled in grad school and earned an M.S. in math. I spent a year as a volunteer teacher in Haiti, then moved to South Carolina to work on a Ph.D. in med-ical statistics. But the teaching bug had bitten, and before long I put my Ph.D. on hold and began teaching part-time at three different local colleges.

I filled my spare time snorkeling and sailing with friends from a church singles group, but I knew I was just filling time to fight loneliness. I dated occasionally, but there were never any sparks, and by the time I turned forty I could almost feel the ticking of my biological clock.

I began to dread friends' baby showers, and every Mother's Day tears coursed down my cheeks when the pastor asked the moms to stand and be recognized. "Dear God, why not me, too?" I prayed, and I was so frantic, I even considered artificial insemination. I backed out at the last minute, though, and I never seriously considered adoption. Raising a child on my own seemed like such a daunting responsibility. Marriage and then a baby—that's the way the world was supposed to work.

But then with a single phone call my whole world was turned upside down.

For years Pam had drifted in and out of contact, and these days she lived in an Atlantic City rooming house with no phone, so I rarely got to talk to her. But recently when I learned Pam's illness was getting worse I called her social worker and gave her my number—just in case.

"Pam can't care for Scarlett anymore, and we need to put her in foster care," the woman told me now. "Can you take her?" she asked. Gripping the phone, my brain reeled dizzily with a dozen reasons why I couldn't possibly.

I was single and living in a one-bedroom apartment. I didn't have medical insurance, or even a full-time job. *What do I know about raising a three-year-old?* I asked myself. But no matter how many reasons my brain listed why I couldn't do this, my heart disagreed.

Pam is my sister, and her little girl needed a loving home. Maybe this was God's way of answering my prayers. Maybe he never gave me children because he was saving me just for this.

"I'll do it," I said, knowing those few simple words would change my life forever.

There were many arrangements to be made, and Scarlett was placed with a temporary foster mom in New Jersey while I filled out reams of paperwork and applied for my foster-home license. I convinced one of my bosses to hire me full-time, and then I went house hunting.

When Scarlet's caseworker sent me her picture I carried it everywhere. But as the magic day grew near I began to panic. *What does a three-year-old eat? What should her bedtime be? What do I do with her when I need to take a shower?*

One day riding with colleagues to a conference I sat in the backseat poring through a parenting book searching for answers. "You're going to do fine, Barbara," my friend Steve told me. "And not because of anything you read in that book, but because you care enough to read it."

Steve's words gave me confidence. But my heart was pounding a few days later when Scarlett's caseworker and I pulled up in front of her foster home. "Hi, I'm your Aunt Barbara," I introduced myself to a gorgeous little girl who was still blinking away sleep from her nap. I stooped and nervously held out my arms . . . and the moment Scarlett hugged me back I could feel the family bond and somehow, I knew we'd be okay.

Scarlett and I were embarking on a wonderful adventure together, but at first the ride wasn't very smooth. I wasn't prepared for the time and energy it takes to care for a toddler. There simply weren't enough hours in the day.

How do other single moms manage? I wondered, dropping into bed exhausted and overwhelmed.

Scarlett had just turned four, but she was developmentally delayed. At day care when she wanted another child's toy she scratched and bit. And there were times I couldn't understand a word she said. "Ma-che?" she asked one night again and again, growing visibly frustrated until finally I got it: She wants macaroni and cheese.

Another night Scarlett refused to leave our cat Zoomer alone. "Let go!" I ordered, snatching away the cat. Scarlett shrieked and stamped her feet, until finally I told her, "Into your room for a time out." But as Scarlett slammed the door behind her I was riddled with doubt.

"How should I have handled it?" I asked a friend from church.

"Exactly the way you did," she told me. "You have good instincts—learn to trust them," she said, and it was the best advice anyone could have given me.

I enrolled Scarlett in speech therapy, and the next time I didn't understand something she said I asked questions until I did. I also told her there would be no more biting or scratching at day care. "If you misbehave we won't go to any of your play dates on Saturday, and on Sunday you'll have to sit with me in church instead of joining the play group," I explained. It was tough, but I held my ground, and after a few weeks Scarlett's behavior slowly improved.

Scarlett and I have been together four years now, and every day I still wake up looking forward to the adventures, joy, laughter and even the challenges of being a mom. Like racing from the university to pick up Scarlett at school so she can do her homework in my office until the end of my next class when it's time for her gymnastics. Or sitting up half the night sewing a Pocahontas costume for a school play, or teaching her to ride a two-wheeler in the park.

"Look, Mommy!" Scarlett cried excitedly the first time she kept her balance and pedaled away. Watching my little girl disappear over the rise I felt like a mama bird watching her fledgling take wing to conquer the blue, blue sky.

Scarlett and I are bound as close as any mother and child can be. But every Monday night we call "Mommy Pam" to tell her about school and ballet classes and singing in the church musical. Scarlett feels lucky because she has two mommies to love her, but I'm the lucky one. Scarlett has taught me the true meaning of love: changing your life for someone else, and not because you have to, because you want to.

Barbara Wojciechowski
as told to Heather Black
Originally appeared in Woman's World

You'll Never Be the Same

When I announced my pregnancy to a good friend, herself the mother of two, the first thing she said was "Congratulations." The second? "You'll never be the same again."

It was to become a familiar refrain during my pregnancy, words I would hear again and again as my body ballooned. Everyone from my mother to the supermarket clerk seemed to take delight in telling me how much every aspect of my existence was about to shift. Even my doctor got in on the act; she waltzed into the delivery room and grinned as I lay moaning on the bed. "Well!" she said. "Your life is about to change forever!"

It was all good-natured banter, of course. The kind of thing people with children delight in saying to those about to join the club. But for me the comments sounded as much like a warning as a promise, and an ominous warning at that. It seemed what people were really saying was that I was about to change, that my core being would alter in some mysterious and fundamental way. And that was a little scary.

My mother raised the five of us alone and at great cost to herself. For years she worked the graveyard shift at the post office, wrecking her sleep, so that she could be at home with us during the day. When she could no longer work, she swallowed her pride and went on welfare rather than give us up.

Every day my mother sacrificed. She fed us before she ate, dressed us first and rarely bought herself anything new. She never had a boyfriend because she was afraid of exposing her daughters to possible sexual abuse. She was a bright, intelligent woman who abandoned her own dreams to guide the five of us into adulthood. It was a grand and noble decision, one I admire deeply. But sacrificing my sense of self on the altar of motherhood was not an action I cared to emulate.

For the longest time I was unsure whether I even wanted children. For one thing, my mother had drummed it into our heads that getting pregnant would mean the end of whatever dreams we had. She meant to scare us out of getting pregnant as teenagers, of course. But for me the dread remained long after I'd graduated from college and successfully launched myself.

Besides, I liked my work, or rather, I liked the things which work afforded me. Being a journalist exposed me to interesting people and allowed me to travel. Most important my career brought me the sense of financial security. I wasn't rich—print journalists do not get rich—but I made a good living. If there was ever anything I really wanted, I could go out and buy it. I reveled in that.

Getting married only deepened my ambivalence. My friends were marrying too, and getting pregnant one by one. After their babies were born, their husbands would disappear for a week or two, then return to the office with a few baby pictures and quickly take up their routine. But my friends, the new mothers, seemed to drop off the face of the earth. One minute they were there, discussing politics with me over drinks in some chic café, and the next minute they had disappeared into a cloud of baby powder. *Poof.*

Eventually my biological clock went off, and my husband and I decided it was time. I was excited and eager about being pregnant, but there remained this nagging sense of fear. I didn't want life, as I knew it, to change forever. I didn't want to walk into the hospital as myself and be rolled out a few days later some foreign, slack-brained creature called a mom.

It has been fifteen months now since my daughter, Samantha, was born, and my life has most assuredly changed. I used to sleep when I wanted, go out when I wanted, enjoy leisurely dinners with my husband over candlelight—all that is history now. We haven't used our alarm clock in so long we don't even know if it still works. A trip to the supermarket has to be planned three days in advance. And my husband and I have learned that it is possible to be in and out of a restaurant in thirty minutes flat.

And, yes, I admit it, I have changed. Or rather, it seems that parts of me have expanded beyond imagining. At night, when I lean over my sleeping daughter and stroke her hair, I know, for the first time in my life, the true meaning of the word *grace*. And of the word *joy*.

But one of the most gratifying discoveries I've made in this first year of motherhood is how much of the core me remains intact. I am a mother now, true. But I'm also still a writer and tennis enthusiast. I still love dancing and french fries and standing beneath a tree in the spring when it rains. I'm still stubborn and grumpy in the morning and sometimes too quick to judge other people.

I've learned that me-the-person needs to make room for me-the-mom, but she doesn't have to let her take over the house. There is room in this life for both. And that's wonderful. Because it took a lot of years to create this all-around person. I'd sure hate to lose her now.

Kim McLarin

5

INSIGHTS
AND LESSONS

The mother's heart is the child's schoolroom.

Henry Ward Beecher

Mother's Lessons Can Last a Lifetime

God could not be everywhere and therefore he made mothers.

Jewish Proverb

I have learned many things from my mother.

I learned where to go for comfort and sustenance as first I suckled at her breast, later climbed into her lap and now sit across the table from her with a cup of coffee.

I learned not to run into the road, not to touch the stove, not to run with scissors in my hand, never to use a BB gun lest I put my eye out, and that young ladies don't make impolite noises in public.

I learned that "please" and "thank you" are the most important words in the language, to respect my elders, to look a person in the eye when I speak, to sit with my knees together and keep my skirt down, and that a body must be bathed on Saturday night whether it needs it or not.

I learned to fry chicken, bake a cake, make sun tea, flip pancakes, can vegetables and wash dishes—by hand. I learned that "casserole" and "crock pot" are the most important words in kitchen language if you have hopes of pursuing any interests in life away from the stove.

Growing up on a farm, I also learned how to reach under the hens to gather eggs, how to avoid the rooster and the goose, how to pull ticks out of dogs, where to find a nest of baby bunnies in the spring, how to call to the bobwhite down by the creek, and to stay away from sows and their litters.

From my mother I also learned to look for the subtle colors of the flowers in her garden, to listen to the mockingbird's song in the morning, to enjoy the fragrance of the lilac, to spot the rainbow-rimmed moon and to play with the ladybug.

I learned, at her suggestion, that when I wasn't able to tell her the things that troubled me, I could write them to her, pouring out my heart on the sheets of a Big Chief writing tablet.

I learned that even though I sometimes hated her in adolescent rage, she always loved me. I learned that she didn't always have the right answer, but she always had the right intention. I learned that, even though the crop didn't do well or the hay barn burned down or the cows got into the neighbor's corn field, you take care of things and go on.

My mother is sixty-seven now. She recently was diagnosed with cancer, underwent surgery and is receiving chemotherapy treatments.

And this is what I'm still learning from her: You can't always choose what experiences you'll face in life, but you can choose how you'll face them. That faith is stronger than fear, that the love of family and friends is powerful, that each day is a gift and that the fortunate daughter never stops learning from her mother.

Vicki Marsh Kabat

Entertaining Angels

An ounce of Mother is worth a ton of school.

Spanish Proverb

It was fifty years ago, on a hot summer day, in the Deep South. We lived on a dirt road, on a sand lot. We were what was known as "dirt poor." I had been playing outside all morning in the sand.

Suddenly, I heard a sharp clanking sound behind me, and as I looked over my shoulder my eyes were drawn to a strange sight. Across the dirt road were two rows of men, dressed in black-and-white striped, baggy uniforms. Their faces were covered with dust and sweat. They looked so weary, and they were chained together with huge, black iron chains. Hanging from the end of each chained row was a big, black iron ball.

They were, as polite people said in those days, a "Chain Gang," guarded by two heavily armed white guards. I stared at the prisoners as they settled uncomfortably down in the dirt, under the shade of some straggly trees. One of the guards walked toward me. Nodding as he passed, he went up to our front door and knocked. My mother appeared at the door, and I heard the guard ask if he could have permission to get water from the pump in the backyard so that "his men" could have a drink. My mother agreed, but I saw a look of concern on her face as she called me inside.

I stared through the window as each prisoner was unchained from the line, to hobble over to the pump and drink his fill from a small tin cup while a guard watched vigilantly. It wasn't long before they were all chained back up again, with prisoners and guards retreating into the shade away from an unrelenting sun. I heard my mother call me into the kitchen, and I entered to see her bustling around with tins of tuna fish, mayonnaise, our last loaf of bread and two big pitchers of lemonade. In what seemed a blink of an eye, she had made a tray of sandwiches using all the tuna we were to have had for that night's supper.

My mother was smiling as she handed me one of the pitchers of lemonade. Then, lifting the tray in one hand and holding a pitcher in her other hand, she marched me to the door, deftly opening it with her foot, and trotted me across the street. She approached the guards, "We had some leftovers from lunch," she said, "and I was wondering if we could share with you and your men." Calling me to her side, she went from guard to guard, then from prisoner to prisoner, filling each tin cup with lemonade, and giving each man a sandwich.

It was very quiet, except for a "Thank you, ma'am," and the clanking of the chains. Very soon we were at the end of the line, my mother's eyes softly scanning each face. The last prisoner was a big man, his dark skin pouring with sweat and streaked with dust. Suddenly, his face broke into a wonderful smile as he looked up into my mother's eyes, and he said, "Ma'am, I've wondered all my life if I'd ever see an angel, and now I have! Thank you!"

Again, my mother's smile took in the whole group. "You're all welcome!" she said. "God bless you." Then we walked across to the house, with empty tray and pitchers, and back inside.

Soon, the men moved on, and I never saw them again. The only explanation my mother ever gave me for that strange and wonderful day, that I remember, was to always entertain strangers, "for by doing so, you may entertain angels without knowing."

Then, with a mysterious smile, she went about the rest of the day. I don't remember what we ate for supper that night. I just know an angel served it.

Jaye Lewis

Trying Times and Dirty Dishes

The best thing to spend on children is your time.

Joseph Addison

I cleared the table and stacked the breakfast dishes on top of the dinner dishes left in the sink from last night's feast of macaroni and cheese with carrot sticks. I braced myself for the cold, clumpy feeling of the dishwater then plunged my hand deep into the sink, searching for the plug.

"Yuk! Why didn't I do these last night?" I asked of who knows who. The only people around to hear me were my six-, five-, three- and two-year-olds and my six-week-old baby.

It wasn't just the dishes. The dryer had gone out that morning and sheets were drying over every available chair and table, to the great delight of my sons who were playing fort-town all over the house. I would have hung the sheets outside but it was ten degrees below zero.

The living room was exploded with toys, and the way things were going, it would be lunchtime before any of us were even close to being dressed. The flu that had run through the family had finally caught me after six nights of little to no sleep caring for each of my children's needs and comfort. It caught me the same day my husband, recovered and healthy, flew out of town on a business trip.

The hot water bubbled up in the soap-filled dishpan, and it encouraged me a little. "I'll have these done in no time. . . ." But before I could finish my pep talk, my new-born began to cry.

I changed the baby's diaper, stepped over the basket of clean clothes that had already sunk into wrinkled neglect, pulled the sheet off the couch along with the full collection of my sons' horses and corral, and settled in to nurse my baby.

Idyllic moment? Hardly. As soon as I sat, books were tumbled into my lap. If Mom was sitting she might as well read to us, was the common thought. So balancing the four toddlers, protecting the baby from their commotion while trying to turn pages with no hands, I began to read.

I read over the phone ringing and over the TV set clicking on and off at full volume because one of them was sitting on the elusive remote control.

I read over my pounding headache, around the errant thought of what to make for dinner and the doorbell ringing. The doorbell ringing! Oh no! All but the baby and I were off the couch to the door before I could grasp a moment of hope that whoever it was would give up and go away never to see me at my unkempt worse.

"Grandma!" The children chorused while doing the Grandma-is-here dance of anticipated hugs and candy.

Grandma coming was always good news for all of us, but it couldn't be my mother! It couldn't be today. She lived three hours away. She never just dropped by. What would she think? I scanned the room and sighed. There was no way to recover this, no way to quickly put things to right.

Cold, fresh air rushed in ahead of my mother making me realize how stuffy and sick my house smelled.

"Cindy?" My mother called my name, startling the baby and making her cry. I could hear my mother's uneven steps as she navigated around and over the things on the floor.

"Cindy?" she said again before spotting me among the Spiderman sheets.

I was stricken. I was embarrassed. I had forgotten it was Thursday in the sameness of each day. I had forgotten that my mother had planned to stop in on her way back home from the city.

"My, oh my, have things gotten out of control around here," she surveyed the room and started laughing when she saw my gowns drying on the bouncing horse with my nursing bra forming a hat over its head, its ears sticking through the drop down flaps.

Her laughter filled the house with the first ray of sunshine to make it through the wintery gray of the last mucky week.

I started to giggle, then to laugh right out loud before I teared up in my fatigue.

My mother cleared a space for herself beside me. "Cindy, weren't you raised in my home?"

I nodded, because no words could get around the choking of my tears.

"Was my house always perfect, always clean?"

I shook my head no.

"Did you think I was a failure as a mother or as a homemaker?"

Again I shook my head no.

"And I don't think that of you. I have sat where you are sitting now," she grinned at me while she reached over and pulled a toy horse from under my hip.

We chuckled together.

"Cindy, I can tell you one thing, and you listen to me," her voice became solemn with the depth of what she wanted to say. "These are the days you will smile fondly on when the years have passed and your time becomes quiet enough to roam the memories of your heart."

I recognized the love and truth in her words. I wrote them on my heart and contemplated them when my mothering days were both calm and sunny and hectic and never ending.

Now, the years have passed and my time has become quiet enough to roam my memories.

And when my daughters and daughters-in-law are pressed in and overwhelmed with the making of their families and homes, I remember and I say to them, "These are the days you will smile fondly on."

Cynthia Hamond

On-the-Job Training

We admire the other fellow more after we have tried to do his job.

La Rochefoucauld

After being on the mommy track for several years, I decided to test the corporate waters and check out the going rate for all the volunteer work I've been doing at home. Translation: I had a bad week and the grass was looking much greener on the other side of the laundry basket. What started as a casual perusal of the local want ads quickly evolved into an interview, and I suddenly needed to update my resume. To include all that I've accomplished in my years at home, naturally, I highlighted the following:

Fluent in Several Languages. Studied Baby-ese, eventually attaining the ability to switch back and forth from this language to Big People Talk with about 75 percent success rate. Current position finds me deciphering shrugs, gestures and other nonverbal communication used by my preteens to answer the questions "Where are you going?"

and "Do you have homework?" Presently involved in teaching these same children English as a Second Language.

Peacemaker. Experience rivaling that of Madeleine Albright. Breaking up drag-outs between three-year-old twins puts me in contention for the Nobel Peace Prize. Have gone through the "share" and "be nice" routine so often that the Barney show could put me on retainer through the year 2025.

Race Car/Stunt Driver. Accomplished in getting from preschool to the dental office to band lessons to basketball practice quicker than one lap of the Indy 500. Only adult in the house with ability to locate various gas stations in town.

Illusionist. Perform more sleight-of-hand and magic acts than David Copperfield at a gig in Vegas. Possess extraordinary home-budgeting skills using this technique. Also able to make broken cookies whole again, re-assemble dilapidated science-fair projects and fit a size-twelve body into size-ten jeans for a brief period of time.

Child Psychologist. Firsthand experience with various psychoses of children. Developed theory that bedtime brings about increased activity in young children measurable in direct proportion to fatigue of parent. Author of the thesis entitled "Because I Said So as the Only Explanation to the Question 'Why?'"

Clairvoyant. Have the uncanny ability to see things even though they are not there. Strengths include finding spouse's car keys, kids' library books, little hands in the cookie jar. Attribute this talent to the fact that I do, indeed, have eyes in the back of my head.

Scholar. Have become proficient in solving fifth-grade word problems involving trains leaving stations at varying speeds, memorization of all the Arthur books ever written, and deciphering the alphabet as it can only be recited by three-year-olds (i.e. the often used "Elmo-and-a-pea" for the middle five letters). Skilled in being successfully quizzed in these areas upon demand so as not to lessen my credibility with children. Can spell hieroglyphics quicker than my own name, have constructed numerous Iroquois villages out of clay and witnessed the miracle of celery stalks turning blue in colored water over thirty-seven times.

Hobbies. Dabbled in cooking, cleaning and laundry in spare time.

I ended up not changing my employment status, mainly because I couldn't afford to replace me. If I wait a few years before confronting corporate America again, I should have no problem keeping my resume fresh with all the experience I'm getting. I only hope I don't become overqualified.

Karen Trevor

Mother's Magic

Mama was my greatest teacher, a teacher of compassion, love and fearlessness. If love is sweet as a flower then my mother is that sweet flower of love.

Stevie Wonder

Ken, the sixth child in our family, was born with cerebral palsy, profound deafness and mild retardation. Though my mother was extremely affectionate and loving, she never babied Ken. She expected him to do whatever we did.

I remember one Christmas we got a new swing set and slide. Ken, who was nine years old, loved the slide from the first second he saw it, but because of the braces on his legs, he couldn't manage the steps. So he spent the holidays watching the rest of us from the ground.

The first day we were all back in school, Mama put Ken in the backyard, this time without his braces, and watched him crawl right over to the slide. For the next three hours or longer, Ken climbed the ladder and fell, climbed the

ladder and fell, again and again. He busted the knees out
of both of his pant legs. His head was bleeding a little by
one ear and so was an elbow.

The neighbor to the back of us yelled at my mother,
"What kind of woman are you? Get that boy off that ladder." Mama told her kindly that if it upset her, she would
have to close her kitchen curtains. Ken had decided to go
down the slide, and down the slide he would go. It took a
couple of days of trying before he could go up the ladder
and down the slide as well as the rest of us, and another
week before he could do it with his braces on.

But to this day, Ken—the boy who was not supposed to
make it to his tenth birthday and is now a forty-two-year-
old man who lives independently and holds down a job—
approaches everything the way he did that slide so many
years ago. What a gift my mother gave him that day by
expecting him to be the best he could be—and never
settling for less.

Mama could also make things easier for Ken. One week-
day morning, the ladies of the church altar society were
seated in our living room enjoying polite conversation
and cups of my mother's coffee. Ken, an adult now, woke
up and took his place at the head of our dining-room table
in the next room. Mother excused herself, served him his
morning coffee and toast, then rejoined the ladies in the
living room. With his breakfast Ken sat with his back to
the open french doors leading into the living room and the
group of ladies. However, just as he raised his coffee cup
to his lips, his arm experienced an involuntary spastic
movement and he threw coffee all over both french doors,
one wall and himself.

Mother rushed to him finding him embarrassed to the
core, his head hanging, face beet-red, apologizing over
and over to her for the mess he'd made. Mama didn't miss
a beat. She looked down in his cup, and seeing there was

still an inch or two of coffee in the bottom, she threw the coffee on the only clean wall, and told Ken with sign language, "Looks like you missed a spot over here." Ken dissolved in laughter forgetting all about his embarrassment and the mess he'd made, and with a gentle smile on her face Mother began to clean up the mess.

Though I often feel I fall short when I compare my mothering to hers, it gives me great comfort to know that her gentle spirit is within me, somewhere—preparing me to make "mothering magic" of my own.

Mimi Greenwood Knight

Gotta Watch the Fish Eat

What you do today is important because you are exchanging a day of your life for it . . . let it be something good.

Anonymous

I did something very daring today. I said, "No." I was at a meeting where I was asked to serve on a committee that would require numerous Thursday evening meetings. And I said, "No."

I declined politely, even graciously, but it wasn't enough. The others just looked at me, waiting. Three long seconds, four, five. Waiting, waiting for my important excuse. They couldn't move on until I had explained my answer.

"You see," I continued, "I really want to be home to tuck the kids in bed at night." Most of the others around the table nodded in understanding. "Well," the chairperson offered, "we can make sure we're done by eight-thirty, so you can be home in time to tuck the kids in." The others murmured in affirmation, and turned back to me, expectantly, waiting for my response.

"Well," I explained, "that's right when we are watching the fish eat." The others weren't impressed. "You see," I continued, "on Thursdays, after I've quizzed the children for Friday's spelling tests, we watch the fish. It's just an important time in our family's week. It seems to set the tone for the next day, and when I'm gone on Thursday nights, Fridays just don't go as well." My words sounded rather weak and almost silly as they tumbled out. No one said, "Oh, of course, Cheryl, we understand!" They were still waiting.

Now, I could have added, "But, you see, I've got a book manuscript due to the publisher in two months that I have *got* to work on." That would have been sufficiently important. After all, that's my career. They would have nodded in understanding, and quickly moved on. But the truth is, I'm not writing between 7:30 and 8:30 P.M. on Thursday evenings. I'm being Mom. I'm reviewing spelling words for Friday's tests. I'm checking math answers. I'm making sure permission notes are signed, book reports are written and weekly assignments completed. And when school work is done, and the children have brushed their teeth and gotten into their PJs, the family gathers on the couch in front of the aquarium to watch the fish eat. We feed the fish every night, of course. But on Thursdays we make an effort to sit together as a family and *watch* them. This is when I heard about Blake's plans to be a paleontologist. It's when I learned about how Bryce handled the bully on the playground. This is when Sarah Jean explained why she doesn't want to wear bows in her hair anymore.

The committee members were still looking at me. Feeling guilty, I almost changed my mind to say, "Okay, I'll do it." But I didn't. Because my reason for saying no is important. On Thursday evenings, we watch the fish eat.

Cheryl Kirking

Dancing for Fireflies

On a Saturday morning a few years back, I made a diffi-cult and irreversible decision. My daughter was at the piano, galloping through *Unchained Melody*. My son was polishing the hallway mirrors, eager to earn a few extra dollars for a new CD. I couldn't decide if it was the warm mug of coffee cupped in my hands—brewed just right for a change—or the sense of harmony that seemed out of character in a house that had become a war zone as of late, but I realized how crucial it is that a home be a peaceful place away from the turmoil of work and school. And, in those moments, a startling thought welled up in me. I sud-denly realized that little by little, I was jeopardizing the greatest source of safety my children can possess: the home that my husband and I have provided for them.

A safe home has little to do with physical elements, even though we judge other people's homes by the crafts-manship of the woodwork or the quality of the drapes. I'm referring to the "atmosphere" of a home—or maybe "soul" is the definitive word. I recall one weekend years ago, visiting a college friend's elaborate home. I was so impressed that each bedroom had its own bathroom with the thickest, most luxurious towels. Yet that detail seemed marred by the chilling silence that existed between her parents—a silence so loud that I still recall it vividly. I also remember a rather ramshackle house on the outskirts of my hometown. The lady who lived there was a seamstress, a kind woman who listened with eyes that smiled through peculiar blue-rimmed glasses. Whenever my mother took me for a fitting, I was never quite ready to leave. One evening when I went to pick up a dress, she and her husband, Eddie, with the oil-field grime scrubbed from his skin, sat at the table with their kids. They were eating peach cobbler, laughing loudly and playing Yahtzee, and on that evening, their home, with its worn furniture and framed paint-by-number artwork, was clearly one of the finest.

Uncontrollable hardships may plague a home's well-being: the loss of a job, a serious illness or even death. But it's the circumstances many of us encounter on a day-to-day basis that often wear us down and more often contribute to the breakup of a home. I know many couples just like my husband and myself. Once upon a time each other's company charmed us. Our infatuation with each other seemed to cast a rosy glow over the fact that we could barely make ends meet as we struggled to balance part-time jobs with our college classes. Our furniture was the cast offs our relatives were glad to unload, we guarded the thermostat with a frugal eye, and tomato soup was a common meal staple. Yet the two of us created a mansion out of our passion. We graduated, found our niche in the working world, bought our first house, and when our children came along, we were even more enchanted with the cozy feeling their wide-eyed wonder contributed to our home. Long walks with the stroller, Dr. Seuss, dancing for fireflies in the warm twilight—we were happy.

But somehow twenty years passed and neither my

husband nor I could account for the past five. Our jobs demanded more of our time, and our passion for each other slipped away so gradually I scarcely noticed. Our children grew older and fought more so we bought a house twice as big where we were soon spending our time in four remote corners: my husband with his work or evening TV, I with my nose in a pile of bills, my daughter's ear glued to the telephone, and my son, depending on his moods, lost in the world of alternative music or ESPN. When my husband and I did talk, it was to argue about how to discipline adolescent angst, or whose turn it was to take out the garbage. What happened to the long walks, "Sam I Am" and the fireflies?

On that Saturday morning months ago, I faced a reality I had been denying. Something I never imagined could happen to me, had happened. I grew dependent on the attention of another man. Despite his graying hair, he's uncannily like the strong-willed but sensitive guy who charmed me almost two decades ago. Our friendship sparkled because we'd never raised headstrong children, never lived together during hay-fever season, and never woken up to each other's foul breath or puffy eyes. We had never experienced any of the tribulations, minor or major, which test and shape a relationship. In the months that followed, visits with him had grown more intense and drew me farther away from my husband, the other anchor in our children's home. In fact, I had actually begun to imagine life without the man I had promised to love until my last breath.

And so, in one of the saddest and most awkward moments of my life, I told my friend that I could no longer see him. I ended a friendship with a person who had begun to matter very much to me. As I struggled to abandon my feelings for him and embrace the logic of closing the door, the days which followed were filled with a frightening revelation: somehow, unthinkingly, when half of marriages end in divorce, I had threatened our home with the most common reason: a lack of commitment. I had pursued a selfish desire to the point that I could no longer distinguish between right and wrong. I had been entrusted with a loyal husband and two remarkable children, yet I risked their well-being with every moment I spent in this other person's company.

After my decision, there was a wave of emptiness that continually washed through me as I moved through each day. I felt it when I laid awake next to my husband who snored peacefully at three in the morning. It came again at work when my mind drifted away from the pile of paperwork in front of me or the discussion at a meeting. It welled up once more as I sat on the front porch with the evening paper and my two kids fought over the basketball in the driveway. Gradually, though, that feeling has been replaced with a sense of relief that, despite my temporary insanity, my family is safe. But a thousand "I'm sorries" will never take away the sting of remorse I feel nearly every time I look in my husband's eyes and they smile back at me. While the passion we first had doesn't always seem as strong, passion is meaningless compared with the qualities he possesses. I hadn't a clue how much I would come to value his integrity, his work ethic or his devotion to our children. It wasn't until I was confronted with the fear of losing the world that he and I had created together, that I recognized the pricelessness of his friendship.

So tonight, on an unusually warm evening for this time of year, my husband has agreed to join me for a walk. As I study the sky from the window by my desk, I see that there must be a thousand stars tonight, all sparkling like fireflies.

Sarah Benson

Nobody's Perfect

Give what you have. It may be better than you think.

Henry Wadsworth Longfellow

After I discovered that the real life of mothers bore little resemblance to the plot outlined in most of the books and articles I'd read, I started relying on the expert advice of other mothers.

Most of their useful survival tips were too insignificant for the pediatric "experts" to bother with, but for those of us stationed on the front lines, they saved countless lives. I remember trying to talk with my friend Joan one afternoon while my older son fussed in his playpen, flinging his toys overboard and then wailing loudly. Undoubtedly recognizing the homicidal glint in my eye as I got up for the fiftieth time, Joan asked if I had a roll of cellophane tape. I immediately thought she was going to tape his mouth shut—a thought that had begun forming darkly in my own mind—but instead, she gently wrapped it, sticky side out, around his fingers on both hands. For the next half hour, he was totally absorbed, testing the tactile surface on his shirt, nose, hair, toes.

"Where did you learn this stuff?" I asked Joan, who possessed a wealth of small but effective techniques for preventing child abuse.

"I don't know," she said. "I guess after five kids, I think like one: 'What would be fun?'"

I also relied on my friends whenever I needed a sanity check. One year, I'd completely lost my bearings, trying to follow potty-training instructions from a psychiatric expert who guaranteed success in three days. I was stuck on step one, which stated without an atom of irony: "Before you begin, remove all stubbornness from the child."

"What's wrong with you?" Joan asked one day. At the rate we were going, I confessed, my younger son would be ten years old and still in diapers.

Joan laughed, deeply familiar with "the guilties." Mothers breathe guilt on the job every day, like germs in the air. She recommended I accept stubbornness as a fact of childhood. ("Powerlessness corrupts," she often said.) She then taught me a game using toilet paper rolls: Darren found it so amusing, he practically moved into the bathroom—and mastered another level of civilization.

Every time I told Joan what a terrific mother she was, she would respond with the story of a "bad-mother" day. She told me about waking up once in the middle of the night, foggy-brained, unable to remember putting her two-year-old to bed. She got up and was horrified to find the baby's crib empty. Racing frantically through the house, she finally found Patty in the kitchen, sound asleep in her high chair. "At least I'd strapped her in," Joan said.

Nobody's perfect, we knew, but mothers are somehow expected to exceed all human limits. This ideal is especially preposterous since mothers are likely to have more bad days on the job than most professionals, considering the hours: round-the-clock, seven days a week, fifty-two weeks a year, no sick days.

Given the punishing rules—and the contemptuous labels for any mom who breaks them—mothers are reluctant to admit having bad days. We all have them, of course, a secret that only makes us feel more guilty. But once my friends and I started telling the truth, we couldn't stop.

One mother admitted leaving the grocery store without her kids—"I just forgot them. They were in frozen foods, eating Eskimo Pies."

Most of our bad-mother stories didn't look so awful in retrospect: some, however, looked much worse. Every one of my friends had a bad-mother day somewhere in her history she wished she could forget—but couldn't.

But however painful or compromising the reality of motherhood, we preferred it to the national game of "Let's Pretend," the fantasy in which we are all supposed to pass for perfect mothers in perfect families.

Once I'd given birth to my sons, there were no guarantees. That first burst of love expanded over the next two decades, along with the growing realization that I could not possess them for long, keep them safe, insure their happy lives. Joy/pain . . . joy/pain . . . the heartbeat of motherhood.

Mary Kay Blakely

A Mother's Letter to Santa

Dear Santa,

Here are my Christmas wishes:

I'd like a pair of legs that don't ache after a day of chasing kids (in any color, except purple, which I already have) and arms that don't flap in the breeze, but are strong enough to carry a screaming toddler out of the candy aisle in the grocery store. I'd also like a waist, since I lost mine somewhere in the seventh month of my last pregnancy.

If you're hauling big-ticket items this year, I'd like a car with fingerprint resistant windows and a radio that only plays adult music, a television that doesn't broadcast any programs containing talking animals, and a refrigerator with a secret compartment behind the crisper where I can hide to talk on the phone.

On the practical side, I could use a talking daughter doll that says, "Yes, Mommy," to boost my parental confidence, along with one potty-trained toddler, two kids who don't fight, and three pairs of jeans that zip all the way up without the use of power tools.

I could also use a recording of Tibetan monks chanting,

"Don't eat in the living room," and "Take your hands off your brother," because my voice seems to be out of my children's hearing range and can only be heard by the dog. But please, don't forgo the Play-Doh Travel Pack, the hottest stocking stuffer this year for mothers of preschoolers. It comes in three fluorescent colors guaranteed to crumble on any carpet and make the in-laws' house seem just like home.

If it's too late to find any of these products, I'd settle for enough time to brush my teeth and comb my hair in the same morning, or the luxury of eating food warmer than room temperature without it being served in a Styrofoam container.

If you don't mind, I could also use a few Christmas miracles to brighten the holiday season. Would it be too much trouble to declare ketchup a vegetable? It will clear my conscience immensely. It would be helpful if you could coerce my children to help around the house without demanding payment as if they were the bosses of an organized crime family, or if my toddler didn't look so cute sneaking downstairs to eat contraband ice cream in his pajamas at midnight.

Well, Santa, the buzzer on the dryer is going off, and I've got to run. Have a safe trip, and remember to leave your wet boots by the chimney and come in and dry off by the fire so you don't catch cold. Help yourself to cookies on the table, but don't eat too many or leave crumbs on the carpet.

Always,
Mom

P.S. One more thing, Santa, you can cancel all my requests if you can keep my children young enough to believe in you.

Debbie Farmer

Momma's Little Surprise

I got a call from a friend the other day, asking me if 7:00 A.M. is too early to start drinking when one must try on mail-order bathing suits. I said, "Hell, *no!* And if I were you, I would start slamming down the tequila an hour prior to ripping into the first plastic bag."

She thanked me and said she knew she could count on my support. "No problem," I replied; we women need to stick together.

Her phone call sent me into shock as it reminded me it was that time of year again and somehow I had forgotten to go on a diet. I'm not vain; I'm fat. Over the past sixteen years, my husband and I gained seventy-five pounds collectively. Sadly, our accountant rolled his eyes at us when we asked if we could claim our girth as a new dependant. I said, "Come on! We've gained the equivalent of a fourth-grader; that's gotta count for something." His answer was a firm *no*.

At any rate, it is time for my annual disrobing and a chance to see what one more year has done to my body.

Worse, by far though, is that this year I need to buy a new bathing suit, and the thought gives me tremors, especially because of what happened the last time I bought a new suit.

I forked over eighty bucks for a catalog swimsuit that promised I would look slimmer, trimmer and younger. Yeah, I know I foolhardily bought into the propaganda, but at this point in my life, I would try voodoo if I thought it would work.

I decided on the black mock tankini that came equipped with a shelf bra and the promise that the steel-enforced fabric would tuck my tummy and firm my fanny. It arrived the day we left for vacation, so I threw it in my suitcase and headed for the beach.

I tugged, I pulled, I sweated. An hour later, the suit was on and, oh boy, did I feel fabulously firm. I walked to the full-length mirror and let out a scream so primal that my kids banged on the bedroom door, asking if they should call an ambulance. I told them no, but then said that maybe they could call the local butcher and ask if he's interested in buying a human sausage link.

The shelf bra worked its magic. It coaxed my normally low-hanging breasts up to my earlobes. I now had what looked like a horrible case of the mumps. Not only that, but some of the flesh decided it did not want to meet my neck and would rather hang out elsewhere. If I didn't know better, I would have sworn someone shoved hotdog rolls under my armpits.

As for the tummy tucker, well there is a little known scientific fact that states, "What gets smushed in, also gets smushed out."

Sure, I had a flat tummy but that's because all the subcutaneous fat pushed itself down and out of the bottom of the suit. I had a sorry case of frontal butt cheeks.

After that, I swore I'd never purchase another swimsuit again until I lost weight, but like I said, somehow dieting slipped my mind. This year, I am trying a new approach to the swimsuit fiasco. I told my husband and children that for Mother's Day I would rather have a gift certificate to the local sporting goods store, instead of the usual dinner out. When they asked me why, I said, "It's a surprise."

This summer, I'm gonna buy me a full-length wetsuit. Whadda ya think about that? Creative huh? No more crying or screaming for me. No siree, this year, I'll be tucked and smooth from neck to ankles.

I've decided against the flippers, though. I do have long, slim toes that I want to accentuate with pink, Day-Glo toenail polish. As for the goggles, I'm still not sure. My impeccable fashion sense tells me that would be overdoing it.

Golly, I just had a fabulous thought. My thirteen-year-old daughter finds my mere presence on this earth an embarrassment to her. Wait until she gets a load of my new beachwear.

Susan Krushenick

Look at Me

"Look at me, Mum."

Jason's shrill voice skimmed across the water. Jen grunted and went on dipping out leaves, jabbing angrily at the water. She had had enough.

It wasn't Jason's fault. Of course he had lots of energy—he was a boy. She just wished he wasn't so constantly demanding. It had been Jen's idea to work from home—she'd done it when Callista was tiny. They just couldn't afford for her not to work at all.

"Look, Mum."

"I'm looking," Jen growled, regretting it instantly. She hunched over, feeling guilty, glaring at the water.

"You're not watching, Mum."

"Okay."

She smiled at him, wiping her hands on her long cotton sundress. He was kneeling up on his little inflatable boat. He couldn't swim properly but he had floaties on his arms, and Jen made sure he stayed at the shallow end where he could stand. The boat was cute—it had a funnel and ropes around it. He could hang on to it and float all round the pool if she was with him.

"Whee!!" Jason leapt and splashed into the water. He

paddled around, whooping breathlessly, until he could grab hold of the boat.

"Good, darling. Really good."

Jen went back to scooping. It was partly her husband, Andrew's, fault. He had promised that if they had another he would stay home. Why should it be her? Why should she have to give up all her chances? There had been the big promotion opportunity—his, of course—and the pay raise they couldn't afford to miss. She would never have agreed to another child if she'd known.

Jen had enjoyed Callista's company so much that she almost missed her when she slept. For three blissful years, from the time Callista learned to walk until the time she went to kindergarten, they did everything together. While Jen worked, Callista would look at books or draw pictures or help in her own way with the housework; they would shop together with endless discussions about what to buy. Callista would tell her when the postman had come, remind her to buy food for the cat, give her a hug when she felt a little low—somehow Callista always knew, even when she tried to hide it.

"Look, Mum! I'm gonna do it again."

"I'm busy."

Jason couldn't have been more different. She couldn't talk to anyone anymore; she couldn't read a book. He was there, constantly demanding her attention, testing her. Nothing seemed to keep him occupied more than a few minutes, and then he was at her again. Why couldn't he entertain himself? Why couldn't he invent something to do? Her attempts at work were an agony, and in the end she always had to do it at night when Andrew was there and she wanted to relax. It just wasn't fair, and the worst of it was that Andrew hated her mentioning it. Jason was always half-asleep by the time he came home. Sometimes she just wanted to go away and leave them all to it. Go away and never come back.

It was the silence that made her look up.

The first thing she saw was the boat. For a moment she thought it was empty, then she realized that Jason's feet were still in it, tucked under the rope. The rest of him was in the water, upside-down. The floaties were stopping his weight from tipping the boat but his head was under.

With a cry, Jen flung herself into the pool. She was a terrible swimmer and hated the water, but in a flash she was tearing toward the boat, not even feeling her long dress around her ankles. As she reached the boat she ducked under. She could see his little face through the water, with his arms waving helplessly. She grabbed him and hauled him free of the boat. She could stand easily here so she picked him up and carried him, coughing and spluttering, to the edge.

She sat clutching him tightly, her mind an utter blank, so scared she couldn't think at all. He was clamped to her and seemed stunned by what had happened, but she could feel that he was breathing normally. With the shock, though, Jen was frozen.

"Mum?" His voice sounded a little strange. "Mum, you're hurting me."

Suddenly she realized she was holding him so tight he could hardly get a breath. Tears rushed down her cheeks at the thought of what had nearly happened. She looked at his bewildered face and suddenly, in a moment, she understood that this little life was the most precious thing she had ever held in her hands.

"Mum," Jason said, frowning slightly. "Why are you crying?"

She smiled at him through her tears.

"Because . . ." she sobbed. "Because you did your biggest trick of the afternoon and . . . I nearly missed it."

He put his arms around her wet dress and gave her a strong hug.

"Don't worry, Mum," he said. "You can look at me again tomorrow."

Jaie Ouens

Mother Love

I tickled his tummy and kissed his sweet toes;
I powdered his bottom and wiped his wee nose.
I raced him and chased him
(and once I misplaced him!)
I rubbed and I scrubbed
('til I nearly erased him!)

I shook from his pockets things living and dead;
I entered his room with a shudder of dread.
I tended him and mended him
(and always defended him!)
I begged and I bribed
(when I should have rear-ended him!)

Oh, where is my baby? Which way did he run?
He's now a teen monster at six-foot-and-one!

Carol McAdoo Rehme

The Last Rebellion—Weddings

*My mother had a great deal of trouble with me
but I think she enjoyed it.*

Mark Twain

My son, now an eminent professional approaching
midlife, has been mostly successful in cutting that infamous umbilical cord after a lifetime of passionate battles
beginning in the playpen. For him, the phrase *guilt trip* was
routine vocabulary when he was barely out of diapers.

"Finish your broccoli; they're starving in Biafra," I'd cry.

"You're trying to give me a guilt trip," he'd reply.

A product of the rebellious '60s and '70s, he caused
episodic disharmony in our home as he fended off leg-
endary guilt trips, while challenging established attitudes
toward sex and marriage, money, religion, recreation,
music, food or appearance. Like my mother before me, I
was an overprotective and controlling parent. My son
taught me "esoteric" philosophy: holding my tongue and
walking on eggs. His battles for independence waged and
won, some resentments lingered. The last arena of

rebellion and confrontation: wedding celebrations.

Halfway into his twenties, David arrived from his home out of state to attend the wedding of my friend's daughter and asked if I would hem his new "wedding pants." I was relieved—and delighted to do so. The invitation had read, "black-tie optional," and I was skeptical about his owning appropriate clothing. My husband and I wanted to buy him an outfit, but fearful of suggesting anything that could be construed as an assault upon his personhood, we remained silent.

The "wedding pants" turned out to be khaki cotton chinos! I do not attribute his choice to rebellion—not that day. Perhaps he was merely ignorant of wedding garb outside his circle of friends who were marrying on the beach, in the woods or on a mountaintop and to whom a new pair of khaki chinos would have been akin to formal attire.

"I see you want to be comfortable, but since this is a dress-up affair, chinos are inappropriate. The choice is yours of course; think about it."

Having incorporated the walking-on-eggs philosophy, that is what I could have said, what I should have said, what I didn't say.

Instead, I roared, "You can't wear those pants to a wedding."

"I can wear whatever I wish," he roared back. "You are trying to give me a guilt trip." The ensuing battle of wills and words was not a tribute to either his maturity or mine. He declined subsequent black-tie invitations from friends and family alike.

When it was his turn to walk down the aisle, acceding to his fiancé's wishes, he prepared himself for an extravaganza crammed with preceremony rehearsals, luncheons and dinners, which relegated black-tie optional to the insignificant. Searching through flea markets and used clothing stores, he found a frayed but dashing Victorian cutaway that assuaged his need for nonconformity. Nevertheless, his marriage began to disintegrate, even before he chimed "I do," during those days preceding the huge gala, as his resentments against pomp and tradition mounted. I believe the wedding gestalt contributed to his divorce not many years afterward.

"Love is nature's second sun," so it was not surprising when, after five years of bachelorhood, his cutaway hanging expectantly in the closet, David declared his intention to marry again.

"The wedding will be small, it will take place outdoors, and the guest list will include intimate friends and immediate relatives only," he informed me. He wanted the most "harmonious vibes." I nodded my head to everything, in total blissful agreement. What occasion in life is more joyful than a child's marriage?

I then learned that a street minister, colorfully attired and barefooted, would conduct the ceremony. David was bored with ritual ceremony, a ceremony with religious and spiritual significance to me. I was distressed, but having at long last mastered the technique of addressing sensitive subjects, I quietly told him how I felt.

"Distressed?" he bellowed. "You cannot feel distressed. It is my wedding and my choice as to who performs the ceremony."

"Distressed?" he repeated. "You can feel distressed if I have a terminal illness. You can feel distressed if I do drugs or sell drugs. You can feel distressed if I rob a bank. You are trying to give me a guilt trip."

Two weeks later, David called and announced that if I could produce a female rabbi, with acceptable vibes, willing to go along with his concept of a meaningful ceremony, he would bow to my wishes. I never knew his motivation. Did he really want to please me? Was he

influenced by his somewhat more traditional fiancé? Was
he acknowledging his heritage? It didn't matter.

Heavy rainfall and storm warnings were predicted for
that memorable day in mid-October. Instead, the sun
peeked out from behind the clouds, then appeared in its
full regalia, glorious and warming. The groom, heeding his
own wedding invitation dress-code suggestions—colorful, casual and comfortable—wore a purple and black
striped knit shirt with his old cutaway. From her closet,
his bride had selected purple dotted tights and a print
blouse that she topped with a white blazer. Together they
greeted their baby-boomer guests, some of them attired in
T-shirts and denim shorts. Under a grand old copper
beech tree, which doubled as a *chuppah,* the young blonde
rabbi with "acceptable vibes" and the elderly black barefoot minister presided over a two-hour ceremony, accompanied by a trio of friends on guitar, bass and drum.

Amid uproarious laughter and buckets of tears, the cus-
tomary seven blessings were presented in the context of a
puppet show, a flute solo, an original prayer, poetry read-
ings, group chanting, a dramatic performance and a love
story told in rap. The young couple, reciting a long scroll
of wedding vows, was united in the presence of God, the
glare of the sun, the scent of marigold, cooing babies and
nursing mothers. I probably laughed the loudest and cried
the most. No guilt trips have been exchanged since.

Ruth Lehrer

Recipe for Life

I stood at the departure gate in Boston, preparing to cross the Atlantic. Although I had made the journey countless times before, it never really got much easier to leave my home and family, and this time was no different. I looked at my mother, our eyes full of emotion, and as we wondered when we would see each other again she handed me a package, saying it might help me feel better. *Typical Mom.* Little did I know that it would not only help me feel better, but would also teach me one of life's greatest lessons.

Through the airplane window I watched the last lonely lights slowly disappear off the North American coast and thought about the fateful day years before that had changed my life forever. I had wanted to see Britain, the land of my family's ancestors, and there I was fatally smitten with a young Swiss girl, whom I later married and with whom I had started a family. Now, back in Switzerland after visiting my parents in Massachusetts, I opened my mother's package. It was a book of recipes; I laughed out loud as I thumbed through it. All the sections like vegetables, soups and breads were empty but the one section on desserts was chock full. *Typical Mom.* Here were handwritten cards bearing names like "Seven Layer Squares" or "Double Chocolate Fudge," many of which my mother had created or named. Then my heart skipped as I noticed that she had written this on the inside front cover:

> *To my dear son: Make some fudge. Think about us. Remember all the wonderful times we have had together, and have them now with your family.*
> *Love, Mom.*

It's okay, she was telling me; we must grow up and lead our own lives, even when it sometimes hurts. But there was more. Recipes in hand, I remembered snowy winter mornings with no school and hot chocolate; Christmases of joy and special homemade treats; afternoons when my mother was always there, consoling me after a rough time with the school bullies by saying, "Let's make cookies!" Now, years later, Mom was telling me about what really matters in life: the only real gifts we can leave behind for our children or loved ones are the appreciation of a full life and the beautiful memories of our time together. Other things will rust or decay or get lost. The things that really matter never will. It is never too late or too early to create beautiful memories and it is now my job to give them to my children.

I sincerely hope that my Swiss-American girls will not do what I did; with luck they will marry the boy next door and stay on this side of the Atlantic. But wherever they may be, I hope that they, too, will one day open my mother's recipes and read her words. And like me, they will find a recipe for life. *Typical Mom.*

Arthur Bowler

6

SPECIAL
MOMENTS

The only way to live is to accept each minute as an unrepeatable miracle, which is exactly what it is: a miracle and unrepeatable.

Storm Jameson

Snow at Twilight

Your day goes the way the corners of your mouth turn.

Anonymous

The sky had been gray all day, and now it was getting darker. Four feet of fresh snow lay over our town, a small city in a southern state that usually doesn't see a foot of snow all at one time, all winter long.

This was an unusual snow, a big snow, to which we had awakened that morning, and which had taken all day to accumulate. Anticipating it, the city had closed schools, and CJ and I had watched through the morning as showers of small grainy flakes were interrupted by windy swirls of large ones. By late afternoon, our mailbox was nearly drifted under and neither foot nor tire tracks disturbed the plane of snow we could see out the front window.

We decided to go sledding. Twilight was falling, but the snowfall had stopped, and the air was perfectly still. Bundled and booted, CJ and I skidded his new red plastic snow saucer behind us down the unplowed streets toward the sledding hill at the neighborhood park.

Slow work it was. Each boot fall cut a fresh break in the snow. We were the only ones out there.

But our snow hill is worth it. A nearly vertical drop that terminates in an open soccer field, it's about fifteen feet from the top of the hill to the wide flat below. The next day would surely see it crawling with kids, while moms in minivans drank coffee from carry-mugs and visited along the residential street at its crest.

"We're gonna have fun," I encouraged my six-year-old as he did his best to power himself through snow that reached, at times, to his thighs. We had to move with as much determination as the snow would allow, or dusk would overcome us before we got there.

But we never got to the snow hill. At least, not both of us.

Children's voices came to us as we approached a side street where a friend of CJ's lives. "Hey Mom, it's Kyle," CJ said. "I want to play with him."

Naturally, a friend one's own age is far more fun than the mom with whom you've been cooped up all day. And Kyle's driveway slopes; that was hill enough for a couple of little boys and Kyle's plastic toboggan. Kyle's mom said she was happy to have CJ come play for an hour before dinner.

So there I was, halfway to the sledding hill, but without my companion. I could have turned around and gone home to a house made quiet for the first time all day. But I didn't want to stop. And that's when I realized that taking CJ to the big hill was my excuse for going there myself.

So I continued.

Four teenage boys were the only ones at the park when I arrived. No other moms, no other kids. Mostly the boys were hanging around and jiving each other. But every so often, three boys watched as a fourth took a snowboard run down the side of the hill.

I might as well have been from another time zone, as little in common as I had with these boys in their neon fleece vests, tasseled knit caps and nylon ski suits. My old sweats and ancient peacoat were no match for fashion, and CJ's unadorned red saucer was a paltry counterpart to the logo-adorned snowboards they carried.

Together, the boys had dragged a tractor tire halfway up the hill, from the playground below where it usually functions as a climbing toy for children. Together, they had packed snow over and around it, to create a mogul for their snowboard runs. And individually, they tried to outdo each other as their snowboards hit the jump and went airborne.

Slyly, they eyed me. What could a mother possibly be doing at the snow hill without a child? I began to wonder about this myself as I folded my forty-one-year-old frame into a first-grader's snow saucer to push off. I hadn't bent my body into these angles in a dozen years or more.

If I end up spraining something, it serves me right, I thought.

But the saucer hadn't yet cut a gully into the snow, so my unhurried first run really required pushing my way down the hill. I hadn't injured any body parts when I reached bottom, but I hadn't really gone very fast. It was going to take another run or two before the saucer would gain any speed.

I picked up the saucer, trudged back to the top of the hill and learned afresh that no step routine at the gym matches the effect of taking oneself up a deeply snow-banked slope. But the second saucer run was more like it.

On the third run, my saucer sped down the hill and went a distance across the soccer field before stopping. Snow spray against my face refreshed it better than any fancy water spritzer at the cosmetics counter. My lungs filled with air that felt absolutely clean.

On the fourth run, the saucer's lip caught some snow on the way down and flipped me upside down into the soft powder. *This is it,* I thought, *the moment I will have to explain to everyone from my neck brace.* But instead, I found myself laughing out loud, sprawled on my back in the snow. My own victory whoops accompanied runs five and six.

The teenagers may have thought I had lost my mind. But no, instead I had found something else I had misplaced through my years of career advancement, motherhood and the advent of my forties: the freedom of going really fast through thin air.

It was nearly dark when I left the hill and made it back to Kyle's house for CJ. My son looked me over: my snow encrusted pants, wet gloves and flushed face. "What were you doing, Mom?" he asked.

"Me?" I answered. "I took myself sledding."

Maggie Wolff Peterson

Picture Day

It was Picture Day at my daughter's preschool, and Nicolle was in tears.

"I'm going to wear my Easter dress for my picture," Nicolle had announced earlier that morning: the one with the frilly, puffy collar, which I secretly thought made her look like a clown. Naturally I already had her photograph fixed firmly in my mind, framed and displayed proudly on the piano. In it, she had adorable pigtail braids, and was wearing the navy blue sailor dress. She was definitely not in the Easter clown dress.

She cried, she pleaded, but although I offered a measure of sympathy, I was unwilling to surrender the image in my mind's eye.

"If I can't wear my Easter dress, then I'll look like *this* in my school picture," she announced, pouting dramatically, her lower lip puffed out like a little strawberry.

Luckily, Nicolle attends afternoon preschool, so I had several hours to pull as many tricks as possible from the proverbial mommy hat. Finally, after deftly maneuvering a little creative compromising, threatening and (okay, I admit it) *bribery*, Nicolle was ready for Picture Day. In a small triumph for the mommy camp, she was wearing the darling navy blue sailor dress. However, as a compromise, she was also wearing her hair down, unbraided—prone to be fly-away and quickly tangled, mind you—but the way she wanted it. I prayed for a photographer who was handy with a comb, and we set off on our carpool rounds.

Usually Lindsey was stationed at the front door, ready to be taken to school, but today when I rang the doorbell, it took a few moments before her mother opened the door. She was trying to anchor an enormous pink bow to Lindsey's hair. I noted Lindsey's pretty pink fingernails and wondered if I should have painted Nicolle's nails too.

After her mother's fussing, Lindsey was adorable in a frilly pink jumpsuit. She also looked like she was ready to burst into tears. "She wanted to wear a dress," her mother confided in a stage whisper. She made a few more subtle adjustments to Lindsey's ensemble, instructed me to make sure the collar on her jumpsuit was straight after she took off her coat, gave Lindsey a kiss, and sent us on our way. As we pulled out of the driveway, I could see Lindsey's mother peering anxiously from the window after us. The drive to Lauren's house was uncharacteristically quiet. Lindsey pouted silently out the window at the passing scenery.

Lauren and her mother were waiting for us on their front porch. As I got out of the car, I could see that Lauren's bangs had been carefully curled and fluffed. *Darn it,* I thought. *I should have curled Nicolle's hair too.*

Lauren scurried toward the car, then slipped and fell to her knees in her shiny black patent leather shoes. Her mother's mouth froze in displeasure, and her eyes rolled heavenward.

"Lauren, come here," she demanded in a stern tone. She kneeled in front of Lauren, took her by the shoulders and spoke into her face.

"Remember what I said. Be careful." Lauren approached my car with her eyes glued to her patent leather shoes.

I found myself struggling to make conversation with the four-year-olds in the back of the car, just to break the unusual silence. In the rearview mirror, I realized Nicolle's hair had picked up static from her jacket, and was clinging to her face. I wondered if she'd let me put her hair in pigtails once we got to school. I wished I'd brought a curling iron with me, and maybe some fingernail polish.

At school, mothers were lingering, adjusting head-bands, tucking in shirts and straightening ties. The children allowed the adults to fuss over them, but as soon as they were released, bolted into the classroom.

I made sure Lindsey's collar was straight, that Lauren's bangs were properly fluffed, tried to smooth the static from Nicolle's hair, then left, trying not to worry.

Later, when I returned to pick up the three girls, I was nearly mowed down by children erupting from the school. Catapulted by pent-up energy, the children were running, jumping, laughing and shouting. Hair was breaking free from ponytails and bows, neckties were merrily askew, collars were crooked and shirttails flapped in the breeze. Nicolle, Lindsey and Lauren were among them, pink-cheeked, uncombed, happy and beautiful.

I wished I had my camera.

Carolyn C. Armistead

Sharing a Bowl of Happiness

My mother's mixer is sturdy and heavy. As I carry it into her kitchen from the pantry where it stays hidden in a closet, I marvel that the frail woman she has become can carry it at all. After placing it on the tiny counter between the sink and the stove, I find I have no room for the flour, chocolate chips and eggs. Efficiency has replaced spaciousness in her retirement cottage. So, for lack of a better solution, I put my cache of ingredients in the sink until I need them and search for a spatula.

Looking into the next room, I see my mother sitting at the table with her head pillowed in her arms. For these past ten years, severe asthma has taken its toll and movement is often a chore, taxing breathing already choked with congestion. She sighs and closes her eyes, spent from a night of coughing. Also, although cooking has never been her passion, I know it pains her to see me puttering in her kitchen, and she is hurting for the days when she could mother me with tasty treats. So am I.

Turning back to the mixer, I lift the towel that serves as the mixer's barrier against the dust of idleness. A nostalgic smell wafts up from the ceramic bowl nestled in the mixer's turntable. It must be the fragrance of my childhood.

Memories come to me of watching my mother use mixer magic to turn ordinary eggs into white mountains for topping tangy lemon pies and plain, bitter baking chocolate into syrupy sweetness for cream-filled éclairs. The whir of the beaters under my mother's direction folded sifted flour mixed with a cup of this and a pinch of that into thick batters that became tall, white angel food cakes, round buttery cushions for pineapple upside-down delights, sugar cookies topped with colored sprinkles, and moist bars oozing with melted chocolate chips.

On summer mornings before the Texas heat built up and the fans worked to move the last of the cool night's air around the kitchen, my mother often did her baking. I remember one special morning, sitting just outside the kitchen listening for the thud of her wooden spoon scraping the last of the beater-whipped batter onto cookie sheets for baking and the clang of the released beaters falling into the bowl. The silence that followed meant that it was time for licking.

If my mother was generous, thick streaks of batter lined the sides of the bowl and the beaters were heavy with whatever she was mixing. That morning, after entering the kitchen and peeking around her apron-tied waist, I saw small mounds of leftover chocolate chip dough that made my mouth water and my mother licking the spoon with guilty pleasure. Fearful of losing even the tiniest nibble of this unprecedented treasure, I tugged at my mother's apron, demanding her attention. "Ah," she said, looking down at me. "Don't worry. I've left some just for you. Would you like to lick them clean?"

Laughing at the greed that filled my eyes, she slid out a chair for me. And there we sat, side by side, me with my tongue curled around a dough-covered beater, and she with a wooden spoon and a smile stained in chocolate. Such a simple pleasure and yet such a bowl of shared happiness.

As I stand in my mother's kitchen looking at her lined face resting on her arms, I wish for that long ago day that is earmarked in my memory. I wish to be sticky with chocolate, smothered by the protection of my mother's love, and jealously guarded against the ravages of disease and pain. But only in our memories are we allowed a way back.

So I retrieve the recipe I found for a chocolate chip cake and begin to create a gift that I hope will bring a smile to my mother's face. Flour and eggs, pudding and oil, a pinch of this and a dash of that. A lot of chips to make round dollops of soft melting chocolate. Then the beaters whir, mixing waves of chocolate that roll inside the ceramic bowl. Taking my mother's spoon, I scrape the batter into the pan for baking and listen to the thud of the wooden spoon against the sides. Something makes me stop, and I look into the next room to see my mother staring at me with the touch of a smile on her face.

In the sudden silence, I see a different way back. Leaving an unprecedented amount of batter in the bowl, I loosen the beaters, letting them clang against the sides. And picking up the bowl, I turn to a mother still beautiful to me, and say, "I've left some just for you. Would you like to lick them clean?"

We sit side by side at the table, bent over a bowl of batter and two laden beaters, both of us with sticky fingers and smiles rimmed in chocolate. It is a bowl of happiness that I greedily share once again with my mother.

Kris Hamm Ross

The Good-Night Kiss

Four feet. Just forty-eight inches. But it might as well have been the Grand Canyon for all the difficulty my mother had in crossing that gap—the space between my little sister's bed and mine. Each night I watched from my bed as my mother tucked in my little sister to go to sleep. I patiently waited for her to walk over to tuck me in and give me a good-night kiss. But she never did. I suppose she must have done so when I was younger, but I couldn't remember it. I was seven now, a big girl—apparently too big for bedtime rituals. Why or when my mother stopped, I couldn't remember. All I knew was that she tucked my little sister in each night, walked past my bed to the door, and, before she turned out the light, turned and said, "Good night."

At school the Sisters said that whatever you ask God for at your First Holy Communion you will surely get. We were supposed to think very carefully over this, but I didn't have to think too long to know what I was going to pray for. This was the perfect time to ask Jesus to make my mother tuck me in and kiss me good night.

The day of my First Communion drew to a close. That

night, as I hung up my communion dress and got ready for bed, butterflies danced in my stomach. I knew in my heart that I was about to get the best gift of the day. When I climbed into bed, I pulled the blankets up around me, but not all the way up. I wanted to leave some for my mother to pull up. The nightly ritual began. My mother put my sister to bed, tucking the blankets around her and kissing her good night. She stood up. She walked past my bed to the doorway. She started to say, "Good night," but then she stopped. I held my breath. This was the moment. "This was a beautiful day," she said softly. And then she said good night and turned off the light.

I quietly cried myself to sleep.

Day after day, I waited for that prayer to be answered, but it never was. My mother's actions taught me that sometimes God answers "no," and though I never knew why my mother couldn't cross that small space to kiss me good night, I eventually came to accept it.

Deep down, though, I never forgot. When I grew up and became a mother myself, I vowed that my children would always know that they were loved. Hugs and kisses were freely given in our home.

In the evening, after tucking the children in their beds upstairs, I usually went back downstairs and dozed off on the couch in the living room. My husband worked the night shift, and as a young mother, I felt safer sleeping downstairs. One night—it must have been after midnight—I was wakened by the sound of footsteps coming down the stairs. At first the footsteps were loud, and then they suddenly stopped. Whoever it was had seen me.

Finally! Now I would find out just which of my children was raiding the cookie jar during the night. No more waking to be greeted by crumbs all over the kitchen table and blank, innocent looks, in response to my accusations. Tonight the culprit would be caught!

I didn't move, pretending to be asleep, and waited for the footsteps to resume. When they did, they were ever so gentle on each step so as not to wake me. But they were not coming down toward me anymore. They were retreating back upstairs to the bedroom. I heard a little scurrying above, then quiet footsteps again, almost imperceptible, slowly tiptoeing back down the stairs.

The steps softly came close to me, then stopped. They did not continue on into the kitchen. *Smart child, this one,* I thought, *wants to make sure I'm really asleep.* Well, I was up to the challenge. I didn't move a hair's breadth. I continued to breathe deeply as if I were fast asleep. I wasn't about to play my hand too soon. I was going to catch this cookie thief in the act. I was already preparing my lecture.

Suddenly, I felt a heaviness settle on me. I didn't move even though it caught me off guard. What was it? Then I realized that this child was putting a blanket over me. Ever so carefully, so as not to wake me, the child covered my feet, then my arms, and finally, with the utmost care, my back. Little hands briefly touched the back of my neck and then the child bent down and, soft as a feather, gave me a loving good-night kiss.

The footsteps retreated—not to the kitchen, but back upstairs. As I cautiously looked to see who it was who had covered me, I was glad that my youngest daughter, Patricia, didn't look back from the staircase. She would have seen her mother with tears streaming down her face.

God did give me what I asked for at my First Holy Communion. Maybe he took a little while, and maybe he didn't answer my prayer in the way I expected, but I was satisfied. Even though my mother hadn't known how to cross that gaping four-foot space to kiss me good night, somehow my children had learned how.

Georgette Symonds

Anticipating the Empty Nest

The two most important things a parent can give a child are roots and wings.

Hodding Carter

Tomorrow is about to arrive. My first child is preparing to leave for college, and the family unit will change forever. This is not a surprise to me, and yet, I am deeply surprised by how quickly this day is speeding toward us. I'm not quite finished with her. I feel betrayed by time.

This is a happy and healthy step in the expected, and hoped for, chain of milestones. She is eager and ready to leave, but I am not nearly ready to let her go. I need to make a few more cupcakes with her, read and recite from *Goodnight Moon,* and maybe create one more fruit basket from Play-Doh. I want to tell her, "Wait a minute!" and have her stand still. And in that time I would hurry to fill her head with the things about life that I am afraid I forgot to tell her. But standing still, she would impatiently reply, "Yes, Mom, I know. You've told me." And she would be right; but I can't help feeling that I forgot something.

Seventeen years ago, as I stood over her crib watching her breathe, I wrote a letter to my four-day-old infant. It said, "These are the days when doorknobs are unreachable, the summer is long, and tomorrow takes forever to arrive." In this letter I told her of the plans and dreams I had for the two of us. I promised her tea parties in winter, and tents in the spring. We would do art projects and make surprises for her daddy. And I promised her experience. We would examine sand and flowers and rocks and snowflakes. We would smell the grass, the ocean and burning wood. I would have the gift of learning about our world once again, as she absorbed it for the first time.

We experienced so much more than I promised on that night long ago. We endured many of life's painful interruptions. When the continuity of our plans had to pause to accommodate sorrow, we grew from the shared hurt and the coping. I never promised her that all of our experiences would be happy, just that her father and I would be there with unquestioning support.

When this tomorrow is actually here, I will keep the final promise I made to my baby daughter. In the letter I told her, "I will guide you as safely as I can to the threshold of adulthood; and there, I will let you go . . . for the days quickly pass when doorknobs are unreachable, summers are long, and tomorrow takes forever to arrive."

As I prepare to let her go, I reflect upon her first day of nursery school, when I, like countless mothers before me, said good-bye to a tearful child and went back to look in the school window a few minutes later. I needed to know if she was still crying. I believe that in September, when I leave this child at her college dorm, she will slip down to the parking lot and find me there, crying.

Seventeen years ago I watched her breathe. Tomorrow I will watch her fly.

Bonnie Feuer

Teddy Bear Tonic

It was my fortieth birthday, an event some women dread, but others celebrate. For me, it was time for my first mammogram. I always made sure I followed the guidelines for preventative health care. This year, the kind woman at my gynecologist's office told me that it was time to add mammograms to the annual checkup.

As luck would have it, the first available appointment was on my birthday. I hesitated. After all, who wants to spend her birthday at the doctor's office? Then I recalled some advice that I'd once heard: your birthday is a perfect reminder for annual physicals.

While I was feeling somewhat intimidated by my first mammogram, the staff made every effort to put me at ease. Just when I thought I was done, however, the nurse came in and told me they needed to repeat the films. There was a thickening, she said. Nothing to worry about though, large-breasted women sometimes needed to be repositioned.

I waited again. The nurse came back and told me that the doctor would be right in. I thought, *That's nice—the doctor takes the time to see everyone who comes in for a mammogram.*

It gave me a feeling of confidence.

But my confidence vanished when the doctor informed me there was a suspicious area that required further study. "Not to worry," she said. "Everything's fine."

So down the hall I marched for an ultrasound. The room was dark. The doctor was serious. Trying some humor, I said, "The last time I had an ultrasound, there was a baby."

But there was no baby this time, and soon I was asking the dreaded question. "Is it cancer?"

The doctor was noncommittal, "This concerns me," was all she said. She suggested a biopsy. Right then and there.

I was not ready for that. My simple mammogram had turned into a six-hour marathon session. I had been shuffled back and forth for one test after another, now culminating in the biopsy.

I drove home on automatic pilot. Luckily, the doctor's office was a mere five minutes from my house. I drove through traffic wearing my sunglasses, which hid the tears pouring from my eyes. I stifled the screams I felt rising in my gut, as I thought, *I am forty years old, too young. It's my birthday. Why is this happening to me?*

Unfortunately, my three kids were already home from school when I arrived. I didn't know how I was going to deal with this cancer scare, but one thing I did know was that I could not deal with the kids at that moment.

I had to pass through the family room to go upstairs to the sanctuary of my bedroom. Hoping the kids were completely enthralled by the television, I went through the room quickly, then ran upstairs and threw myself on the bed, unleashing all my pent-up rage and fear.

A knock on the door heralded the arrival of my oldest daughter, fourteen-year-old Robyn. I couldn't let her in because my distress was too obvious. "I'll be right down," I shouted through the door.

Robyn went away, and I breathed a sigh of thanks.

It seemed just a few minutes later when the door opened. My husband, Paul, walked in, and looked on helplessly as I dissolved into a puddle. He gathered me in his arms to offer what comfort he could.

"Robyn called me. She thinks you have breast cancer," he said simply.

How could she possibly have known? It turned out that resourceful little Robyn had not been convinced by my assurances that I was okay. She had known something was wrong when I walked through the house with my sunglasses on. Evidently the sound of my wracking sobs had scared her. (I thought I'd muffled them so that no one would hear.) Young Detective Robyn then consulted my Day-Timer and noted that I had been to the doctor's office. Not recognizing the name of my usual physician, she looked the name up in the phone book. The large advertisement for the breast center told her all she needed to know. Fearing the worst, she called her dad at work.

I told Paul the whole story of my six-hour ordeal, and he suggested we better face the troops. Letting their suspicions grow would be worse than the truth.

We both went downstairs, and Paul lined the kids up on the couch. It was our first family summit. I cleared my throat. *I can do this,* I told myself.

Then I looked at the fear plastered all over the young faces of my three children: Robyn, on the brink of womanhood; John, a brave soldier, not quite twelve; and Lisa, still my baby at ten.

I couldn't do it. Paul took over. Sitting next to me, clutching my hand, he explained very succinctly that I was having a problem. Yes, breast cancer was suspected, but we wouldn't know until the results of the tests came back.

Robyn, so resourceful and perceptive in spotting the problem, didn't say a word. She has always been hard to read. John was full of questions; he needed the details. Lisa cried, clinging to me.

Somehow we got through a hastily prepared dinner. It was all I could do to retain my composure. Afterwards, I made an abrupt retreat to my room.

After a while, there was a timid knock on the door. Robyn, my quiet one, entered, clutching the teddy bear she'd had since childhood. She sat down next to me on the bed and handed me the teddy bear. "He's always made me feel better," she said.

Such simple words, such heartfelt sentiments. My daughter was trying to comfort me in the only way she knew. I opened my arms to receive the token of my daughter's love. And yes, that teddy bear *did* make me feel better at the end of that long and difficult day.

During subsequent days, I traveled a tortuous road. The diagnosis was indeed cancer, but I made it through surgery, chemotherapy and radiation.

Although Robyn is now too old to give me teddy bears, Lisa, our youngest, still bestows familiar bear-shaped tokens of love on me, with pink ribbons attached.

I call it Teddy-Bear Power. It really does make everything all better.

Bonnie Walsh Davidson

The Day Mama Went on Strike

I knew something was wrong as soon as I opened my eyes that frosty Saturday morning. No one had turned up the heat for one thing. That is, Mama had not turned up the heat. And I did not smell any breakfast smells. Something was definitely wrong. So I ran to the hall, quick-switched the thermostat to sixty-five and jumped back into bed.

But I couldn't stop wondering what was wrong. I jumped out again and went to the kitchen. Nothing. No crumbs, no coffee.

Even if it was Saturday, Mama always got up early anyway. My sister, Althea, was still asleep in our room. I knew this because no one was in the bathroom, and Althea was always either asleep or in the bathroom. That was her whole life.

So I went to look for Mama. And there she was on the living-room sofa. That's where she always slept because we had only one bedroom. Sometimes Althea or I said, "Mama, you come on and sleep in here, and we'll take turns sleeping on the couch," and Mama said, "With all that giggling and snoring in there? Uh-uh. No thanks."

Anyway, I went to look at Mama. Mama was not asleep. She was looking back at me. She was looking at me with both eyes. "Don't bother me," she said. "I am on strike."

"What do you mean, Mama?"

"I mean I am on strike, girl, and you better leave me alone." She threw back the covers. She picked up this sign, you know, like you see people on TV marching around with that say ON STRIKE.

"That's not funny, Mama," I said. "Where'd you get it?"

"No, it isn't funny, and I made it myself."

"Are you going out somewhere on strike then?" I gave a little laugh.

"No," she said. "I am on strike right here."

I went to wake up Althea. I didn't know what else to do. Althea was older, but she mostly didn't know anything. Still, maybe together we would have an idea.

We went to the kitchen, and I told Althea what Mama said. "And I'm hungry," I finished.

"So," Althea said, "eat." She looked at herself in the mirror, rearranging her bangs.

I stuck my head into the living room. "Mama," I said, "are you going to make corn cakes this morning?"

"Definitely . . ." Mama said.

"Oh, good," said Althea.

". . . not," Mama finished.

"Are you going to make anything at all?"

"I am going to make tracks. Nothing but tracks."

She stood up and started slowly circling the room, carrying her sign and chanting.

"What's Mama saying?" Althea asked.

We listened hard. It sounded like: "I don't know, and I don't care. Going to spend the day in my underwear."

"Man," I said. "Mama has gone bananas."

Althea looked scared. "What'll we do?" she asked.

"We'll have to bring her to her senses," I said. I sat down at the table and wrote a note:

Dear Mama,

Now cut that out. We will make our bed, if that's what you want . . . right after we eat. But you should not go on strike. It could be bad for us. We are only little children and we need a mama to take care of us.

Lilly and Althea,
Your only daughters

I took the note to Mama. Mama read it. She took a pencil out of her pocket and wrote an answer. She folded it and gave it to me. In the kitchen Althea bent over my shoulder, and I unfolded the note and read what Mama had written.

"HA!" it said.

"Is that all?" asked Althea.

"That is all," I said.

"What is the matter with Mama? I didn't do anything." Althea looked around, waving her hands over the dishes in the sink, her books and papers on the floor, her left boot under the table.

I said, "Neither did I. Except that night when I wouldn't set the table, and we had to eat on the floor."

Althea said, "I liked it. It was like a picnic. And all I did was, I was late for dinner."

"Five times."

"Well, that's better than six."

"Mama sure got tired of sending me down the street looking for you," I said. "And I sure got tired of going too."

"So what are we going to do?"

"I don't know." I pushed the laundry basket aside and sat down. "First, let's eat."

We poured milk over cereal, and I spilled some, and Althea put her finger in it and wrote a bad word on the table, and I told her to stop that, and we had a very small fight right there.

Mama started chanting louder and louder and stamping her feet while she was walking around on strike.

"Man," Althea whispered. "We better be quiet."

So we went into our room to think about things. Well, I did. Althea went into the bathroom and looked into the mirror. When she opened the door it was all steamy and a big cloud followed her out and she said, "Is Mama still— you know?"

"Yeah," I said. Althea had her hair in this new 'do, and she asked me if I liked it.

"I don't know," I said, and Althea said, "You can never make up your mind about anything," and we had another very small fight.

And then Mama started chanting again. Louder. And with new words: "I don't care, and I don't know. I'm on strike and ready to blow."

I peeked out into the living room. "Wow," I said. I turned to Althea. "She has on the green dress!"

"Oh, man," Althea said. "This is serious."

This green dress was one Mama got from a friend, and it was so shiny you could almost see yourself in it, and Mama had green shoes too, and you could see your face in them if you bent over, and she was leaving.

"Mama," I said, "where are you going?"

"Out," she said.

I was cool. "Out where?" I asked. "In case someone calls."

"No one will call. But I left a note just in case."

"Oh. What does it say?"

"It says I went out." She pulled on her wooly gloves.

"That's not telling us very much, Mama."

"Strikers do not have to tell everything they know."

"I don't want to know everything you know, Mama. I only want to know where you are going."

"I told you. I am going out. Do not worry. I've checked with Mrs. Watkins upstairs. She will be home all day if you need her. The icebox is full of food, and the drawer is full of socks. You'll be okay." She went out. And she slammed the door.

I looked at Althea. Althea looked at me. Althea looked in the mirror. We looked at television. There was nothing good on, but we watched till we couldn't stand it any more.

"Well?" I said.

"Well, what?"

"I don't know," I said. "I feel lonely, and you're right here."

"Me too," Althea said. "I feel lonely and awful. In my stomach, right here." She put her hand on her chest, right where mine was hurting.

"Mama is mean," I said.

"She is?"

"She left us, didn't she, without a word?"

"Well, yes."

"I don't think she's mean. I miss her, and I love her, and I'm going to cry."

"No, you're not. No crying!"

Althea's chin quivered, and her voice shook, and she hollered at me. "Yes, I am. I'm crying. I want Mama to come home." Big tears came out of her eyes and rolled down her face.

I said, "Here now, listen to me. We should keep busy. That will help the time pass faster."

"No."

"Yes it will. Before you know it Mama will come back and you'll say, 'Oh, Mama—back already?'"

"I will not."

"Yes you will. Now come on." I took Althea to our room by the hand. "Here," I said. "Separate the clean stuff from the dirty stuff."

"If it's on the floor," she said, wiping her eyes, "it's dirty."

"No, no. There's a difference between floor-dirty and wearing-dirty. Now do it."

Althea made piles of stuff as I threw it out to her, her head in the closet, like a dog digging a hole and throwing dirt up behind him. I gave Althea fifty cents and the bag of laundry and she came back for fifty more, and then she ran to the Laundromat. While she was gone I made the bed. Althea had 51 books and 6,789 crumbs in her side. I also swept the floor.

Althea came back and said that she was not busy any more and the time was not either passing fast. "It's only two o'clock," she said. She started quivering her chin-skin again, and I put both hands up.

"Wait!" I hollered. "Don't do that. We'll cook!"

Althea looked at me funny.

"You know. Like bake."

So we did, and I made a cake, and it smelled chocolaty in the oven, and the icing was warm and sweet. Then I set the table and Althea made the tacos, and we went into the living room and sat.

At five o'clock Mama came in.

Althea jumped up. "Oh, Mama," she said. She threw her arms around Mama. "Where've you been?"

"Well, I went to the library and got a book about voodoo and then to the art museum, to look at watercolors, and then I bought something at the Emporium."

"What did you buy?"

"A new green dress."

I stood up and went to the kitchen. I turned on the oven for the tacos.

Mama put on her apron and made a salad. Althea brewed tea, and I grated cheese.

Mama pulled her new green dress out of the bag. We stood around her and said how pretty it was.

And it was, too.

Nancy West

The Peach-Colored Crayon

In the summer of 1958, when I turned seven years old, my mother became active as a volunteer for an organization called the Fresh Air Fund, which provided "summer vacations" (actually a couple of weeks living with a suburban family), for inner-city children, most of whom were black. That year, we had the first of what would be several regular yearly visits from a little girl named Viola, who was exactly my age and lived in the Bronx.

Since the plethora of toys available in the stores was still a phenomenon of the future, all of the little girls in the neighborhood had the same kind of doll. My mother bought one for Viola, and we spent hours playing "house" and "school" with our dolls. My mother went to the five-and-ten store in town and bought a pattern, and sewed several identical doll dresses, one for each little girl on the block. The morning that she finished the dresses, I went with my mother to deliver them. We started at the house next door, and presented the dresses to each delighted child.

The last dress was intended for Celeste, who lived across the street. Her family had moved into the neighborhood only recently, so I didn't know her very well yet.

When Celeste's mother opened the door, she just stared at us. My mother started to explain about the doll dress, and held it out to Celeste, who reached for it eagerly. But before she could take it, her mother pushed her hand away. "She doesn't need it," Celeste's mother said firmly. My mother was puzzled. But Celeste's mother glared at us. "You have no business bringing a Negro child into this neighborhood. "She slammed the door, leaving my mother and me speechless on the doorstep.

I suddenly realized that Celeste's mother was talking about Viola. It occurred to me just then that somewhere along the line, I had stopped thinking of Viola as "a Negro child." The other kids and I had been somewhat suspicious of her when she first arrived, since none of us had ever met anyone who looked like her before. But Viola had certain talents and abilities that quickly endeared her to us: she knew how to braid, and she could jump rope better than anyone on the block, including the two fourth-grade girls who lived at the end of the street. By the second or third day that she was with us, Viola was just one of the kids. But Celeste's mother didn't know her the way we did, so to her, Viola was just "a Negro child."

But that same afternoon was my friend Karen's birthday party, so I all but forgot about the incident with Celeste's mother. We wasted no time trying out all of the new toys Karen had received as birthday gifts. One of the most intriguing was a box of sixty-four Crayola crayons. This was the top-of-the-line, most expensive box of crayons there was, the one with the sharpener built right into the box, and we were all envious. Karen brought the precious crayons and stacks of paper out into the backyard, and we crowded around the picnic table, perusing the colors. We marveled over "burnt umber" and "periwinkle," and the subtle difference between "blue-green" and "green-blue."

But when we came to the crayon named "flesh," I looked

at Viola. I knew what the word "flesh" meant, and I knew that the name was wrong, but the other kids paid no attention. After all, they didn't know Viola the way I did. Viola hadn't lived in their houses, hadn't shared their bedrooms. And she hadn't run barefoot on the beach with them, and discovered, as Viola and I did one afternoon, that the soles of her feet were exactly the same color as the sun-browned tops of mine.

I told my mother about this misnamed crayon. "It's not fair!" I complained. My mother agreed, and, always the social activist, she suggested that I write a letter to the Crayola Company. With my mother's help, I carefully wrote the letter out in my very best handwriting, addressed the envelope, and put on a stamp.

What I wrote in that letter was the truth, as I saw it, the summer that I turned seven: that "flesh" can't be just one color, because my "flesh" and Viola's "flesh" were different all over our bodies, except for the soles of her feet and the tops of mine. I knew that the name of this crayon wasn't fair to Viola. I knew this because we were friends, and we played and ate and slept and swam together.

I never received a reply to my letter.

Viola came and stayed with us for four or five more summers, until she got too old for the program. My mother stayed in touch with her and her family for a few more years after that, but eventually we lost contact. I grew up and moved away and had my own family. I don't know what became of Viola.

But when my own daughter turned five, she had a birthday party, and someone gave her a box of sixty-four Crayola crayons. It was the top-of-the-line, most expensive box there was, the one with the sharpener built right into the box. After the party, after I had gathered up all the torn wrapping paper and thrown away the paper plates full of melted ice cream, I opened up the box of crayons. I looked through the box until I found the crayon I wanted, and I pulled it out of the box and held it up. The label read "Peach."

I don't know when, or why, the Crayola Company changed the name of that crayon. And I don't know if my letter had anything to do with that. But I like to think that it did. After all, they say that you can't really understand another person unless you walk a mile in their shoes.

Or run on the beach together, with bare feet.

Phyllis Nutkis

7

MOTHERS AND DAUGHTERS

*The apple doesn't fall too far from the tree.
Like father, like son. Like mother, like
daughter.*

Anonymous

The Bike Trip

My mother's life was one huge story, and a major chapter was "the bike trip." In 1956, my mother, June, rode a three-speed Schwinn from New York City to California, not because she wanted to be a wild girl, not because she wanted to prove anything, but because she wanted to see the Pacific Ocean.

As a child, I'd sit on my mother's lap and say, "Tell me the stories."

And she'd start with the beginning: about how she couldn't afford a plane ticket or a train ticket to see the country, so she decided to ride her bike. About her girlfriends thinking she was crazy; girls didn't *do* those things; it was unsafe. About convincing a Girl Scouting friend, Teri Foster, to ride across with her. "We didn't really think we'd do it, riding bicycles across the country! But then Schwinn sponsored us, and then the *Today Show* heard about us, and then we had to. It was a lark, really, something to make my friends laugh, and now here we were, two girls on bicycles wanting to ride to California."

"What did you have to pack?" I said, leaning back into her.

"I didn't know what I'd need, so I brought along a little of everything." And she'd describe how she packed a bathing suit, cocktail dress, high heels, pearls, some shorts and shirts, red lipstick and a Bible. "A bathing suit for hot days, an old wool sweater for cold and always my saddle shoes because they were the *best*. They held up in the heat, stayed warm in the rain and still looked nice at the end of the day."

She still has them.

"But why'd you bring a cocktail dress and high heels?" I asked, and this would always make her laugh, make her pull out red lipstick from her shirt pocket and smear it on her lips.

"Back then, you couldn't go out to eat in shorts or sandals. You dressed for dinner, and we were invited out quite often. By cowboys, businessmen, but usually preachers from the local churches. We were celebrities."

There was no talk about fear or worries about the unknown. She simply got on her bike and rode. She didn't have an itinerary, no specific route, other than pointing her bike west and riding.

"They didn't have motel chains back then, so we just asked farmers or preachers, mayors or policemen if we could sleep in city parks, front yards or barns." The towns they passed through called them "celebrity girl cyclists" and they were given keys to cities, parades and new tires. "Sometimes we got to sleep in an extra bedroom of a kind person, but usually we requested camping under the stars. We had our sleeping bags and always made a campfire. We invited anyone who passed by to sing Girl Scout songs with us."

She sang in hoedowns in Colorado, and was a chambermaid in the Grand Canyon "when money got low. I didn't have a credit card, and there were no ATMs back then for money." And she talked about the West being some place dyed in red and rock, with sunsets that held the sky.

My favorite part was watching her face when she talked about California. "We finally got there; we were set up on blind dates. Guess who my date ended up being?" she'd always ask, and I'd always answer loudly, "Dad!" They were married three months later.

I came along six years after that.

And always, I craved being inside her stories. I wished to run my fingers over the edges of the Rockies, along the glowing yellow fields of Iowa, wished to splash inside the ponds of New England under stars. I wanted to touch her life, know her inside this special place she called her "adventure of a lifetime."

As I grew older, I stopped sitting on my mother's lap, listening to the old stories of her three-speed, her bicycle bell, the steak and Manhattan dinners in her cocktail dress, that ride across the country. I had other things on my mind, places to go, people to see and didn't have time to listen to her past. I moved away from home after college and traveled in my Chevy Malibu, this lime green dream of a car that held six and went fast, always on the highway. I had my life, or so I thought, until trips back home were filled with worries: Dad with another stroke, Mom counting her blood pressure pills, organizing doctor visits and falling asleep in her old rocking chair, the one that held us together when I was a child. I'd go into the garage where her dusty bike leaned and ring its rusty bell, the old flag still hung lopsided from the handlebars.

On one trip, I found her journal, and I sat with the deteriorating pages, closing my eyes after reading her descriptions of sunsets, early morning hill climbs, cowboys wrangling broncos, aspen trees in fall, how she rode each hill with a friend in mind. And I became her journey. I was the celebrity girl cyclist in her words. I held that journal tightly in my hands and decided then that I needed to go. I would ride my bike across the country.

But no one wanted to go. Friends, coworkers, cousins shook their heads at me, called me loony. "Take a car!"

"You'll be run off the road!" "Why do you want to waste time doing that?" they said. It took me three years to find someone to go with me. I met Brian at my brother's house, this man with curly hair and green eyes who played a guitar and had a dream to ride across the country on a bicycle. When I found out he knew bike maintenance, we had to get married. We started our life together making plans not for children but for bike routes, bike gears, tires and high-performance Lycra. It was all so very romantic.

In 1996, Brian and I started off on our trip, packed for fifty-five days of riding on 24-speed Schwinns. We'd trained for months up mountains in Utah, up and down elevations that would leave us spent and excited at the same time. We didn't know if we'd have our jobs when we got back from the trip, we had nothing saved in the bank, we had mortgage and college loans to pay for, but it didn't matter. We had credit cards. We were ready to go.

Mom was there for the first day of our trip. Of course she had comments.

"Why are you wearing all that rubber stuff?" Mom asked. "I didn't wear that when I went." We were standing in Rockefeller Plaza after our appearance on the *Today Show* with Bryant Gumbel, for our send-off. People walked past us in suits and heels, staring at us in bike shorts and helmets. Mom was coiffed like I'd never seen her before, her usual green eyeshadow and red lipstick replaced by sculpted pink cheeks and lined eyes, hair blown up and over her forehead.

"I told you before Mom. It wicks the sweat away. It's Lycra."

"So wear your bathing suit. I did."

"I don't want to wear a bathing suit."

"You're going to fall off your bike with those shoes."

"They click on and off. I've practiced."

"They frighten me."

"Lots of things frighten you."

"Like now. This," she waved her hand around at the bustling city of New York. "The world has changed from when I went."

"We'll be careful," I said. "We're staying in motels every night."

"I camped. Why aren't you camping? Just ask a nice policeman to guard you in a city park."

We stared at each other, her lined face to my expectant one, and then we laughed with her holding the handlebars. The day was like us, brilliant blue and then blown clouds, and I see how love can be between mother and daughter—this confusing place between rain and sun that often goes unnoticed until it's there in your face.

"I love you," I said, hoping she didn't think that I was canceling out her comments.

"I love you more."

"I'll call you."

"Every night." Her eyes were hard, and I knew then as I know now that she sits by the phone sometimes waiting for me to call.

"Absolutely."

And we were off, in a blaze of tears and blessings and thrown rice from a passerby as if it were a honeymoon we were going on instead of a cross-country ride.

As we rode, there were times when I wanted to give up: in the humidity of the East, my eyes covered in sweat; when the wind in Nebraska blew me straight across the road; through food poisoning and 130-mile days; a blizzard in Colorado and men throwing empty beer bottles against our bike frames. But I didn't. I'd see her face, fragility balanced out with spunk and spice, and keep pedaling on. I couldn't give up or give in because I was her girl; I'd heard the bike trip stories so many times that they were inside my veins, running in and out of my heart, these stories a heartbeat that pounded me over the Poconos, across the fields and plains, up the Rockies, the Sierra Nevadas to the Pacific Ocean. These stories were whispered urgings, prayers uttered in my mother's name to finish, keep at it. I could do it, and would do it.

San Francisco Bay was beautiful on our last leg of the trip, sailboats careening past the bridges, the city in the haze of an indigo sky. The fact that my mother was singing "She'll be comin' round the mountain" at the top of her lungs did not deter us as we dipped tires into the Pacific Ocean. As Brian went up to the boardwalk to drink celebratory wine, Mom and I stared out past the breakers to the sun dipping toward the sea.

"It's all just beginning, isn't it?" she asked. And I didn't know if she was talking about my life or our lives together, this new shared story of time. I didn't want to ask because to me, it didn't matter.

"We did it," I said.

"We sure did." And I knew she was talking about us, mother and daughter. I realized that life is not about accomplishing or finishing but experiencing moments like these and holding them close—my mother's hand in mine, her long gaze over my face as if wanting to memorize me, and the waves rolling over us and up the beach, leaving our feet covered in sand.

I hope my six-year-old daughter finds a road. It might not be along her grandmother's route of 1956. It could take her away from the back roads Brian and I took in 1996, and in fact, maybe she will want her own path apart from ours. But the important thing is the journey, the adventure, a favorite story you want to repeat aloud at night over and over again until it threads itself, a colorful quilt of love, around her heart.

Peggy Newland

The Piano

Three summers ago, I flew to my parents' home in New Jersey to help them prepare to move to a new house. My mother had suffered a series of small strokes, and although the physical damage was slight, she was having trouble going up and down the stairs. So my parents bought a comfortable ranch house in a nearby suburb.

My parents had lived in the old house for forty years. This was the house I had grown up in, the only home I could remember. My mother had redecorated more than once since I'd left. There were new drapes and carpeting in the living room, different furniture in the den. But the basic pieces, the big, solid ones, were still there.

That first night at dinner, we sat at the same dining-room table that we had gathered around for countless family meals and celebrations. And later, when we had finished eating, I played Bach on the grand piano that no one ever played, but which had taken up nearly half of the living room for as long as I could remember. My mother sat on the sofa and smiled as she listened to me play the familiar melody, the one she had heard me practice endlessly, and that she always asked me to play whenever I was there. She'd always been completely tone-deaf—as a child in school music classes, she was told that she should be the "listener"—but she always hummed along when I played this piece.

I woke up early the next morning and got right to work. I decided to start in the attic, since my mother couldn't get up the steps any more. Besides I was already feeling nostalgic about this old house, the house that held our family history in its dusty cupboards and dark closets. The attic, I knew, would have been the least disturbed over the years. If I were to find any of the old, familiar things from my childhood, that's where they would be.

All day long, I sorted through piles of crumbling papers and filled numerous trash bags with stuff that could only be described as "junk"—pieces of broken toys, old magazines that had become decayed and moldy, remnants of mildewed carpeting. But I also found some treasures— several boxes of family photographs.

I carried the boxes downstairs and piled them on the dining room table. After dinner, my parents and I began to sort through the pictures. Many of them were familiar, but others were of people and places that I didn't recognize. I asked my parents about them, but my mother had trouble remembering. The strokes had damaged her memory and her ability to call up the words she needed to express herself, so she was often silent. Every so often, when I came across a particularly intriguing photograph, my mother would start to speak, but before she had gotten very far into the sentence, she would stop with a sigh. It was as if she could only grasp the memory for a few moments, and by the time she was able to find the words to describe it, it had already begun to slip away. Sometimes her eyes filled with tears, and she turned away. I thought that she must have been frustrated, lonely, sad, grieving for the person she had once been. I know I was.

The movers came the next morning. My brothers and I helped my father load some of the more fragile items into the cars, and then they followed the moving truck in a small, slow caravan to the new house. I stayed behind to take one last look around. I hadn't even seen the new house yet, and I wanted to make sure I fixed the old one in my memory while I still had the chance. But the house was empty now. All of the things that had made it a home had been taken to the new place. All I could do now was follow them.

By late afternoon, when the movers were almost finished, I walked around the new house, exploring its spaces, its as yet unfilled closets and empty cupboards. Gradually, as the things from the old house were settled in their new places, the house began to take on a character of its own, one that reminded me of the old one, but with its own personality. The final piece to be brought in was the piano. After the movers left, I sat down and began to play Bach. As I started to play, I realized that because of the bumping and jostling during the move to the new house, the piano would need tuning. But there would be time for that.

We gathered around the dining-room table for dinner that night, my brothers and my parents and I, just the way we used to when we were growing up in the old house. Everyone talked at once, just the way we always had, except for my mother. Now she just listened to the voices of her family. At first it was awkward and odd, the rest of us having to carefully negotiate the gaps my mother had always filled in. But gradually we had found a rhythm, a new way of including my mother in the conversation without her having to speak.

It didn't take long for my parents to settle in to the new house. By the time I visited them again at Thanksgiving, the closets were organized, the books were arranged neatly on the shelves, the pictures had been hung on the walls. There were still a number of cartons in the basement that hadn't yet been emptied, but my parents didn't seem to be in a hurry to finish unpacking these last boxes.

They hadn't had the piano tuned, either. When I sat down to play, I had to try to ignore the notes that were slightly off-key, and concentrate on the melody, the way I remembered it. It sounded a little different, but still, the music was beautiful.

It's been three years since my parents moved. My mother seems less anxious, less sad these days. When her words fail her, her eyes no longer fill with tears. Instead, she shrugs her shoulders. "Oh, well," she says smiling wryly. And I've learned not to be so anxious about her speaking. Sometimes, when I call her on the phone, I just talk about my children or my job. Sometimes, when I am there visiting, we just sit on the couch without saying anything, and she holds my hands. And sometimes she just sits on the bench next to me while I play the piano. It still hasn't been tuned, but my mother hums along anyway. I don't know if she remembers that she is tone-deaf, or if she even realizes that she is humming off-key. But even played on this slightly flawed piano, the rhythms are familiar, the melody still soothing.

Maybe my parents will have the piano tuned one day. Or maybe they won't get around to it. It doesn't really matter. We've all become accustomed to this new way. The music sounds slightly different, but it's still perfectly beautiful.

Phyllis Nutkis

Don't Cry Out Loud

All, everything that I understand, I understand only because I love.

Leo Tolstoy

Why do you let him talk to you like that? I felt like saying.

My teenage brother had just mouthed off again and peeled out of the driveway in his Mustang.

"He's going to get himself fired with that attitude," my mom would begin explaining to Dad when he got home. "I'm so worried. . . ."

My exhausted father showed no support.

"Would you just stop worrying? Good Lord, do you have to be upset about everything?"

My mother and I were exact opposites. I took after my father: strong, fearless and happy to take charge of any situation, while my mother was a pleaser and a server whose motto in life was "Don't rock the boat!" She never spoke up for herself and would never dare send back a steak in a restaurant. She would rather eat around the raw parts than have to confront a waiter. In fact, her favorite phrase was, "It's fine. Let's not make a scene."

My mother was a domestic goddess, and as she proudly called herself, "an efficiency expert."

"Look!" she said grinning proudly one day when I arrived home from school. "I made a swimming suit!"

"How do you make a swimming suit, Mom?"

"Stretch & Sew class," she announced. "I can sew anything!"

I could never even find a swimming suit that fit, let alone sew one from scratch!

My father once dropped her off at the door of a crowded restaurant to put their name on the list while he went and parked. He walked up and found her pulling weeds in the planting area.

"Shirley, what in the world are you doing!"

"Well, I was just standing here waiting, and I looked down and saw all those ugly weeds next to those pretty flowers, so I just decided to pull them myself!"

"Shirl, come out of there!" he said, pulling her out of the bushes.

When I grew up and got married Mom loved to come over and pick me up for a day of shopping.

"I'll be down in a minute!" I would call while frantically tripping over the pile of laundry strewn about the floor of my bedroom. I would gallop down the stairs, and there she would be in my kitchen mopping the entire floor.

"Mom, you don't have to do that!"

"Oh, it's nothing, honey. I had a few minutes while you were getting ready."

Actually, it was delightful having her there to help me when the laundry pile got too much, or it was time to wallpaper, scrape old paint, or do anything involved with housework. Mom ironed her sheets and folded them like tissue paper before placing them in their assigned positions in her linen closet. I remember the first time I walked into a bed and bath store. *This reminds me of something,* I said to myself. *All these perfectly folded linens, lined up according to color. Oh yes—Mom's closet!*

Mom saved small boxes to organize her drawers ("This is the perfect size to stack gloves in!") and never had one empty hanger in any of her closets. ("Each outfit has a hanger. You shouldn't need extra ones if you've organized your closet correctly!") My drawers looked like a bomb went off in them. I still had my wrinkled college T-shirt shoved in the bottom under the hot pink spandex pants that went out in the late '80s.

Mom was my greatest helper, but when I wanted to have deep, transparent discussions, she was afraid to talk about her feelings. Girls of her era were trained to smile, be charming and never, under any circumstances, let anyone see them cry. As a result, my overbearing father would get upset with her, and she would drive off to the mall crying, but always in secret . . . behind her sunglasses.

Mom never learned how to speak up for herself, but somehow she knew how to speak up for me. Maybe that is the real bond between mothers and daughters. She didn't give herself permission to follow her own dreams, but she certainly gave it to her daughter.

"Did you read Carla's latest story?" my sister-in-law asked her during a visit. My mother responded the way she always responded to any of my work: "Isn't she marvelous? Isn't she talented? She could write any kind of book she wanted to! She could accomplish anything!"

The last time I moved, my mother came over to do what she had done for me all her life: clean, organize and get the task done. For some reason, while we packed and swept that afternoon, Mom started to open up.

"Your sons have been given a gift," she said. "You are the greatest mother they could have had."

I scoffed. "Oh, Mom, I don't even know how to cook. I still stare at the butcher counter and ask the guy what in the world you do with meat! I've never even made a roast before!"

"That doesn't matter, dear. They can eat out. Housekeepers can be hired, dishwashers can do dishes, and turkey dinners can be bought at Boston Market. But what you have given those boys is something I never knew how to give."

"What do you mean, Mom?"

"You show them your emotions. You teach them how to feel. You share the deep things in life with them. I wasn't much good at that, I guess. You touch them emotionally, and that is the most important thing of all."

Seven days later Mom died of a sudden, unexplained heart attack. Like the efficiency expert she was, even though perfectly healthy, her funeral had already been arranged, paid for, and a separate checking account set up with instructions typed out in her bottom drawer. There was one more thing though, that she couldn't have planned for: her last laundry pile. I was afraid to touch it. I was in shock, denial, stumbling around her empty condo grief-stricken and overcome with sadness. *Who was going to do it?* Not my brother. I had no sister, no daughter. The one who always said, "Here honey, I'll do it," was gone. It was *my* job now. I loaded the washer and poured in her Fresh Scent Tide and then fell to the ground, weeping in front of her washing machine. I sat there on that spotless laundry-room floor grieving the woman who had defined her life by tasks, but who actually had been the greatest *emotional* support of my life. Every time she did a load of my laundry she was saying, "I love you." And every time she listened to my poem, story, or song and told me I could do it, she was teaching me to feel my feelings and express them without fear. The woman who couldn't show her emotions had touched mine deeper than anyone.

Carla Riehl

First Love

As far back as I can remember, I was the loud, adventurous and mischievous daughter; she was the quiet, traditional and ladylike mother. I always blamed our problems on our age difference. She was thirty-eight when I was born, and at that time, in the late '60s, that was old to have a baby. Though I was never embarrassed that I had the oldest parents in my group of friends, I felt that their advanced age accounted for their being so strict and conservative.

It was inevitable that the "loud" daughter and the "quiet" mother would clash. In my early teens, we argued a lot and it created an ever-growing wedge between us. One major problem was how strict she was when it came to boys and dating. We argued until we were blue in the face about when I would be allowed to date. Finally, the magic number was determined . . . sixteen.

In no time I was sixteen and dating. She didn't talk to me about it directly, but I could tell my mother was very concerned. I couldn't understand why. Didn't she realize I was a responsible, intelligent girl who would never date a jerk? I assumed it was due to her "old-fashioned" ways.

She was a strict "older mom" who just didn't understand today's world.

Then toward the end of my first year of dating, I met him. He was a great guy. My parents liked him instantly, though I could still see a look of concern on my mother's face. Was she *ever* going to trust me? My boyfriend and I were in love and after going together steadily for a year, I started college. Anyone who has experienced first love and then a sudden separation knows the chances of staying together are slim to none. When we broke up, so did my heart. I was devastated. This eighteen-year-old know-it-all suddenly didn't know what to do. I immediately ran to my "mommy" and cried on her shoulder like a baby.

Did she lecture me? Did she say, "I told you so"? Not once. Instead, she slept with me in my bed, held my hand and even kissed me on the forehead just like when I was a little girl. She never made me feel stupid or ashamed. She listened to my sad story and watched silently as the tears rolled down my face.

After a while, although I was feeling better, I was still very confused and didn't quite understand what had just happened to me. I was very angry, and I expressed my concerns to my mother. I was surprised at the tone of my voice. It had a harder edge. I wasn't so trusting or naïve; I felt older and more tired.

My mother gently explained the reasons she had been so concerned during my courtship, opening up to me like she never had before. She had always been so conservative with me about sharing her emotions that I sometimes wondered if she had ever been a teenager. Now, she told me about her first love and how she'd felt when it was over. Her heart had been broken, and the tears hadn't stopped for weeks. When it was all said and done, she'd felt just as hopeless as I was feeling. She told me that in time her pain went away, becoming only a faint memory.

She assured me that one day I would meet the man I would marry, and when I thought of my first heartbreak, I would smile. I would forget the pain and only remember the love.

I was surprised, shocked and relieved all at once. Surprised that my father wasn't my mother's first love. Shocked that she had actually shared this story with me. And relieved that my mother was not only a mom, but also a woman who had experienced the same kind of pain I had . . . and survived. It was then that my mother became my best friend.

After that, I shared all the challenges and problems in my life with her. College, dating, career and of course, more heartbreaks. But none ever seemed as serious as the first. I loved how close we were. Even my friends commented on our relationship. It made us both very happy and proud.

Then one day, many years later, I met him: my future husband. The first thing I did was call my mom and tell her all about him. During the phone conversation she asked me if I remembered my first heartbreak. Giggling, I answered yes, wondering why she'd asked.

I could hear the tenderness in her voice as she responded, "Are you smiling?"

Sophia Valles Bligh

It's a Date!

"Should I meet him there Saturday night?" she asked.

"Of course not. You know the family rule," I said. The cold pork chops hissed against the sizzling skillet. "Your date must always . . ."

"It's *not* a date," she interrupted.

". . . come right to the door," I chanted without missing a beat. We had rehearsed this very conversation before. A slight pause followed. "Where is he taking you?"

"Out for supper and maybe somewhere afterwards." Panic peppered her voice. "A whole evening together—alone. What will we talk about?"

"Knowing you, you'll talk about anything and everything. Since when have you been at a loss for words, anyway?" I joked, handing her a short stack of stoneware salad plates.

"But this is different. I hardly know Tom."

Brushing aside crisp kitchen curtains, I peered into the deepening dusk. A gentle rain blurred the boundaries, skewing the scene like a photograph out of focus. "Well, there's always the weather. Better yet, get him to talk about himself. Ask your boyfriend . . ."

"He's *not* my boyfriend."

". . . about his interests. And, by the end of the date . . ."

"It's *not* a date!"

" . . . you'll know each other better and probably have lots to say," I encouraged. After all, I was experienced with this mother-daughter thing. I had raised four teenagers—all at one time—in the not-so-distant past. Could this be much different?

"Well—if you're sure." She paused. "It's just that . . ."

"Yes?" I coaxed, a little impatient with her hesitancy, my mind racing ahead to the details of dinner.

But the voice that answered had slowed, softened and deepened.

"Do you realize how long it's been?" Her words hung there, suspended, unsupported in the sudden silence. Reaching across me to the stove, she flipped the pork chops and turned down the heat.

". . . how long it's been," she cleared her throat, "since I've dated, I mean? Fifty-five years! With your dad gone so long now, I think . . . maybe . . . well . . . maybe it's time. Why, Carol, I was seventeen the last time I went on a date."

I turned—once again a daughter—and winked. "Oh, but Mom . . . it's *not* a date!"

Carol McAdoo Rehme

My Daughter, the Musician

*F*urnish an example, stop preaching, stop shielding, don't prevent self-reliance and initiative, allow your children to develop along their own lines.

Eleanor Roosevelt

When people I don't know ask me if I have children I say, "Yes, a daughter and a son, both in their twenties."

"Oh, really? What do they do?"

"One works in television production and the other in a rock band," I say.

Invariably, the next question is: "What instrument does your son play?"

I smile. "My son is a television producer and a photographer. My *daughter* plays lead guitar. She's also the vocalist and writes all the songs for the band," I add.

Almost as invariably, the next question is: "Ah—an all-girl band?"

"No, she's the only woman in Bell (the name of the band)."

"Oh."

I wish all those people were with me right now, sitting in this audience, in this theater in Seattle, watching my daughter on stage; playing, singing, strutting and, in general, doing, as it were, her thing.

"Is she good?"

"She's great! But it is possible I am the wrong person to ask."

You see, Vanessa was not born with what you might call a God-given singing voice. I was not surprised. She came by it naturally. All my life I have been musically challenged. When I was in elementary school, we were made to try out for the school chorus. The song each of us had to sing was "Bicycle Built for Two."

I can still remember the humiliation of having to get up in front of my class and warble, wobbily, "Daisy, Daisy, give me your answer do!" At the second extremely flat "Daisy," there were audible snickers. However, the school rule was that if you wanted to be in the chorus, you got to be in the chorus, so I was asked, somewhat diplomatically, if I would mind just moving my lips instead of actually, well, singing.

Of course, I was hurt, but I let it go. After all, I could draw pictures and write stories better than the other kids. And later, so could my daughter, which may help to explain why I pushed her in those areas and gently (I thought) steered her away from music.

Didn't work. The more I pushed in one direction, the more determined Vanessa became. Stubborn as a mule (I don't know *where* she gets it), Vanessa devoted hours to her guitar. She listened, watched, studied, practiced, learned. Same with the singing. She would not give up. We fought. I tried to discourage her. I lost.

Now, with the release of her first album, reviewers are calling her voice "strong," "gutsy," "true" and "soulful."

They say the same thing about her songs. And so I sit in a theater next to all these strangers, bursting with pride. Do I say, "Wow! That's my daughter up there"? Yes, but only to myself because I have been forbidden to say it to everybody else.

Heading backstage, I am ashamed of myself. I had actively tried to keep my daughter from pursuing her love, her music. I thought I knew best. I didn't want to see her hurt. "Follow your dreams," I would say, when what I really meant was, "Follow my dreams for you."

In one of her songs, Vanessa writes, "Give me something to hold to/ give me something to reach/ and I can take on anything and shine like the sea/ But ask me to live without that/ I can't make it work—can you?" No, I guess not.

And it doesn't really matter whether Vanessa becomes tomorrow's singing sensation or fades quietly away into obscurity. What does matter is that my daughter stood up to her mother and followed her dream—and her mother, old dog that she is, learned a new trick. It's called humility.

Linda Ellerbee

She Came Back Bearing Gifts

The time is always ripe to do right.

Martin Luther King Jr.

My daughter, Carey, was never really like other children. She began talking in sentences by the time she was a year old. She was extremely inquisitive and always too mature for her age. She excelled scholastically and showed signs of musical talent at an early age. She was inducted into our state's program for gifted and talented children and was invited to be a violinist in the local Youth Symphony. Awards for outstanding achievement in academics and music lined the bookcase in her bedroom. Her stepfather and I couldn't have been more proud.

Then, slowly and dramatically, everything changed. Carey's appearance changed. She started running around with a new group of "friends." She dropped out of the symphony and sports. Truancy notices and reports of her absences from school became commonplace. She became sullen, withdrawn, belligerent and, at times, violent. She scoffed at any form of discipline, crept out of the house in the middle of the night, and often stayed out all night. She ran away from home three times. Carey had discovered drugs.

I fretted, worried, and spent many sleepless nights anticipating a call from local police telling me she was in jail or, worse yet, dead. I lamented over the things I must have done wrong in raising this child and wondered what had become of the moral and emotional foundation I thought I had provided her. Little did I know that this was just the beginning of the end of my dream of a "normal" family with a perfect life.

Over the next two years, my primary goal was to "fix" Carey. I asked a police friend to "scare" some sense into her. I arranged a private "tour" for her of the juvenile detention center. I put her into private counseling. Last, but not least, we moved away from the city, away from the bad influences. Carey loves horses, so we bought three, one for each of us, thinking that if we shared her interest as a family her problems would get better. It was a good plan and it did work . . . for a while. Before long, it all started again.

Just when I thought things couldn't get any worse, my husband confessed that he was seeing someone. We separated on Memorial Day weekend. I'm not sure how I made it through the first few months. I was scared and lost. I couldn't sleep, forgot to eat, worked twelve-hour days between two hours' driving time, and did my best to keep up with three horses, two dogs, fifteen cats, three acres of yard work and normal household chores. As you might guess, Carey's contribution was, at best, minimal. I felt hopeless.

Then came Christmas. I had always loved Christmas, a time that would bring back sweet memories of childhood surprises, family truces and special traditions. But this year there was nothing to celebrate, no reason to even drag out the Christmas decorations.

On Christmas Eve, I worked until noon. If I could have, I probably would have worked right through to the new year. The hour drive seemed longer as I imagined my cold, empty house . . . very much like my heart. I pulled into the drive, reluctantly got out of the car, obligingly petted the dogs and grudgingly walked toward the back door. Suddenly a sweet aroma wafted toward me, beckoning me forward. As I opened the door, a potpourri of tantalizing scents enveloped me. I first identified the smell of food . . . not ordinary, quick-fix food, but festive, only-on-holiday food. Then I recognized the sweet smell of scented holiday candles. If my nose was merely delighted, my eyes were in awe! This house I was entering had been transformed from the drafty, colorless old farmhouse I had left behind that morning into a warm and glowing Christmas fantasy, a joy to all my senses! Soft Christmas music playing on the stereo relocated from Carey's upstairs bedroom gently competed for my attention to the holiday décor as I floated through each neatly groomed room. When I reached the living room, Carey was sitting in her holiday finery, complete with an apron and a childlike smile I remembered from long ago but hadn't seen in several years. She said, "Sit down and relax. Christmas dinner will be ready soon."

I'm not sure what I said to her then to let her know how much I appreciated what she had done, but no words could have adequately described the way I felt. I just sat and allowed the sights, sounds and smells to fill my senses . . . and my heart. Over Cornish game hens stuffed with cranberry-orange dressing, homemade sweet potatoes (not from a can), rice pilaf and creamy chocolate pudding, we laughed as we talked of Christmases passed.

Lying in bed that night, I thanked God for giving me my daughter. The daughter whom I thought I had lost had just blessed me with the most wonderful gift I have ever received: a much-needed reminder of the true spirit of Christmas . . . love and hope.

Luann Warner

The Pink High-Tops

It was late November. We wandered the mall, shopping with the multitudes during the pre-Christmas rush. My two little ones and my mum moseyed along, taking in the holiday gala.

Then I spotted them, a pair of pink high-top sneakers.

I delighted in their pastel cockiness, gentle pale pink on aggressive high-tops. I had found my Christmas present. "That's what I want Mum, those sneakers," I said.

She looked at me as if I had lost my mind. I am sure she had expected me to suggest a cashmere sweater for Christmas, but instead I had found an inexpensive but delightful bit of fun.

A week later, when I returned from a conference in Washington, D.C., the pain in my lower back was unbearable. I went to the hospital, underwent some tests and was admitted. Surgery was scheduled for the next day. *No big deal,* I thought. *Take out three discs, be home in four days, a few weeks off. We'll manage.*

Something went wrong.

I vaguely remember waking in the recovery room screaming in pain. I remember my mother sitting beside my bed and saying her rosary. In a stupor, I could only begin to imagine what character-building events lay ahead.

While I lay in the hospital, my husband, Tom, had to shop and wrap. My father visited faithfully every day and watered my miniature Christmas tree. Two days before Christmas, with much pleading, I was released from the hospital and taken home heavily sedated, bent at forty-five degrees on a walker.

The words from the day before kept ringing through my head. My husband was sitting nearby, incredulous. The surgeon, my nemesis, chart in hand, spoke. His words were crisp, clear and delivered unemotionally: "You will never walk unassisted again. But with therapy, we can help straighten you some, and with time the pain will gradually subside until it can be managed."

Who is he talking to? He can't mean me. All I kept thinking was, *I have two young children. I'm only 31 years old. Of course I'll walk upright again.*

At home I felt as if I were in a fog shrouded in pain. The tree was up. Presents were piled beneath it. I was laid in a recliner on an egg crate mattress. The recliner accommodated the bend in my body. The codeine and other drugs helped block the overwhelming pain and fear.

On Christmas morning, Mum and Dad came for breakfast. As the gifts were being opened, Mum said, "Tom, you did a fine job. Everything looks lovely." I noticed the sparkle of the paper. Looking closer, I saw that everything was wrapped in "Happy Hanukkah" paper. I couldn't laugh. It hurt to just turn my head. Poor Tom, he'd tried. But the paper—what a kick. Our Hanukkah Christmas is still a wonderful memory.

The little ones helped me open my gifts. And there they were, a pair of pink high-tops; I'd forgotten all about them. I started to weep, loving them yet wondering whether I would ever be able to wear them. I wept uncontrollably.

The kids didn't have a clue what was wrong. Tom rushed them to the kitchen for blueberry pancakes, the annual Christmas fare. My mother, unflappable as always, just looked at me without as much as a question and said, "You'll wear them."

Three weeks later, my beloved dad died unexpectedly—another bad dream—and I was back in the hospital for the first of the many tests and hospitalizations to follow. I was put into traction and finally a full-body cast, and slowly I worked my way back to some semblance of an upright position.

At first, I was bent at the waist, face to the floor. I wore weights on my ankles and a body cast. I moved on a walker. There were no high heels, no fancy dresses. There were only sweat clothes to fit over the body hardware, but my feet were dressed in pretty pink. Everywhere I went I wore my pink high-tops. For the first year, they were truly all I saw when attempting to learn to walk again.

It took three full years of pain, perseverance, faith in God and a deliberate belief in myself. It took family support, but I learned to walk and endure and to stand tall. I finally had to part with the worn and cracked pink high-tops. They were tossed reluctantly. Oddly enough, they had been a part of a time in my life I didn't want to forget.

Time went full circle, and I moved into my mother's home to tend to her during her last few years. On the eve of my mother's death, before she slipped into a morphine-induced sleep she said to me, "How lucky I was to have had my family and to have shared yours." She dozed momentarily. When she woke, while stroking my hand, she quietly said, "We had a special relationship. You are not average, Dotty. Don't ever forget. You are extraordinary. Always stand tall, just as if you're wearing your pink feet." She said little else that night as I sat by her side and remembered every nuance of our lives together.

Now when I put the pink angel on the top of the tree, I always stretch tall and straight and remember that terrifying Christmas and the faith and love evident in my mother's gift to me. It was a basic message, one of courage and strength, emblazoned in a simple pair of pink high-tops.

Dorothy Raymond Gilchrest

8

LETTING GO

*We do not get over grief.
But over time, we do learn to live
with the loss.
We learn to live a different life . . .
with our loss.*

Kenneth J. Doka

To See You

Many say their most painful moments are saying good-bye to those they love. After watching Cheryl, my daughter-in-law, through the six long months her mother suffered toward death, I think the most painful moments can be in the waiting to say good-bye.

Cheryl made the two-hour trip over and over to be with her mother. They spent the long afternoons praying, soothing, comforting and retelling their shared memories.

As her mother's pain intensified and more medication was needed to ease her into sedation, Cheryl sat for hours of silent vigil by her mother's bed.

Each time she kissed her mother before leaving, her mother would tear up and say, "I'm sorry you drove so far and sat for so long, and I didn't even wake up to talk with you."

Cheryl would tell her not to worry, it didn't matter; still her mother felt she had let her down and apologized at each good-bye until the day Cheryl found a way to give her mother the same reassurance her mother had given to her so many times.

"Mom, do you remember when I made the high-school

basketball team?" Cheryl's mother nodded. "You'd drive
so far and sit for so long, and I never even left the bench to
play. You waited for me after every game and each time I
felt bad and apologized to you for wasting your time."
Cheryl gently took her mother's hand.

"Do you remember what you would say to me?"

"I would say I didn't come to see you play, I came to see
you."

"And you meant those words, didn't you?"

"Yes, I really did."

"Well, now I say the same words to you. I didn't come to
see you talk, I came to see you."

Her mother understood and smiled as she floated back
into sleep.

Their afternoons together passed quietly into days,
weeks and months. Their love filled the spaces between
their words. To the last day they ministered to each other
in the stillness, love given and received just by seeing
each other.

A love so strong that, even in this deepened silence that
followed their last good-bye, Cheryl can still hear her
mother's love.

Cynthia M. Hamond

Mama's Hands

A few days ago I stood outside an intensive care unit, a stranger looking in, and saw my mother for the first time in five years. I watched as she lay there so helpless and fragile and tried to remember what had made us turn our backs on thirty-three years of love. Later, when I was sure she wouldn't know, I went to her bedside and touched her hand. Even after five years I could have picked that hand out of a thousand. I have felt the love in her hands so many times . . . when they brought me out of emergency surgery, she laid her hand on my cheek and I knew in that instant, without opening my eyes, that she was there. I knew that everything would be okay. When my father was dying, Mama's hands reached across his bed and gave me the strength to face what lay ahead. Mama's hands were always there to nudge me when I hesitated and to catch me when I fell. Of all the hands in the world, I knew hers. There was a lifetime of love and strength and giving in those hands. To feel Mama's hands reach for me just one more time and to give back to her all that she had given to me, would calm the storm that raged in my heart.

My mother had suffered a massive aneurysm. She was

semi-conscious and could not speak. On the night before she was to have surgery, she indicated she would see me. As I approached the bed, I was so afraid of hurting her, but I had to connect with her just one more time. Standing by her bed holding her hand, I believe she knew it was me by her side. She squeezed my hand tightly, and tried to sit up as if she were reaching for me. When she lay back, a single tear escaped and slid down her cheek, bearing silent witness to all that we had lost.

I hope she heard all the things I told her in the last three days that we were together. I held her hand and told her how foolish we were to let pride destroy the extraordinary bond that we had shared as mother and daughter. But most of all I told her that I loved her, and that I had never stopped loving her. When I held her hand to my cheek and closed my eyes, all the noises and smells of the hospital faded and I was a little girl again. Sitting on the bed watching my mother paint her nails, I knew in my little girl's heart that she was the most beautiful mother in the world and that I did not have to be afraid as long as she loved me. But when I opened my eyes, I was afraid because I knew I was losing her and I was never going to feel the love in Mama's hands again.

Families in the ICU form a common bond born of sudden pain, sorrow and sometimes, tremendous loss. Usually when your eyes meet theirs, all you can give is a quick smile before you look away. It is just too much to hold their gaze and see your own reflected pain.

The day my mother died, a new family came into the ICU. It was apparent that their tragedy was untimely and heart wrenching. Their story was told in the lost expression on the little girl's face clinging to her grandfather in confusion, not understanding why her mother was there. When her frightened eyes found mine, I did not turn away. I could hold the gaze of that little girl, because in my heart that night, I was that little girl.

As we stood in the hallway, her grandfather stopped to talk to us, his eyes wet with tears; it was his daughter, the little girl's mother, who was fighting for her life. Yet he put aside his pain to offer comfort and to pray with us. Through the night, if he saw us outside the doors, he would stop and ask how my mother was, and to see how we were doing.

Sometime during the last six hours we were together, Mama's hands showed me the way again. I realized that whatever had kept us apart for all those years didn't matter, we had never stopped loving each other. Our lives had come full circle. Mama's hands had welcomed me into this world and guided me through all the years of my life. Now, holding her hand to my cheek, my tears washing over it, I sent with her all the love of a little girl and the grown woman I had become, as she moved on. At last, I felt the storm that had raged for so long in my heart grow still.

As I fled the ICU, I ran straight into the arms of my husband. Blinded by tears, I did not see the little girl's grandfather approach and put his arms around us both. Not long after, I heard a terrible cry in the hallway, and I knew another little girl had lost her mother that night.

I hope that two souls met on their way to Paradise that night: One a sixty-seven-year-old woman who had seen life come full circle, and the other a twenty-six-year-old woman for whom the circle had been broken, so that Mama's hands were there to guide and give strength for the journey that lay ahead.

Beth Crum Sherrow

The Fragrance of Chanel

Time is the only comforter for the loss of a mother.

Shane Welsh Carlyle

Today my mother came to visit, totally unannounced. It was during the morning hours as a winter's sunlight forced its brilliance through the bathroom blinds and on to the Hessian carpet beneath my bare feet. Nail polish bottles crowded the window ledge and a curling iron, slowly cooling down, reclined on a nearby train case. One by one I replaced the eye shadow, blush, mascara and lipstick back into a zippered makeup bag, alternately checking in the mirror to see if I had left anything undone. As a finishing touch, I reached for the cologne.

Near the sink lay a bone china dish, full of cologne samples from a bridal show. One finger-search through the dish and there I stood, surprised to find myself holding a tiny glass vial of Eau de Parfum in the palm of my hand, distinguishably labeled Chanel.

Holding the sample over the sink, I cautiously removed

the tiny black stopper and let the sweet-scented Chanel
run over my fingertips and onto my neck. Working
quickly, I splashed a small amount on my wrists and massaged them together, releasing a fragrance that quickly
filled the sunlit bathroom.

It was at this precise moment that my mother entered
the room. It wasn't that she had knocked, or even visibly
appeared, but she was definitely there . . . in the room with
me. I couldn't see her . . . nor could I reach out and touch
her . . . but I could close my eyes and smell her . . . and it
had been so long . . . so very, very long.

As suddenly as the burst of Chanel filled the room, a
picture of Mama came to mind, a private moment that
never made it into our family album. It was her ritual on
Sunday mornings. First she bathed, followed by a generous dusting of bath powder. Next she put on her hand-
washed bra, panties and slip, followed by a skin-tight
girdle with four rubber clasps. Finally, she took out her
nylon stockings, neatly stored in the original cardboard
box, and held them up to the window light in search of
runners. Not until she laid out her shoes, however, did she
make a decision between her two favorite shades of
nylons—Barely Black and Barely There. She was determined never to put on her dress (only to get it wrinkled)
until it was time to walk out the door, which left her no
option but to complete the essentials and wait. And my
mother waited in elegance. Her stockings were the best
she could afford—Hanes. Her slips and bras were top-of-
the-line—Vanity Fair. Her shoes? Nothing but Aeigner.
Her choice of perfume? Chanel No. 5.

I watched through the mirror as she applied her
makeup, standing there in her high heels and underwear,
a fan oscillating on the floor. One by one she replaced the
face powder, rouge and lipstick back into the middle
drawer, alternately checking in the mirror to see if she had

left anything undone. As a finishing touch, she reached for the cologne.

Holding the bottle in her hands, she removed the black cap and let the sweet-scented Chanel run over her fingers and onto her neck. Working quickly, she splashed a small amount on her wrists and massaged them together, releasing a fragrance that quickly filled her sunlit bedroom.

I thought of her often throughout the day . . . heard her laughter, felt her near me. I breathed in the essence on my wrists and she was there . . . in the room beside me. And although she hadn't knocked, nor could I reach out and touch her . . . I could close my eyes and smell her . . . and it had been so long . . . so very, very long.

Today my mother came to visit . . . totally unannounced . . . in the fragrance of Chanel.

Charlotte A. Lanham

Signs of the Times

For years, whenever I drove to my mother's house, I always went past a small country church. Each time I went by, I would read the church's marquee and think that at least one Southern Baptist had a sense of humor because there were always pithy little sayings rather than quotes from scripture.

One day, two months after my mother died, I was driving to her house and passed this church. That day, however, I was in a funk and not in a mood for rural quips. I just wanted to know where my mother was and why she hadn't contacted me. Her house was there, her hand-stitched quilt was still spread carefully over the bed, the sheets unchanged, but she was gone.

I was feeling more alone than I'd ever felt in all my years of being single. My mother had been widowed twice, so she knew all the ins and outs of being alone, but she wasn't here anymore, and I was having a real problem with that fact. What I really wanted was to have her back, maybe for five minutes, and conscious. (She had been in a coma before she died.) I'd just say, "You okay?" And she would answer yes, that she was fine, that she was happy and she loved me.

If I couldn't have her back, I wanted a sign. Maybe I was greedy. I had already had a sign when I returned home from the hospital after her death on that tenth day of the tenth month (and in the tenth hour). On my wall hung a calendar opened to October. Each month displayed a different personal photograph. A friend (who knew nothing about my family) had compiled it for me as a gift and had "coincidentally" placed a picture of my mother, two sisters and me taken on October 10, 1992, the last time we were all together before my sister died. Now it was October 10, three years later, and my mother had just died. Well, I wasn't born yesterday. I know a sign from God when I see one.

But I always want more, and I asked for more signs. How about a rose blooming in the snow? How about my mom's face in the clouds? Or okay, couldn't she call me on the interdimensional phone? I knew these things happened. I wanted a lot of them to happen to me. *Now.*

Grief is a taskmaster who will not be denied. You can repress grief for a while, and you can try to ignore it. But it will have its day. I could not predict when it would come over me like some uncontrollable seizure. I did come to the place where I could feel the signs of it and withdraw into a private place. Over and over again I was surprised by its strength and tenacity.

On that bright, cold day in December, I could feel grief creeping up on me and I needed something to hold on to, a scrap of comfort, however small. Then I rounded the curve, and the sturdy little church came into view on my right. The marquee said: "You asked for a sign from God. This is it."

In a moment of sudden clarity, I realized I didn't need any more signs. I was doing everything that needed to be done. I was grieving my loss; I was taking care of my mother's house and her affairs; I was consoling relatives; and I was going on with my life, just as my mother would have wanted me to, just as she would have done.

I laughed through my tears all the way to Mother's house.

Bonnie Michael

Light in the Dark

This is a true story of a town within a larger city. Beacon Terrace is the name of the square of townhomes settled just on the edge of Springfield, Massachusetts. The square had just the right mix of young, middle and older folks, rich and poor—worldy and not. We were young, on a military stay with many others in this complex. We all made family of each other because all our families were so far away.

Overwhelming joy came to our home when our daughter, Stacey, was born on November 15, enlarging our "town family" and our own individual family. I remarked to Mother, "God has blessed me so! A wonderful daughter and son! My family is complete."

Devastating grief followed four days later, when our five-year-old son, Peter, was killed by his school bus. "Hard" is an understatement of how difficult that time was for us. Our beloved Peter—dead. Gone.

We managed to keep going, taking care of a newborn and surviving Thanksgiving, though we were numb with shock. We went about life as best we could.

It was an evening two weeks before Christmas when

Mother came to my husband and me. "Dears," she said, "I love you both so much and wouldn't hurt you for anything. But I must make you see something." We, Tom and I, looked blankly at each other. We did a lot of that "blank" looking at that state. "What is it Mother? Tell us."

"Come to the window, both of you, and tell me what you see," Mother said.

We looked out into the darkness and then at each other. We said we saw nothing.

"That's what I have to show you. It is Christmas week, and there is nothing to show it in the square. Everyone loves you both, and their hearts are so sad for you; they don't want to hurt you in any way. Dears, you must, no matter how hard it is or how much it hurts, you must give these good, kind neighbors their holiday back." We were so into our own grief we hadn't noticed that life for the square had come to a stop.

The next day, we went out and bought a Christmas tree, decorated it, and put it right in front of the windows, to be seen by everyone in the neighborhood.

As Mother said, "Once you let life back into your home, everyone will know it's all right to celebrate Jesus' life in their homes."

The next evening, it was as if a switch had been turned on. Trees and lights had gone up everywhere. Doorbells rang. Fruitcakes and cookies were passed round and round. Peter's classmates came to see us.

Beacon Terrace surrounded us with love during a very difficult time of our lives.

Our journey back had begun.

Betsey Neary

Tomorrow Is Not Promised

Walking would save my sanity. I just knew it. The hope of escaping lunacy prompted me to drag my exhausted, grief-stricken limbs out of bed each morning and hike to keep walls from closing around me. As I trod toward a nearby park, I replayed the events of the prom-night loss of my son, Shawn, to a drunk driver. Other thoughts strayed to a favorite quote from an assistant-principal friend. After the loss of both his parents within one year, he often reminded me that *"tomorrow is not promised."* Nothing in my life's story of stress and challenge as an urban high-school principal had prepared me for this tragedy. If only I had spent more time with my son prior to May 1. If only I had been more tolerant of his maturation process during his senior year.

My admiration and enjoyment of other families' relationships with their children had turned to bitterness and anger. *Why were their children still here to enjoy and my child so forever gone?* This truth brought my steps to the edge of the park where a young Shawn had flapped his arms in a swimming pool and launched his skinny hiney down a slide. I watched a father and two small children. They ran

as only excited youth can run—with total abandonment—
across the mud and grass of the park toward playground
equipment.

A bright new BMW was the only car in the parking area.
Withdrawing into my thoughts, memories of my son
returned, and I tramped on, vainly attempting to find
comfort in the flowers and sunshine of a spring day. When
reaching the corner where I planned to stop and head
home, my body turned as if on autopilot, and with lagging
footsteps I passed the park again. Playtime was over. The
children and dad moved toward the new Beemer.

The father's voice rose a shrill octave when he yelled
directions at the smaller boy, "Son, don't run across the
wet ground. You'll get mud all over Daddy's new car."

My hands itched to grab him by the neck and throttle
him until he became a symbol for shaken-adult syndrome.
Didn't he know the importance of time spent with those
two small children? Weren't the treasured memories they
would build together worth more than the cost of vacuuming out a little mud? My fantasies grew as I rehearsed
a myriad of biting words to arrest his attention and cause
him to rethink his approach. None of the words reached
my lips. I hiked past the park and back home.

The experience served as directive to my grief-stricken
heart. I had two choices on handling the rest of my life. I
could serve as a watchdog when witnessing parent-child
problems of this nature—issuing stern warnings of future
consequences; or I could pursue a softer approach by urg-
ing parents to spend more quality time with their children. I chose the latter.

A clearer understanding of my anger and jealousy—
concerning parenting situations—began to emerge. I realized the foolishness of resenting others' relationships with
their children. They had not caused my loss. A drunk driver and my son's decision to leave the safety of his hotel

were the culprits. How could I resent time others spent with their kids regardless of weak parenting skills? Grieving for loss of time spent with my son didn't mean they couldn't enjoy theirs. Grabbing this new reality by the throat resulted in a new dimension of walking through hot coals of guilt and anguish.

Attempts to analyze each new parenting situation began to bear fruit. I realized my words today carried the added weight of a *grieving mother*. Now when friends complained of problems with their teenagers, I attempted to give solace and understanding. Communicating stories of my own soul-searching through similar problems became the norm, instead of caustic be-glad-you-still-have-them words.

The greatest progress made in my healing quest occurred two years later when addressing junior- and senior-high church youth groups prior to prom week. Telling my story in the hope of saving a youngster's life did more for me than for them. Interacting with each bunch prior to the meeting quenched some of my thirst for quality time. Receiving their warm hugs afterwards gave me comfort beyond measure.

*   *   *

My husband and I sat at a local Sonic drive-in enjoying a Sunday evening hamburger. We watched a picnic table where a young family ate burgers with their two small children. The older child bore a strange resemblance to our son at age six.

Hyperactive, with small cheeks stuffed with fries, he quickly got into trouble. We tuned in to the event when we heard him whine, "Please Daddy, I promise to be good." The father smiled and gave him another chance.

Turning to my husband in the car I said, "Doesn't that

sound like Shawn at that age?" We couldn't resist playing peek-a-boo with him. He joined into the rhythm of the activity, miming faces and hiding behind his kid-meal sack. His parents seemed to enjoy the game as much as we did.

For just a moment the old resentments flared to see a child so full of life, and I gulped back the sob forming in my chest. But grief homework from the last few months held me in check. Words of my assistant-principal friend galloped through my mind. Tomorrow is not promised. The promise of tomorrow thrives with helping others.

Rita Billbe

$\overline{\underline{9}}$

A GRAND-MOTHER'S LOVE

If your baby is "beautiful and perfect, never cries or fusses, sleeps on schedule and burps on demand, an angel all the time . . ." you're the grandma.

Teresa Bloomingdale

A Dance with My Grandmother

When I married my wife, Martha, it was the most beautiful day of my life. We were young and healthy, tanned and handsome. Every picture taken that day shows us smiling, hugging and kissing. We were the perfect hosts, never cranky or tired, never rolling our eyes at pinched cheeks or embarrassing stories from friends and loved ones. We were as happy and carefree as the porcelain couple on our towering wedding cake.

Halfway through the reception, in between the pictures and the cake and the garter and the bouquet, my grandmother tapped me gently on the shoulder. I hugged her in a flurry of other well-wishers and barely heard her whisper, "Will you dance with me, sweetheart?"

"Sure, Nonny," I said, smiling and with the best of intentions, even as some out-of-town guests pulled me off in their direction. An hour later my grandmother tried again. And again I blew her off, smiling and reaching for her with an outstretched hand but letting some old college buddies place a fresh beer there instead, just before dragging me off for some last-minute wedding night advice!

Finally, my grandmother gave up.

There were kisses and hugs and rice and tin cans and then my wife and I were off on our honeymoon. A nagging concern grew in the back of my mind as we wined and dined our way down to Miami for a weeklong cruise and then back again when it was over.

When we finally returned to our new home, a phone message told us our pictures were waiting at the photographer's. We unpacked slowly and then moseyed on down to pick them up. Hours later, after we had examined every one with fond memories, I held one out to reflect upon in private.

It was a picture of two happy guests, sweaty and rowdy during the inevitable "chicken dance." But it wasn't the grinning couple I was focusing on. There, in the background, was my grandmother, Nonny.

I had spotted her blue dress right away. Her simple pearls. The brand-new hairdo I knew she'd gotten special for that day, even though she was on a fixed income. I saw her scuffed shoes and a run in her stocking and her tired hands clutching at a well-used handkerchief.

In the picture, my grandmother was crying. And I didn't think they were tears of joy. That nagging concern that had niggled at me the entire honeymoon finally solidified: I had never danced with my grandmother.

I kissed my wife on the cheek and drove to my grandmother's tiny apartment a few miles away. I knocked on the door and saw that her new perm was still fresh and tight, but her tidy blue dress had been replaced with her usual faded housedress.

A feeble smile greeted me, weak arms wrapped around me and, naturally, Nonny wanted to know all about our honeymoon. Instead, all I could do was apologize.

"I'm sorry I never danced with you, Nonny," I said honestly, sitting next to her on the threadbare couch. "It was a very special day and that was the only thing missing from making it perfect."

Nonny looked me in the eye and said something I'll never forget: "Nonsense, dear. You've danced enough with this old broad in her lifetime. Remember all those Saturday nights you spent here when you were a little boy? I'd put "The Lawrence Welk Show" on and you'd dance on top of my fuzzy slippers and laugh the whole time. Why, I don't know any other grandmother who has memories like that. I'm a lucky woman.

"And while you were being the perfect host and making all of your guests feel so special, I sat back and watched you and felt nothing but pride. That's what a wedding is, honey. Something old, something new. Something borrowed, something blue.

"Well, this OLD woman, who was wearing BLUE, watched you dance with your beautiful NEW bride, and I knew I had to give you up, because I had you so many years to myself, but I could only BORROW you until you found the woman of your dreams—and now you have each other and I can rest easy in the knowledge that you're happy."

Both of our tears covered her couch that day—the day that Nonny taught me what it meant to be a grandson—as well as a husband.

And after my lesson, I asked Nonny for that wedding dance.

Unlike me, she didn't refuse. . . .

Rusty Fischer

Mended Hearts and Angel Wings

I broke the angel's wing the year my grandmother died. I was ten, Nana was eighty and the angel was older than both of us put together. Nana had lived with us for as long as I could remember, and that was fine with me because she had neat stuff like tiny cases of perfume and powder and a sewing box with fancy buttons and bits of lace, and she let me play in her room whenever I wanted to. I was the youngest in my family and usually in the way or trying to tag along with somebody. Nana was special because she was the only one who actually wanted me around.

Breaking the angel's wing and Nana being sick enough to die, both seemed impossible to me. I knew how easily things could break, and I knew that people died, but I was certain something as precious to Nana as that angel could never break, and someone as precious to me as Nana could never die.

Nana's angel was a Christmas angel, a gift from her grandmother long ago. Each year when the decorations were brought down from the attic, we opened the angel's box, carefully unwrapped the tissue paper and the angel would emerge, pure and sparkling to take her place behind the cradle in the crèche.

She never stayed where we put her though; she moved around as if she could really fly. She sometimes landed next to the telephone, where nervous hands fingered her delicate wings while talking, or she perched on a desk to watch over an anxious teenager studying for exams. Sometimes she would alight on the windowsill by the kitchen sink where my mother scrubbed and whispered prayers for a daughter or a son or, the year Nana was sick, for her mother.

That year *everyone* was praying for Nana. Christmas approached but not nearly as gaily as it usually did. I unwrapped the angel by myself that year, and she wasn't the same either. Her china white gown, her crystal blue eyes and the gold ribbons around her waist still sparkled, but somehow she seemed like a fake angel, not a real one. She sat in the crèche forlorn and untouched.

Nana stayed in bed night and day and our house got quieter and quieter. One morning I brought the angel up to her. She held it in her soft wrinkled hand and stared at it for so long that I started to feel bad because it seemed to make her sad, and I thought she might cry. But she turned to me and smiled and in a whisper I could barely hear she told me to take good care of her little angel. I wondered if she meant me, but before I could ask her, she drifted off to sleep. She never spoke to me or to anyone else again.

Nana died before Christmas came that year. Everyone said I handled it well. They talked to me about death, saying how it's a part of life; they told me how good I had been to Nana and how God needed her to care for little children in heaven as she had cared for all of us. They said it was okay to miss her, and it was okay to cry. I listened and nodded, but their words made no sense to me because none of it was real. I couldn't grasp that Nana had really left me. Until I broke the angel's wing.

Christmas was over, and I was wrapping the angel gently in extra folds of tissue paper when my brother threw his new football at me, shouting, "Catch!" a second too late like he always did. The ball hit my arm, and the angel fell in slow motion down onto the kitchen floor where her wing broke away from her white china gown and shattered into pieces.

I cried then. Loud, aching sobs that I had hidden inside came tumbling out as I realized for the first time how final death is. How real and how wrong that Nana, my best and often only friend in the whole world, was gone forever.

Everyone made a big fuss over me then and sent all sorts of cards and gifts trying, I guessed, to fill the giant empty space in my heart. Time did ease the pain, but sometimes all it took was a whiff of perfume or the sight of an old white head in a church pew, and I would feel an aching tug in my heart.

I forgot about the angel until the next Christmas. As I slowly unwrapped the tissue inside her box, I began to imagine that if the angel was healed, I would be too; maybe all those tugs on my heart had been Nana sewing it back together up in heaven. Just as she had mended my torn clothes, she had been mending my broken heart with those memories and signs, telling me she wasn't gone and never would be.

I don't know who fixed the angel, and I never tried to find out, because it would have stolen the precious wonder and peace I felt when I held the mended figure in my hand. It was my first glimpse of the tremendous power of love and faith that is so much stronger than death.

Many Christmases have passed since then, and many stages of my life: from child to woman to mother to grandmother, and my belief in that power has never dimmed, but strengthened, just as surely as the angel's beauty has never dulled, but brightened.

I have seen Nana's eyes in each new baby I've held, felt her touch in each gentle embrace I've shared, and spoken to her and been answered in every prayer I've whispered. I feel her hand on mine every year as I unwrap the angel. And when I tell the story, I know that she's listening and watching and smiling with me.

Anne S. Cook

Sacred Cows

A child can ask questions that a wise man cannot answer.

Source Unknown

Last weekend my grandson noticed for the first time the cow skull I have hanging on the living-room wall. As a longtime admirer of Georgia O'Keeffe, painter-laureate of the Southwest, I came home from Santa Fe several years ago with one of those bleached skulls that have become a trademark, of sorts, for her and her desert art. It hangs on the wall just to the left of my front door, and I use its horns as a hat rack.

One day I walked into the room and found four-year-old Bennett standing stock-still beneath it, a dead-serious expression letting me know his little mind was whirling. So I stood by him, not saying a word, just to give him moral support wherever he was going with this new discovery.

It was a full minute before he turned to me and asked: "Did you kill it?"

Before I could say a word, he shot a mouthload of more

questions: "Did you shoot it with a gun or stab it with a knife?"

"How did you get the skin off?" And, finally: "Why do you have dead things on your wall?"

I tried to explain, going into way too much detail, about Georgia O'Keeffe and how she painted pictures of the desert; and because deserts are so dry, lots of cows and other animals die in the heat; and the sun beats down on the bones and turns them white and blah blah blah.

Bennett didn't get it.

"Did a cow die in your yard and turn white, and so you picked it up and hung it on your wall, so you could think about O'Creep?"

One of the things Bennett and I like to do together is drive over to the pasture about half a mile from my house and visit the cows. Occasionally one of the cows in that pasture gets loose and wanders around in the neighborhood. He and I had found one in the middle of the road and had to go knock on the owner's door to tell him to come get his cow before somebody ran over it. Bennett's question was not all that far-fetched.

I explained that actually I'd bought the cow skull at a flea market, that out West there are lots of cows, and people sell their skulls to tourists as a kind of souvenir of the desert. We then made a short detour in the conversation while I explained what a flea market was. He wanted to know why there were no fleas at a flea market, but there were cows. Why wasn't it a cow market?

"Good question," I said.

"I live in the West," says Bennett when we got back on the subject of skulls, "and we don't have cows."

"Well," said I, "Houston is not the desert. The cows I was talking about were desert cows that died in the sun and a famous artist painted them as a symbol for her part of the country—its austerity and its beauty."

"I don't think a dead cow is very beautiful," Bennett says.

"I think it's really sad." He looked up at me, such a mournful expression in the drop-dead beautiful eyes he got from his mother and grandfather. "I think you should take it down and bury it in the backyard and put a nice sign over it so God can take it up to heaven with all the other cows."

I was stumped. What's a grandmother to do? Should I rip it off the wall and have a cow funeral? I hate to admit it, but the skull cost me eighty dollars. It makes a great hat rack, and to me it really does represent a part of the country I love for its hard edges and sun-baked magic. To me that landscape is about life, its challenges and sacrifices. I think of it as the workshop of creation, with its blazing lights and fearful clouds, its muscular, bone-bare mesas and flowers that surprise with their audacity to bloom where they are planted, no matter what. That skull means a lot to me. Besides it makes a great conversation piece.

Except in this case.

"When you get a little older, you'll understand," I said, wanting to kick myself the minute I said it. I had hated that phrase when I was a kid. "When you grow up you'll understand" was a cop-out for adults too lazy or too dumb to explain things properly. But leave it to Bennett to get the last word. "My daddy's a grown-up and he wouldn't like dead cow heads hanging on the wall. . . ."

If you're curious as to how this situation worked itself out, well, I don't know if I did the right thing, but I didn't take it down. He and I met several more times under the hat rack to chat about it—like where the eyeballs were and what happened to all its teeth, and is that why his mom puts sunscreen all over him when he goes to the beach— so he won't get bleached and his skin dry up and fall off?

But the only thing I convinced Bennett of in all my explanations was this: his grandmother is slightly crazy.

Ina Hughs

Gran

*A grandmother is a babysitter who watches the
kids instead of the television.*

Author Unknown

When I was a young mother my grandmother, who was
lonely after my grandfather's death, visited me every
month for a few days. We'd cook together and talk, and
she'd always babysit, so I could have time to myself.

By the time she was ninety-five, practically deaf and
very frail, I was working part-time, and two of my three
children were in school. Gran would come to our home on
days when I wasn't working. Once when she was visiting,
my older children were in school, my eighteen-month-old
was sleeping, and Gran and I were having coffee. I always
felt protected and relaxed when we were together. Then I
got a telephone call that there was a crisis in my office—
would I please come in for an hour or two. Gran assured
me that she and Jeff, the eighteen-month-old, would be
fine, and I left.

As I drove to work, I panicked. I'd left my deaf, elderly

grandmother with an eighteen-month-old she was not strong enough to pick up and could not hear if he cried. But Gran inspired so much confidence that I felt it would be all right. And perhaps, if I was lucky, my son would sleep the whole time I was gone.

I returned two hours later and heard happy sounds coming from Jeff's room. He'd awakened, she'd dragged a chair next to his crib, and she was reading him a story. He sat there, enchanted by her voice, unperturbed by the bars of the crib that separated them. And our German shepherd lay at her feet, also completely content.

The drama of that day did affect Gran, who later admitted that communicating with an eighteen-month-old presented some problems. Unlike adults, if he'd needed something and wanted her to know about it, of course he couldn't write it down. The next week she enrolled in a lip-reading course at a local college. The teacher was a young intern, and Gran was her only student. After the first session, the teacher made the trip to Gran's apartment each week, so Gran wouldn't have to travel to the college, changing buses twice. By the end of the semester, Gran's ability to lip-read had greatly improved, and she felt infinitely more comfortable with Jeff and with the rest of the world.

Gran continued to communicate with Jeff in this way until she died, a few days before her hundredth birthday—leaving an unbearable void in my life.

Mary Ann Horenstein

Little Bits of Letting Go

I sit at the picnic table on an early morning visit to my grandma's farm. From here I can see most of her twenty acres, lowland pasture cut by the muddy waters of the Snohomish River, and the barn, red paint long since faded into rough wood siding. The wind rushes up from the river and sends me deep into the wool lining of my coat. It carries on its swirling back the sounds saved up from all the years: laughter of children running through the corn and Grandma's chuckle as she accepts another fistful of field flowers. Her presence echoes across this land—but Grandma isn't here. The heart of this farm is now in a "home" in town.

It has been four years since Grandma's stroke, four years of visits to the home and quiet conversations while Oprah keeps the others company. The sudden grasp of illness, added to long years working her farm has used up Grandma's legs. In the afternoon I find her in bed, propped up with pillows to keep the weight off her bottom. The cushion of her wheelchair aggravates a sore that won't heal. She pulls her sweater around her shoulders and assures me, "I'm doing fine. Just have to lie down awhile." I wipe a tear and make a comment about a darned summer cold.

Grandma's family settled here more than eighty years ago. They made their first home on Mill Street, across the railroad tracks from a German family with two daughters about the same age as Grandma and her sister Margit. Gram tells me about Norma and Alice. "They were the first friends we met. We walked right past their house on our way to school." Now Norma and Alice reside in the corner room, down the hall, two more old women confined to chairs with wide spoke wheels.

I imagine them climbing School House Hill together. Grandma in a plaid dropped-waist dress, black socks stretched to the hem, her thick, dark hair pulled back with a wide cloth bow. "One, two, buckle my shoe . . ." skipping songs in mixed notes fill the air as the girls swing their book straps.

Grandma sips her tea and talks about Grandpa. "We found a justice of the peace in Montesano, and that's where we got married. We lived at Copalis by the ocean."

I've got a postcard that Gram sent home to her folks. Old growth evergreens tower in the background. Two dogs are pictured by the new road to Pacific Beach; Grandpa was on the construction crew.

She looks at the collage of family pictures arranged on the nightstand. "He had a cold, so he told me to sleep upstairs." There is loneliness in Grandma's voice. "I should have stayed with him. That's when he died." Thirty-five years disappear in a sigh.

Grandma was a gardener. Rows of sweet corn and snap beans were harvested and preserved in clear Ball jars. Her peonies, like fancy ladies in ruffled bonnets, danced beneath the lilac hedge. In October, Grandma's homemade ladder leaned into the apple trees that lined her driveway.

Peonies brighten the walk to my back door. Gram gave me a start one spring for my new home. "Plant them where they can stay, they don't like to be transplanted." Her back was straight as she dug around the tender shoots.

Grandma smoothes the satin edge of her blanket. "When I get home, you and your daughter will have to come, and we'll sew a quilt. We can clear the dining-room table and spread out the layers. We'll pin it with those nice, big safety pins you brought me."

"I bought those at Sprouse." Small talk seems to help my cold symptoms.

I hold my grandma's warm hand, tracing the wrinkles that testify to her long life. I want to gather her up, go back to the farm, pick apples, pin quilts. But the yards of oxygen hose and the emergency call button around her neck ground me in reality. Gram is safe and comfortable. She squeezes my hand and smiles. My eyes are dry now. I know my tears are just little bits of letting go, as frame by frame, I recount our good times. My heart is full. I wear my grandma's love like a golden locket, and I am rich. For I have loved her too.

Lynda Van Wyk

Porch-Swing Cocktails

A grandmother is a mother who has a second chance.

Anonymous

This is not one of those "when Grandma was alive she used to . . ." stories you often read. No, my grandmother is alive and well and kicking at eighty-four and so, I guess you could call this one of those "let's see if *my* memory is as good as hers" stories:

When I was growing up, my parents went out on Saturday nights and my grandmother babysat for me. For their big night out, Dad always wore a shirt with a very 1960s ruffled collar and puffy sleeves and had neatly trimmed sideburns. Mom dressed in a miniskirt and shiny white go-go boots. It was the only night my parents were free to go out and have some fun for themselves, but I knew I had just as much fun as they did.

My grandmother went all out for my weekly visits. Shortly after Mom and Dad dropped me off, dinner would be served. I loved her carrots. Sliced thick and never mushy, they swam in a sea of butter and melted in my mouth like candy. "Orange wheels," I called them, which always made her laugh.

Grandma's other specialty was a steaming platter heaped with succulent chicken and rice. Being a five-year-old boy, I was too young to know that this was the only meal of the week Grandma actually cooked anymore. With her arthritis, it was hard just to open the can of Campbell's mushroom soup, which she stirred in the rice to give it that special "oomph." And skinning and deboning the chicken breasts (they were cheaper that way) was a nearly Herculean effort for the little old lady who spent the rest of the week zapping Lean Cuisine dinners and sipping tea with blueberry muffins for dessert.

Grandma had a special set of dishes she'd purchased, one dish a week, at the local grocery store. They were white and covered with blue windmills and little wooden shoes. Grandma told me that she had bought them just for our special dinners, and that I was the only person she ever used them for. This always made me feel ten feet tall. (It was years later before she finally confessed that the real reason she only used them with me was that she'd skipped a few weeks down at the grocery store, and the set was incomplete.)

Dinner was usually over by the time "The Lawrence Welk Show" came on, and even though it was her favorite show, Grandma said she preferred spending time with her "little man." So we'd retire to the wooden porch swing.

Grandma's husband, my grandfather, had died years earlier. The two of them had spent countless hours in this very porch swing, rocking back and forth and admiring the Florida sunset while the neighbor children played, dogs barked and flowers bloomed. Now it was my turn to sit next to Grandma and help her while away her lonely Saturday evenings. It never felt creepy, taking my grandfather's place in that creaky, old porch swing. To me, it just felt right.

While champagne music bubbled through the screen door from the TV, Grandma and I would sit and swing, swing and sit. Sometimes I'd draw, and she would sew. Other times, we'd just talk about the neighbors or what each of us had done that day. She'd share stories about growing up in the Great Depression until the closing strains of champagne music were corked for yet another week. Then it was time for dessert, which, in the best of all grandmotherly traditions, was something Mom would never give me at home: a bottle of Coca-Cola, the short kind that fit perfectly into a young boy's hand, and a can of fancy mixed nuts. Grandma showed me how to drop the salty Spanish peanuts inside the bottle and watch the soda foam, then take a sip, chomping the slimy nuts and tasting the salty sweetness of the fizzy soda.

Grandma called this concoction our "porch-swing cocktails," and not only were they delicious, but they made me feel grown up. Imagine a five-year-old drinking a cocktail!

When the Cokes were gone, we'd chomp on cashews and almonds and listen to dogs bark in the distance. Grandma would light a citronella candle to ward off the mosquitoes, so big and plentiful that she called them "Florida's State Bird"!

As the night got darker, the tempo of our rocking would gradually slow down, until our feet just dangled in the warm air. We hardly moved at all, simply enjoying the smooth ocean breeze from the beach flowing over us. Living half a block from the Atlantic Ocean, there wasn't a night of her life that Grandma didn't enjoy falling asleep to the sound of ocean breakers crashing against the sandy beach. She said she wouldn't trade that sound for anything in the world. . . .

So you see, this is not a "boy, I miss my grandmother"

story. It's a story about good times past, but still possible today. I think I'll call Grandma and tell her it's time for some porch-swing cocktails. And even though I'm old enough now to enjoy an alcoholic drink, I'll go buy some Cokes and nuts—and get ready for my favorite Saturday-night date.

Rusty Fischer

10

TIES THAT BIND

One generation plants the trees; another gets the shade.

Chinese Proverb

Another Mother

When my mother, hospitalized for a simple flu, died of a heart attack at sixty-five, I would have given the world to have her survive so I could care for her in my home. But she was suddenly, irreparably, devastatingly gone.

That was twenty years ago. Since then I have heard the many woes and worries of friends with aged parents. I feel some relief that this task will never be mine (as my father has married a much younger woman who will assume this responsibility), and yet I also experience wistfulness, even envy. To have my mother—or an older version of her—back with me for just a day!

So the decision we made that afternoon three weeks ago wasn't difficult. My husband and I live in Sweden. That afternoon we had stopped by his mother's fifth-floor apartment in Old Town Stockholm to check on her before enjoying a movie and dinner out. At eighty-eight, she was gradually weakening, and for years has longed to join her husband in death. Her 1600s-era home has no elevator, and the steep, winding flights of stone steps had become Mt. Everest. That day she seemed, as the Swedes say, *svagg* or very weak. "Come home with us," I heard myself saying.

And surprisingly, this very independent woman did. While I quickly ransacked drawers for nightgowns and necessities, she went into her husband's long-empty bedroom and closed the door. Only his large picture propped on the bed knows what she said. Then, clutching a grown grandson's arm with one arthritic hand and with the other a plastic bag of underwear and medicine bottles, she shuffled slowly down the steps in her slippers and robe.

Life for all of us changed.

We gave her our ground-floor bedroom with its adjacent bath and set up dining-room chairs to lean on for the few steps it would take to reach her walker. Upstairs in the guest room, my husband and I, mature but still enthusiastic newlyweds, shoved two single beds together and reconciled ourselves to a crack that seemed like a chasm. We learned to use the toilet quietly and to brush our teeth in the kitchen sink.

I discovered that once a mother, always a mother— even if one's "child" is a nearly ninety-year-old mother-in-law. Once on the alert for babies, I'm now attuned to her. I also learned that even my perfect doctor-husband—like the average man—hears *nothing* in the night.

The days now unfold in slow motion; my self-directed days no longer are. I'm sometimes summoned awake before I'm ready, and just-for-me moments don't come until my husband arrives home, and I can consciously clock out. Mealtimes are regular and seldom vary: butter-thick bread and tea for breakfast, soured yogurt with lingonberry and a few cereal flakes for lunch, and please, a potato for dinner? And don't forget the small pitcher of water for the too-warm tea, heating the bowl for the too-cold yogurt, the small white pillow for the chair back, the light blue blanket for her shoulders, the lamb-skin rug wrapped around her feet. Remembering each item before she does becomes a game.

Yet Eivor is easy. Grateful. Sweet.

Often we talk as women over tea. She tells me, "There were supposed to be two more babies, but I had trouble, so I have just the one child." "Was I a good mother?" she wonders. Look at how your son turned out, I assure her. "And now a professor. His father would be so proud," she says. "I think I spent too much time cleaning," she says of what seems to me the Swedish indoor sport. "People are more important," she adds. I nod, and resolve to sit until she has finished her tea before I pop up to load the dishwasher.

Other days, conversation is scant. I prod her with questions and choices, but her only answer is "I don't know. I am a wreck. This is so terrible. Why can't I die? Each night I pray to God I can be gone."

But when tomorrow comes, she is still here. And I am glad. For Eivor is teaching me much.

For the first time, I know the intimacy of helping to bathe an adult. Standing naked as she lowers herself into the lawn chair I have wrestled into our small shower, she is as unselfconscious as I am slightly embarrassed. I test the temperature of the water before handing her the nozzle. I shampoo her newly permed white hair. As she stands dripping at her walker, I towel her dry then apply gardenia-scented lotion, warming it first between my palms.

How many times have I bathed my babies, my grandbabies? It's not so different, only one doesn't grab the rubber duck or camera. And it is every bit as tender. But time has replaced soft, sweet curves and dimples. The hips which conceived and bore and lost babies are wide, the years have lichened her body with the thickened brown spots of old age. No airbrushed, magazine advertisement this, yet there is beauty here. And history: the playing child running free, the young mother cradling the babe who will become the man I love, the passionate wife, the outstanding cook and hostess, the old woman bent over her sick husband.

As a woman well into middle age, I look at my mother-in-law and acknowledge the preview of my own body, should the movie of my life last as long as hers.

I've come to enjoy our physical contact as much as she does. Such simple pleasures: the warmth of the blow-dryer on pink scalp, the feel of my fingers in her still-heavy hair. The slipperiness of her perpetually cold hands as I smooth lotion into the gnarled knuckles, willing warmth into them. Her satisfaction at a fresh nightgown and clean robe. Her white head against my chest—suddenly, surprisingly, as precious as the soft downy heads of my babies.

She may not know it, but Eivor bears many gifts. Oh, not her nightly, "Thank you for today, Jann," nor her instruction on the proper folding of used plastic bags, nor her lesson on the Swedish custom of welcoming spring by wiring colored feathers to birch branches and placing them in water until the "mouse ear" green leaves appear.

No, she's also teaching me the importance of patience: the grace of eating and drinking and moving more slowly, the importance of expressing gratitude regularly, the delight in a snowy day or the sight of a vase full of tulips close-up or the enjoyment of children at play in a nearby yard.

Eivor is teaching me that my own body—which looks to me so unattractive at nearly fifty-nine—is really quite young and agile in comparison. She's teaching me that death needn't be feared if life has been savored. But most of all she's teaching me that it's never too late to learn more, to love more.

Eivor's blue-veined hand in mine is not my mother's. And yet it is. It is my mother's hand and my mother's mother's hand—and her mother's before that. It is the hand of Eivor's mother and her grandmother. Just as someday, it will be my hand. Or your hand.

May the universe provide us all with another hand to hold.

Jann Mitchell

Recapturing the Joy

My husband, John, loaded parcels into our van while I brushed off a half-inch of new snow from the windshield. John's usual patience was wearing thin as we headed to yet another shopping mall.

We had made our list and checked it twice, so we knew exactly what to shop for. But as the day wore on, we felt increasingly frustrated. Our teenage and young-adult children had made very specific requests. Now we were taking a grand tour of half the malls in the city to fulfill them.

As John searched for a parking space, he thought of the time we ordered a coaster wagon with our hoard of Green Stamps. "They sent that red pedal-car instead, which was worth several more books. The kids played with that car for years."

"Remember Angel and KimSue?" I asked. "We gave those dolls to the girls when they were almost too old for dolls. But they became the most treasured dolls of all. There was something special about those Christmases, John—more excitement, more uncertainty. I liked them better."

"Yes," my husband replied, "a lot more uncertainty. Twenty years ago a teacher's salary hardly paid for a decent Christmas."

Laughing at our shared memories, John and I headed into the mall. We hunted for a sweater for Marjorie, our oldest, who was twenty at the time. Kristin, nineteen, wanted a coffeemaker for her dorm room. We probably would buy the ever-popular jeans for Tim, our fourteen-year-old son. Melissa, eighteen, needed lamps for her first apartment.

Lights, tinsel, music. The stores were sparkling with holiday cheer. But I noticed none of it. I was thinking about the surprise and joy on my kids' faces when they were small as they ran to the tree on Christmas mornings. No one was ever surprised now. Suddenly, John said, "This is no fun. I want to buy toys!" He had read my mind. *Of course,* I thought as I stuffed the list in my purse, *That's the magic we're longing for. Toys!*

We talked a mile a minute about what to buy for the kids. "What about Melissa's boyfriend?" asked John. "He'll think we're crazy if everyone gets toys."

"Let's just do it!" I said.

We erupted into laughter as we made our choices. Tim would like something mechanical. We put a robot-type toy in the cart. We hoped Melissa's boyfriend wouldn't be embarrassed with the truck we picked out for him. A Dressy Bessy doll would be just right for Kristin. Melissa would get a pull-toy telephone. We remembered how much Marjorie loved jack-in-the-boxes and bought her one.

Without being quite aware of it, we also purchased the sweater, the lamps and all the other everyday gifts.

As soon as we returned home with arms full of bags, everyone knew something was afoot. The secrecy and smiles seemed like those wonderful Christmases years ago when our kids were little. John and I just grinned when questioned. Everyone, no matter how blasé their attitudes had been, began to be very enthusiastic about Christmas. The tree lights burned a little brighter. The twenty-year-old crèche figures seemed less shabby. The growing pile of wrapped packages was intriguing after all.

Our family gathered on Christmas morning with rolls, coffee and juice. By this time John and I were experiencing equal parts of anticipation and anxiety. What if they all thought it was a dumb idea? Maybe they had been adults too short a time to appreciate being a kid again.

John gave each child a single gaily-wrapped package. On the count of three, I told them, the gifts should be opened. The kids looked at each other as if to say, "What gives here?" But within minutes the floor was littered with wrapping paper and ribbons.

The scene that unfolded brought tears to our eyes. At once the truck was zooming across the floor. Kristin was playing with her doll. The jack-in-the-box was both delighting and terrifying Marjorie. Melissa was pretending to talk to her boyfriend, Ryan, on the toy phone. Tim was taking the robot apart just as he had always disassembled every other toy. We were astounded and overjoyed by their reactions. That childlike magic had returned.

The "toy" Christmas became an instant tradition in our house. Now, ten years later, our family has spread across the country. Sons-in-law, a daughter-in-law and grand-children have enriched our circle. Still, the requests for toys are at the top of everyone's lists. One year Kristin asked for a favorite book from her childhood. The success-ful search for that out-of-date book was an exciting adven-ture in ingenuity rather than drudgery. The coffee table in Marjorie's Victorian cottage holds a small train and track. Dressy Bessy sits on the bookshelves in Kristin's California house. The toys given to Melissa and Ryan over the years now make their home in our grandchildren's rooms. Tim has moved several times, but the carton labeled "toys" has never been lost.

Who would have thought that the act of giving toys to our grown-up children would bring such excitement, joy and closeness to our holiday and our family? We never know just where or when we will find magic. Sometimes, I suppose, it simply finds us.

Lee Sanne Buchanan

In the Eyes of the Beholders

The older you get, the more you need the people who knew you when you were young.

Mary Schmich

The staff at Assisted Living has Mom ready, just as I asked. I take Mom's hand and say, "Come on. This is going to be fun."

My smile says we are going to fly kites or eat banana splits. She follows me, a slight drag to her step. I open the car door and remind her to sit. I have to press on her shoulder so she remembers what to do. I drive carefully, watching to make sure she is not fiddling with the locks. Time before last, she got the door open while we were driving. Dad fell apart when he heard about it. "Do you think she's trying to commit suicide?" he wanted to know.

"An adventure," I say, swinging Mom's hand as we walk into the beauty salon.

The woman directs me to three pink, vinyl-covered chairs and a glass-top table that holds a worn copy of *People* and a large thick hardback called *Style*. I guide Mom to a chair and open the big book. Each page gleams with a large picture of a pixie, vixen or sexy woman from the neck up. One has moussed hair that looks like the prow of a ship. Another has curls as still as marble and another's hair waves like it's in a wind tunnel. I hold the book close to Mom and point at each picture. She likes pictures. The largeness amuses her.

We have looked through all the picture books, and I can feel Mom getting restless. At the nursing home, Mom has refused to bathe, refused to let them wash her hair or trim her fingernails. "She gets combative," the nurse told me. "We've got to let her get past this." My father went to intervene—he would bathe her himself. But Mom fought him as well. Meanwhile, her hair has grown long and greasy, her nails are gnarly and yellowed. She looks like the crone in the old fairy tales, the kind of witch who will take your bread and water and give you a valuable secret that might save your life. As much as I enjoy fairy tales, I want Mom to look like her old self, not some disguised heroine.

"Frances?" a stocky woman wearing a green smock over black pants stands before us. "I'm Kim. Pleased to meet you."

I take Mom's hand and lead her to a chair in the center of a long row. I hold her hands while Kim puts a smock over her.

"So how do you want it cut?" Kim asks.

Mom is swiveling in the chair.

"She usually wears it short," I say. "We need to be quick, because I don't know how long she will last."

Kim nods and gets out her scissors.

I kneel and hold Mom's hands. Mom smiles. Locks of Mom's silvery hair float down on my knees, at my feet. Mom has always been her own barber, until last year when scissors no longer made any sense.

This is only Mom's second time in a beauty parlor. The first time was when her niece got married, and all the women went together to get a hairdo. My mother got her first dose of rollers, hair dryers and hair spray. She was introduced to the idea of protecting hair, like it was an endangered species, wrapping toilet paper around the set so it wouldn't deflate during careless sleep, sleeping in a chair, so her head wouldn't loll unnecessarily.

I sit on the floor, hold Mom's hands and talk to Kim about the pictures of her grandchildren, four of them. The hairs blanket my legs and the floor. I have never knelt before my mother and it seems like I should be saying, "Thank you for birthing me, for raising me, for being such an interesting and constant person in my life." It seems I should be thanking her for my very being, instead of saying to Kim, "Let's try to wash her hair while we're here."

We lead her to the sink. Mom giggles when Kim sprays warm water on her head, then lathers. Kim is quick and when Mom emerges, she looks like the woman I know, clean, with glorious naturally curly hair.

"Is there a manicurist available?" I ask. "One who could do Mom's nails very quickly?"

Isabelle is available. She speaks with a soft Spanish accent. I sit right beside Mom as Isabelle puts Mom's hands in soaking water, then shows her colors of nail polish. Mom picks up a bright red bottle, one that a younger Mom would have warned me against, as being too bold. But when you're in your eighties, you can be bold. Mom doesn't want to let go of the bottle, so Isabelle works on Mom's other hand, using a similar color. Mom watches for a while. When it's time, she unfurls her fingers and Isabelle quickly transforms the other hand.

In her real life, my mother never had her fingernails polished. She thought it was vain and unnecessarily flirtatious. Perhaps she would still think that now. But that simple sparkle of color and elegance adds to Mom's presence, gives her an extra vibrancy.

"I add some lipstick and blush. For free. Your mother, she is a beautiful woman," Isabelle says.

When my aunt got feeble, her one despair was that she couldn't make it to her hairdresser. This hairdresser lived across town.

"Why don't you go to the salon in your neighborhood?" I had asked Aunt Ann. "It's so much easier and closer."

"It's not the same. I'm used to my hairdresser."

Every week, I drove her to the hairdresser. Though I saw how happy she was, emerging with her hair freshly set, tinted, her nails glowing pink and her lipstick freshened, I still did not understand how being coifed and groomed could make such a difference.

Until now. Now that Mom looks like she used to, I feel a sense of ease and hope. The dread of seeing Mom with dirty old-woman hair melts away. Back at my house, we sit on the sofa and I hand her a cookie that I had stashed in my pocket, ready to bribe her into stillness if needed. She holds it like it is jewelry she doesn't own. "It's to eat," I tell her, moving her hand towards her mouth.

"Where is . . . ?" Mom can't find the next word, but I know she is asking about my dad.

"He'll be here in about an hour," I tell her.

We eat cookies and look at pictures in magazines. It feels like after school with a beloved child.

When my father arrives, his eyes fill with tears when he sees Mom's hair. "What happened?" he asks. "Did you get her to take a bath?" His voice is low and awestruck.

"We went to the beauty parlor," I told him.

We look at her, as if she is a brand-new person, pretty and full of possibility.

Her hair changed. Her fingernails got polished and cut. She looks pretty again. Maybe that means she will be able to button her clothes again, remember my daughters' names again and recognize a Hershey bar. Maybe something else will change. For these few moments, we believe anything is possible.

Deborah Shouse

Sunday Afternoons

When I was a child living in suburban New Jersey, we saw my father's parents every other Sunday afternoon. We usually went to their apartment in Queens, but occasionally they would come to us instead. My mother's relationship with her in-laws wasn't what you would call warm and loving. It was more like a truce called by two countries at war. The two parties—my mother and my grandparents—grudgingly tolerated each other for the sake of my father and the grandchildren. But they remained suspicious of each other, and from time to time, there would be skirmishes. One of these happened shortly after my youngest brother, Jerry, was born, when I was almost seven.

On this particular visit, my father was working in the attic when my grandparents arrived. Our house had only two bedrooms, and now that there were three children, we needed more room. My father had finished framing out two new bedrooms and the doorways, but he hadn't put the floor in yet. There were just narrow joists with pink fiberglass insulation between them.

My grandparents were eager to see the new baby, so

my mother took them into our bedroom, where little Jerry lay sleeping peacefully. Suddenly, loud banging sounds began coming from the attic.

"*Oy gevalt!*" my grandmother exclaimed in her thick Yiddish accent. "*Vas is dis?*"

My mother explained about my father's remodeling project. Immediately, my grandmother turned and walked out of the room and headed for the stairs.

"Selma, wait, you can't go up there," my mother called, hurrying after her. But my grandmother paid no attention. She started up the steps to the attic as quickly as her arthritic legs could carry her, which actually wasn't that fast. But what she lacked in speed, she made up for in determination. My mother followed after her, becoming more adamant by the moment. She even grabbed my grandmother's arm to try to stop her, but my grandmother shook her off angrily.

"Leave me!" she insisted. "I just want to see, is that so terrible?"

We were all about to see just how terrible it would be. When my grandmother reached the top of the steps, she peered around the corner, but she couldn't see my father. He was working in the other end of the attic, just out of view. The fact that there was no floor didn't deter my grandmother. She stepped onto one of the joists, and began making her way gingerly down the hallway, as gracefully as you'd expect from an overweight, arthritic sixty-five-year-old grandmother. Needless to say, she lost her balance and fell. Her foot went right through the insulation and through the ceiling below.

My brother Richard and I were still in the bedroom, drawing with crayons, when my grandmother's leg came plunging through the ceiling. We jumped up and ran to the steps. My father hopped from joist to joist until he reached his mother, and then he and my mother and my grandfather struggled to hoist her back to her feet and guide her down the steps. She cried and complained the whole way down. My mother was furious. She must have said, "I told you not to go up there" fifty times. But she got even more angry a few minutes later when she went to check on the baby. He was still sleeping peacefully, his tiny thumb tucked into his pink little mouth. And lying on the sheet, right next to his soft, downy head, was a ten-pound chunk of plaster that had fallen from the ceiling where my grandmother's leg had come through, right above the crib.

"You could have killed him," my mother hissed through her teeth.

My grandmother waved her hand dismissively. *"Ach, he's fine,"* she said.

My father took my mother aside and pleaded with her until she cooled off a little. But my grandparents decided not to stay for dinner.

My mother was still angry, though. It took her a couple of more days before she could even discuss the incident without steam practically coming out of her ears. But nevertheless, when Sunday rolled around, we all piled into the car and drove out to Queens.

My grandparents lived on the sixth floor of an apartment building on a busy street. My brothers and I weren't allowed to play outside, and there wasn't much else for us to do there, except watch TV. There weren't any children's programs on during the afternoon, and none of us were interested in watching baseball, so we usually had several hours of being bored and restless in the cramped apartment, hours we typically filled by whining and fighting. "Walt Disney's Wonderful World of Color" came on at 7:00 P.M. and after that, there was "Lassie," but all too often, my parents decided it was time to leave just when Lassie was about to rescue Timmy from the abandoned well.

Understandably, we didn't exactly look forward to these visits. We didn't really understand why we had to go, especially since my parents didn't seem to enjoy it much, either. My mother typically spent the entire afternoon engaged in a heated political argument with my grandfather, whose newspaper of choice was the *National Enquirer,* which my mother said she wouldn't even use to wrap fish. My mother's and my grandfather's political views were completely opposite: my mother was a passionate, strident liberal, and my grandfather was, basically an extreme conservative, suspicious of the government and resentful of racial minority groups. It didn't occur to me, as a young child, that since he had started out as a poor Jewish immigrant himself, my grandfather should have been a little more understanding of the plight of other minorities. But although his marginal command of English was no match for my mother's quick and brilliant facility with words, he outshined her in pure stubbornness. The arguments would become louder and angrier. My father, unwilling to take sides, retreated unhappily behind the newspaper. I hated hearing the arguments, all of the yelling and the obvious fact that this was more than just a political disagreement, it was also a personal attack on both sides. I begged my mother to stop, and I told her that I didn't want to go to my grandparents' house any more. But she refused to listen to my complaints.

I suspect that, in some strange way, my mother actually enjoyed these arguments. She was supremely confident and utterly convinced that she was right, of course. And perhaps she believed that, if she kept chipping away at my grandfather long enough and hard enough, he would eventually come to his senses and agree with her.

But he never did.

Gradually, my grandmother's arthritis worsened. Various medications and treatments were tried, but a year or so later, she was in a wheelchair, and by the time I was a teenager, she was completely immobilized. She lay in bed, unable to move anything more than her eyeballs without suffering excruciating pain. I was frightened, afraid of hurting her, uncertain of what to say and how to act. But my mother insisted that we talk to my grandmother. My brothers and I would tiptoe into the bedroom and stand at the foot of the bed so she could see us without having to turn her head.

"Oh, *mein kinderlach!*" she would exclaim, her eyes filling with tears. "Come, come closer!"

We would inch towards the side of the bed, and my grandmother would slowly raise one finger, grimacing with pain as she reached to stroke our hands. Even at our young ages, we somehow knew that it was worth it to her, that no amount of pain could stop her from touching us.

In the living room, my mother would be arguing vociferously with my grandfather over a political candidate or a social issue. But after a while, they would just stop. My grandfather went into the kitchen to prepare my grandmother's meal. I watched as he fed her lovingly with a spoon, gently wiping the food from her chin and bending the straw so she could drink.

It wasn't until I was an adult that I understood why my mother had insisted on those seemingly endless visits to my grandparents. I realized that, under the cover of those intense political debates, my mother believed in the value of a family, the invisible bonds that hold people together. I learned that politics and money and egos and everything else that family members disagree about were just on the surface, and that underneath this rough exterior were the things that really mattered: Devotion. Faithfulness. Love. Even when those family members were stubborn and argumentative. Even when they were opinionated and rude. Even when they did something stupid and dangerous and almost killed a sleeping baby. Even if they did all of these things, they were still family—still important and still loved.

Phyllis Nutkis

Baked with Loving Hands

Our son, Tobey, has always had a generous spirit, as well as a *very* independent nature. Like many small boys, he liked to show his affection for someone by doing a kind or helpful thing.

"I'm going to make Vanessa's cake," he announced proudly at age nine when his sister's birthday was just a few days away. Somewhat surprised, I was eager to encourage this decision, as well as his interest in cooking. He was tremendously fond of his big sister and wanted to do something very grown-up in honor of her special day.

At the same time, I was a little worried about how he would accomplish this while also accommodating the demands of his twelve-year-old sister's *very* specific taste. She had big plans for how her birthday would be celebrated with her sixth-grade classmates that year, and was quite specific about exactly what kind of cake she hoped to have for the big day.

Tobey's food-preparation experience was limited to peanut butter sandwiches and microwave popcorn. However, he insisted that this first baking effort, his gift to Vanessa, was something he wanted to do entirely by himself, "With no help from you, Mom." (I would, of course, be allowed to drive him to the store and help him find the necessary baking supplies.)

My confidence in this project was a bit shaky not only because of the limits of Tobey's experience and the size of his sister's expectations, but because my own cakes are not usually the prettiest things to behold. Fortunately for Tobey—and for me—the cake his sister most desired was available as a boxed cake mix. It included brightly colored sprinkles that baked right into the cake and the instructions certainly didn't sound too difficult.

Tobey and I made a trip to the store to buy the mix along with the other things we needed for the birthday party. On the eve of Vanessa's birthday, he raced through his homework and then excitedly began assembling an assortment of bowls and utensils for his project. As if to reassure me, he sat down first and read and reread the instructions on that package until I'm sure he had them memorized. Then he opened the box and got started.

In a game of parental stealth, I tried to monitor the activities of this young chef without appearing to hover over him. I found a dozen reasons to rummage in the kitchen for things as he went about his task.

Brows knit together, lips pursed in concentration, he carried out the list of instructions carefully. He broke eggs into a bowl for the first time and measured out the other ingredients as though he were handling priceless objects. I was impressed by the fact that he made virtually no mess at all. His eyes darted back and forth to check the instructions constantly.

When it came time to use the electric mixer, he granted me permission only to check that all the parts and pieces were connected properly, then thanked and dismissed me as the beaters began to whir away. He mixed the ingredients into a rich, golden batter. He had only to add the sprinkles and then it could all be poured into the baking pan he'd greased laboriously. Soon the smell of baking cake would scent the house.

Encouraged by his progress, I went to answer a phone call and was horrified to return a few minutes later and find him wrist-deep in cake batter, working his hands in the bowl. I wanted to shout, "What in the world are you doing? Are you crazy?" but thankfully, sheer astonishment kept these words tangled up in my throat unable to escape. I'm so glad I choked on my surprise rather than blurt out something I'd have regretted later.

When he saw my contorted expression, he immediately assured me that he'd washed his hands thoroughly—very thoroughly—before taking this highly unusual step.

Then he gestured with his head toward the empty sprinkles packet on the counter beside him and said, "Can you believe it? I thought it seemed kind of goofy myself, but it's exactly what the instructions said: 'Add sprinkles and mix by *hand*'!"

I had to agree with him, as I explained the role of spoons in this process, that it might have been helpful for the instructions to mention them. I'm sure that cake tasted even better for the laughter that followed as we waited for it to bake.

The cake—which turned out beautifully—was a smash! Vanessa, who was as surprised as she was thrilled by Tobey's loving gesture, gave him a big hug, right in front of all her "Eew—boys are yucky" friends.

A young man now, Tobey has become an accomplished cook who still likes to show his generosity by feeding others good food. But now he knows to approach at least some of life's instructions with just a grain or two of salt, along with all the other ingredients.

Phyllis Ring

The Intent of the Heart

My grandmother loved her kitchen and hated her house. As a young woman, she and her new husband lived in an old farmhouse near a small town in the Kentucky hills. What fed her unhappiness with the house was the narrow doorways and small windows. Even though the house had been built in that way to conserve heat she felt constrained by the halls and doorways through which she had to constantly move every day doing her work. And because she was a woman who loved light, the awful, tiny windows that made the rooms so dark, distressed her.

She tried not to complain about the house too much because my grandfather had been lucky to find anything livable for them to begin their lives together. It was poor country and people who had houses kept them for their entire lives. My grandfather was a country doctor and had to have enough land to graze his two horses as well as raise enough food for his family.

But although she understood their circumstances, my grandmother began to complain. Eventually, my grandfather would leave the house when she began to vent her feelings. And, as a result, over the next year and a half they began to grow apart. She tended the house she hated, and he did the work he loved as best he could.

Often he would disappear in the evenings with his rifle. He would tell her that he was going to hunt raccoons, but he had only one dog, and she knew it was not good for much except sleeping and begging for food.

He began to be tired quite a lot of the time, and at first she was worried about his health, and then she began to be convinced he was up to something, and no good could come of whatever that might be.

She began to try to stay up until he came home, but after doing her sewing and reading for a time, she would inevitably fall asleep. When she woke she would find him in bed. She looked for the signs of guilt on his face and saw only peace.

So, uncertain of what to do, she tried to stop complaining about the house. But that produced the most peculiar result. If she did not bring up her unhappiness for a week or so, he would bring it up.

My grandfather would ask if she had gotten comfortable with the house or say that she must have grown used to it. That would always provoke what she called a mean face from her and the small noise of disgust that communicated itself so well. To her considerable consternation this often made him smile. And she decided that whatever it was he was doing away from her gave him unacceptable pleasure.

Finally, she could contain her growing anger no longer. At dinner one night she told him that he could not leave her alone in the evenings. She said that she was frightened to stay in that terrible house by herself, that she knew he was up to no good, that she expected him to keep his marriage vows and that she would not put up with his treatment of her any longer.

My grandfather looked at his young bride and said, "Tomorrow will be the end of it. I promise you."

She went to bed that night inconsolable, certain that her husband had been unfaithful to her. He was telling her as much. She imagined the woman he'd been seeing, she imagined him telling her that he'd decided not to break his marriage, she imagined the tears and the parting. She was not able to sleep that night.

She did not speak to him at breakfast the next morning. The first cool weather had settled in on the mountain valley. The leaves had begun to turn, and she watched from her kitchen window as he saddled his horse and strapped on his two black satchels in which he carried medicine and instruments.

Then he turned back to the house and told her to come with him. When she asked him why, he told her that he expected to have to deliver a baby at the Wakin's place, and he expected it to be a difficult birth. "I need you," he said and smiled that wide disarming smile that had won her heart in the first place.

He helped her up on the saddle behind him and she put her arms around his waist. She had not touched him so intimately in quite a while and was surprised by the strength she felt in his body. They rode about four miles though the autumn woods, through the leaf-filtered light. He hummed a song he liked called "In the Gloaming." She wondered what made him so happy about going to deliver a baby. But he loved children, and she attributed it to that.

At Sandy Creek he pushed his horse into a trot, and as they came to the crest of a gentle rise of land she saw, directly in front of them, the most beautiful house she'd ever seen.

"Oh my," she said. "Have the Wakin's built them this place?"

"No," he said, "my darlin'. I built it. Me and a couple of men from Ashland. We built it. It's for you."

He helped her down from the horse, and as she walked she said, "It's as if I weigh no more than a milkweed seed." He led her through her house with its many windows, its light-filled rooms, its lovely veranda and its wide, wide parlor doors. It was in that house they lived all their lives, raised their four children. And it was that house to which the entire family always came for celebrations, partly out of respect, but mostly because everyone had a better time there than any place they'd ever been.

My mother, to whom my grandmother confided this story once, asked her why the house felt so blessed. And my grandmother said, "It's because he loved me. And because I loved him all of my life. Even when I thought I didn't."

My mother never forgot that, and neither have I.

Walker Meade

Mother's Silver Candlesticks

My mother saw the candlesticks displayed on a shelf in the rear of a secondhand store in the tenement district of New York City. They were approximately ten inches tall and heavily tarnished, but a surreptitious rub revealed their possibility, and a glance at the base showed the magic word "sterling." How did they get there? What poor soul had hocked them to survive? Mother ached to buy them, but we had come to exchange the shoes I was wearing for another pair to fit my growing feet. First things came first.

New York, where we settled upon entering the United States, and the area where we lived bore little resemblance to the *Goldene Medina,* the golden land that many immigrants had envisioned in their dreams. However, it was a land of opportunities, where all might achieve their aspirations if they worked hard toward their goals.

"We can swim, or we can sink," declared Mutti, as I called my mother, "and I have always been a strong swimmer."

And swim we did! Dad peddled caramelized almonds, which we made each evening and packed into cellophane bags, up and down Broadway. Mother went to school in the morning to learn to be a masseuse and did housework for various families several afternoons a week. I attended school at PS-51. My sister, Lotte, went to the Institute for the Deaf in St. Louis, where she worked in an exchange program to learn English. Nights, Dad worked as a night watchman, Mother sewed leather gloves for a manufacturing firm, and I strung beaded necklaces for the Woolworth store for one cent apiece.

The fifth-floor walk-up apartment we shared on 150th and Riverside Drive was hardly what my parents had been used to in their native country, Germany. It really wasn't a walk-up—it had an elevator—but the man who ran it held out his hand for tips each time anyone wanted a ride. Who could afford donations? We walked upstairs.

The place consisted of a kitchen, bathroom, living room and one bedroom. My sister and I shared the double bed in the living room, until she went off to school. When we first viewed the apartment, my mom blanched at the filth of the place. But with determination and elbow grease we made it habitable.

During one of our nightly chats while working together, Mutti told me about the candlesticks.

"Let's see if we can manage to buy them. I think they could look good once we clean and polish them."

Together we schemed how to save enough money to purchase them for Daddy's birthday. Thinking back, it was not the gift my father would have chosen to receive. He was more interested in the war, what of his property he could salvage, and how we would eat and pay the rent. But Mom was desperate to have something of beauty in our dingy flat.

The candlesticks cost three dollars. We conceived our plan in March and discussed money-saving strategies.

"I'll see if I can talk our three elderly neighbors into

letting me carry their trash down to the basement," I offered. "Plus, I could make money stringing necklaces."

"I'll buy large eggs for Daddy, and we'll eat the smaller and cheaper ones," said Mom.

In addition, she purchased three-day-old bread, instead of day-old, saving seven cents a loaf. A friend told her that wrapping a damp cloth around the bread and heating it in the oven would make it taste fresh again. It worked!

We turned saving pennies into a game. At the end of April, we made a fifty-cent down payment on our treasure. By September 23, 1940, we proudly "paid them off," and the proprietor even threw in some used candles.

We rubbed and polished the silver. Mother cut the used candles and scraped the outside until they looked almost like new ones. I will never forget the first Sabbath Eve when we lit the tapers. Tears ran down my mother's face as she recited the blessings. Despite the hardships, we were grateful to be together and, most of all, to be safe and sound.

When I married and moved to Wyoming, my mother gave me the candlesticks as a wedding gift, so that I might always share in their beauty. "You helped to buy them. You know how much they mean to me. I want you to have them and to someday pass them on to your daughter," she said.

The candlesticks now stand on top of the piano in my living room. We have used them at every memorable occasion of our family's life, both happy and sad. One day, I will pass them on to my daughter, as they were passed along to me. The Sabbath candlesticks are, and always will be, much more than candlesticks. They are symbols of faith, courage and love.

Liesel Shineberg

Baby Steps

The hardest lesson in life we have to learn is which bridge to cross and which bridge to burn.

Ann Landers

It happens in every family: angry words between parent and child, heated arguments between brother and sister, somebody walking off into the night.

And the family tie is broken.

It happened in my family without an argument.

I still don't know what triggered it. I just know my oldest son married, moved to Hawaii, and stopped calling or returning phone calls.

It took a child to break the silence.

So proud he could burst, my son had to call and tell me about Travis Hannelai Haas, born a year ago. Gradually, hesitantly, we started talking again. Photographs arrived of a chubby, blond, blue-eyed baby with Asian eyes. What a hunk!

"Come to Travis's first birthday," my son said in a telephone call. "Please come."

Baby steps could close the family circle once again.

"Go," my aunt said. "Life's too short."

Even my neighbor offered advice. "Go," he said. "I wish I were so lucky," he added, referring to a similar unfathomable rift in his own family.

"Go," said my husband, pulling the suitcase from the closet.

Tom was late meeting me at the airport in Maui. We both were nervous. After five years of silence, neither of us knew where to start. We had to find neutral ground somewhere. The baby became safe territory.

At the restaurant, Travis sat beside his mother, eyeing me from a safe distance. He slapped the table. I slapped the table. He slapped the table again and caught my eye. One, two, three times we played the game. Then he looked away, made a pout just like his dad's, turned and slapped both hands on the table, trying to catch Grandma napping.

That was the moment when I finally understood what being a grandma is all about. Travis was no longer a photograph. He was a wonderful, bright and beautiful boy.

I brought a toy piano to the birthday party two days later. Sure, it was a grandma gift. I wasn't going to be around to hear Travis pound away at two some morning.

He loved it. It makes lots of noise.

Guests at the party all talked about family. Most had left relatives on the mainland. "I don't like L.A.," one guest said. "I hate to go there, but I sure do miss my family at birthdays and Christmas."

The next day, Tom drove me to the Haleakala Crater for sunrise and along the fifty-three-mile Hana Highway, past waterfalls and sacred pools. He made a point of helping me down the moss-covered stairs leading to the ocean. It was comforting to have a guide who is 6 feet 5 inches tall and built like a rock.

The water is crystal clear. It's impossible to hide here.

We healed somewhere among the 617 turns and 56 single-lane bridges on the Hana Highway that day.

We healed without talking about the past. Instead, we talked about the future, his plans and dreams and ambitions for himself and his family.

Travis is walking now, circling the backyard in Makawao.

At the art gallery in the Grand Hotel, I got into a conversation with the saleswoman. She moved to Hawaii a few years ago from Laguna Beach. "Maui is a wonderful place to raise children," she said. "They are safe here."

My son says he will never let the family tie break again. "I missed you, Mom," he said.

I wanted to ask, "Why didn't you call months ago?" I wanted to ask, but I didn't.

Life's too short.

Jane Glenn Haas

The Mother's Day Gift

It was a beautiful spring day in early May when I picked up my two little daughters from my mother's house. I was a single working mother and Mom was kind enough to babysit for me. Putting a roof over my children's heads and food on the table were major expenses and ones I worked very hard to cover. The bare essentials were the focus of my paycheck.

Clothes, gas money and an occasional repair of our car left little for discretionary spending. Thankfully, I had a wonderful mother who was always there for us.

As we were driving home Debbie, my six-year-old kindergartner, asked if we could go shopping for a Mother's Day present for Grandma. I was tired and had many things to do at home, so I told her I'd think about it, and maybe in the morning we would. Both Debbie and her four-year-old sister, Cindy, decided that was a definite plan, and they were very excited about it.

After putting the girls to bed that night, I sat down and went over my budget. Putting money aside for the rent, gas for the car and new shoes Cindy needed, I had fifteen dollars for food till the next payday in two weeks. Grandma's present would have to come out of the food money.

The girls were up bright and early the next morning and willingly helped me clean and dust—the usual Saturday chores. The talk centered on what gift we should get for Gram. I tried to explain that we didn't have much money to spend, so we would have to shop carefully, but Cindy was so excited she had a list a mile long.

After lunch we drove to town. I had decided that the only place we might find something I could afford was at the five-and-dime. Of course, this being Debbie and Cindy's favorite store, I immediately made a hit with them. We walked through the store, carefully going up each aisle looking at anything that might be appropriate. Cindy thought Grandma might like a pair of shoes too, (we'd found her a pair of blue tennies for $1.99) but Debbie saw a white straw handbag she said would be, "Just perfect for Grandma to take to church!" Again I explained that we only had a few dollars to spend, so we would have to look further.

After going past most of the counters, we came to the back of the store and were ready to turn down the last aisle when Debbie stopped and pulled me over to a display of small potted plants. "Mom," she said, tugging on my arm. "Look, we could get Grandma a plant!" Cindy started to jump up and down with excitement. "Can we?" she asked. "Grandma loves flowers!" They were right. Mom had a beautiful flower garden and had vases of cut flowers in the house all summer. There was a large selection of plants in 2" pots for fifty cents. We could even pick out a pretty, little pot and some potting soil and plant it for her. That decision made, we now had to select just the right one. They finally settled on one with shiny green leaves with white variegations—a philodendron.

That was a special Mother's Day. Both the girls helped repot the little plant and eagerly told their grandmother all about it. Grandma was pleased and placed it on her kitchen windowsill over her sink, "Where I can watch it grow while I do the dishes!" she told them.

The little plant thrived under Mom's caring hands, and my sister and I got many a cutting from it over the years. Time sped by, and the girls grew up to be lovely young women, married and had babies of their own.

One day when Debbie and Cindy stopped by to visit, Deb spotted my philodendron that was hanging and twining all around my kitchen window. "Mom, is that plant new?" she asked. Both girls wanted to know what kind of plant it was and where I bought it. I explained that you just had to break off a short stem from one and place it in a glass of water and let it root. Grandma always had several glasses with philodendron rooting in them, sitting on her kitchen windowsill. Didn't they remember that they had given Grandma that philodendron for Mother's Day all those years ago?

"You're kidding," they both said in wide-eyed wonder. "You mean this is all from that same little plant?" I assured them it was and suggested they go ask Grandma for some cuttings and start their own plants.

Later that day, Cindy called to let me know she and Debbie had gone to visit Grandma, and both of them now had several pots with philodendron planted in them. "Grandma had loads of them, most of them with real long roots," she said. "And Mom, did you know that she still has the original plant Debbie and I gave her for that Mother's Day when we were little?"

It was just a little Mother's Day gift—a very inexpensive gift at that—but now forty years later, we see the beauty of it. A philodendron is like a human family. You break off a little stem from the mother plant and reroot it somewhere else. And it grows and spreads in its own unique pattern that still somehow resembles the plant from which it came. As our family goes its different ways, the philodendron we all have has become a symbol for us of how connected we all are. Through its silent daily reminders, the philodendron has brought us closer together as a family.

Mom and dad presently live in a Care Center close to me. The largest remnant of that philodendron plant now graces my front entry, and yes it is still giving of itself. I always have a vase with snippets of its rooting in my kitchen for the homes of my granddaughters. These plant snips are the descendants of that one little plant bought from the Five and Dime by two children for a long-ago Mother's Day gift.

Joan Sutula

The Quilt

Every seaside cottage and summer cabin should have indestructible leather couches and a quilt. Only the former will do for wet bathing suits, sandy bottoms and little feet with pine needles stuck to them. Only the latter will do for the goose-bumped and almost blue little bodies that duck into the house for a breather late in the day, shivering and shaking because the sun has dipped behind a cloud, but not quite ready to give up the idea of one last round of cannonballs off the pier.

For years, the hunched little forms of my children would line up on the old leather couch at our summer home on those late afternoons, wrapped in damp beach towels, catching a quick cartoon while they took a warm-up break from the endless outdoor activities that all seemed to center around cold water. In the evenings, the same band of four would drag blankets from nearby beds and share a huddle on the couch as the North Woods night chill crept through the wooden cabin. When it was time for lights-out, beds and blankets always ended up in tumbles as damp as the children's suits.

Then I made the quilt.

I must have been in my Suzy Homemaker stage of motherhood, before career responsibilities later fast-tracked our lives. That one lazy summer—the same summer when we made dandelion wine and learned to waterski on canoe paddles—I took the pile of old jeans, too beat up to be handed down one more time, and a scrap of crimson calico and made a patchwork quilt for the couch.

These were special jeans I just hadn't been able to let go of. Jeans with memories. Some were stained with droplets of khaki-grey paint from the year we had tried to match the cabin color to the surrounding pine-tree trunks—and the munchkins had all insisted on helping us paint. Some jeans had silly patches on them that had once seemed funny but were now embarrassing: "Don't swim in lumpy water." Some had been accidentally tie-dyed with too much bleach and were now beyond fashionably funky even for kindergartners. But I still loved them all.

With the old Singer that had come with the cabin and the old pinking shears, over many quiet nights after the children were in bed, I cut and pieced together those squares that had meaning for me. Randi's back pocket; Mike's torn knee piece from the time he fell off his bike on the gravel; Kelly's embroidered old favorites that had backed into a wet paintbrush; Eric's favorite hippie jeans, ruined for school forever by the oil stain near the crotch.

The quilt, when it finally came together, was perfect. The patches were worn and soft, like old jeans always are. But impervious. The sand flicked off in the mornings with a quick flap against the porch rail, and any dampness the quilt might have acquired was burned off by the sun before it was needed again late in the day. For almost twenty years the quilt hung waiting each summer afternoon for cold, wet kids to come cuddling.

Of course, the children grew. The quilt was big, but it

would only cover one teen adequately. And even though they professed to hate each other for a while and would share nothing else under the sun, I'd catch them on occasion, two, even three big kids, squeezed together watching a rerun, warming up beneath the quilt for half an hour, turf wars forgotten.

But families change. Ours did. A divorce happened, the children's father got the cabin, and years later it was sold, all furnishings included.

I had long since moved on and made my peace with the cabin's loss. The lifestyle we had there was indelible and everlasting, and so there was no loss, not really, not with such good memories. I wondered about the fate of the quilt, but only as you wonder nostalgically about a dear old friend you've lost touch with.

Fast-forward to Mother's Day this year. Two thousand miles to the south, another indestructible leather couch holds a huddle of children. The Baja beach where I now live is nothing but sand waiting to cling to everything. Wet bathing suits are now salty from the Pacific, not just damp from the fresh inland waters of Wisconsin. Little pieces of seaweed instead of pine needles stick to feet. But the lifestyle is much the same. And now grandchildren snuggle on the couch, warming up for a few moments while watching SpongeBob—wrapped in the quilt.

Where did it come from?

My children missed it. One of them drove four hundred miles to see if it was still there, at the cabin someone else now owns, to ask if they could have it back, and to bring it home.

It was a surprise, my gift this Mother's Day. And on the crimson calico squares, between the denim, one of them had written, in black Magic Marker that will stay forever:

Dear Mom,
>*You will never know*
>*how much I*
>*remember and treasure*
>*all that you did*
>*and all that*
>*you taught me*
>*as I grew up.*

>*I love you forever.*

The signature is on a favorite denim square with a little dancing frog stitched on—a frog that once frolicked on the jeans of a six-year-old. Of course it has a paint stain.

Paula McDonald

More Chicken Soup?

Many of the stories and poems you have read in this book were submitted by readers like you who had read earlier *Chicken Soup for the Soul* books. We publish at least five or six *Chicken Soup for the Soul* books every year. We invite you to contribute a story to one of these future volumes.

Stories may be up to twelve hundred words and must uplift or inspire. You may submit an original piece, something you have read or your favorite quotation on your refrigerator door.

To obtain a copy of our submission guidelines and a listing of upcoming *Chicken Soup* books, please write, fax or check our Web site.

Please send your submissions to:

Chicken Soup for the Soul
Web site: *www.chickensoupforthesoul.com*
P.O. Box 30880, Santa Barbara, CA 93130
fax: 805-563-2945

We will be sure that both you and the author are credited for your submission.

For information about speaking engagements, other books, audiotapes, workshops and training programs, please contact any of our authors directly.

Supporting Mothers and Children Around the World

In the spirit of supporting mothers and children of the world, the publisher and coauthors of *Chicken Soup for Every Mom's Soul* will donate a portion of the proceeds from this book to:

Free the Children
233 Carlton Street
Toronto, Ontario M5A2L2
Canada
Phone: 416-925-5894
Web site: *www.freethechildren.com*

Free the Children is an international children's charity founded in 1995 by the international child rights activist, Craig Kielburger, when he was twelve years old. Today, Free the Children is the largest youth empowerment organization having impacted the lives of millions of youth around the world. Their mission is to free children from poverty and exploitation and the idea that they are powerless to affect positive change in the world, and to improve their lives and those of their peers. Free the Children was nominated for the 2002, 2003 and 2004 Nobel Peace Prize.

Here are some highlights of Free the Children's remarkable record of achievement:

- Provided direct leadership training and spoke to youth groups comprising over 1.25 million young people across North America and around the world.
- Built over 400 primary schools in 15 developing

countries, providing education to over 35,000 children every single day.

- Distributed over 200,000 school and health kits to children in need.
- Shipped over $8 million worth of medical supplies and built primary health care centers directly impacting the lives of over 500,000 people in 40 countries.
- Empowered poor women to be economically self-sufficient by providing them with productive resources, such as milking animals, small machines and arable land, allowing them to remove their children from dangerous working conditions and send them to school.

Please contact them directly for more information. We invite you to join us in supporting this extraordinary organization.

Who Is Jack Canfield?

Jack Canfield is one of America's leading experts in the development of human potential and personal effectiveness. He is both a dynamic, entertaining speaker and a highly sought-after trainer. Jack has a wonderful ability to inform and inspire audiences toward increased levels of self-esteem and peak performance. Jack most recently released a book for success entitled *The Success Principles: How to Get from Where You Are to Where You Want to Be.*

He is the author and narrator of several bestselling audio- and videocassette programs, including *Self-Esteem and Peak Performance, How to Build High Self-Esteem, Self-Esteem in the Classroom* and *Chicken Soup for the Soul—Live.* He is regularly seen on television shows such as *Good Morning America, 20/20* and *NBC Nightly News.* Jack has co-authored numerous books, including the *Chicken Soup for the Soul* series, *Dare to Win* and *The Aladdin Factor* (all with Mark Victor Hansen), *100 Ways to Build Self-Concept in the Classroom* (with Harold C. Wells), *Heart at Work* (with Jacqueline Miller) and *The Power of Focus* (with Les Hewitt and Mark Victor Hansen).

Jack is a regularly featured speaker for professional associations, school districts, government agencies, churches, hospitals, sales organizations and corporations. His clients have included the American Dental Association, the American Management Association, AT&T, Campbell's Soup, Clairol, Domino's Pizza, GE, Hartford Insurance, ITT, Johnson & Johnson, the Million Dollar Roundtable, NCR, New England Telephone, Re/Max, Scott Paper, TRW and Virgin Records. Jack has taught on the faculty of Income Builders International, a school for entrepreneurs.

Jack conducts an annual seven-day training called Breakthrough to Success. It attracts entrepreneurs, educators, counselors, parenting trainers, corporate trainers, professional speakers, ministers and others interested in improving their lives and lives of others.

For free gifts from Jack and information on all his material and availability go to:

www.jackcanfield.com
Self-Esteem Seminars
P.O. Box 30880
Santa Barbara, CA 93130
phone: 805-563-2935 • fax: 805-563-2945

Who Is Mark Victor Hansen?

In the area of human potential, no one is more respected than Mark Victor Hansen. For more than thirty years, Mark has focused solely on helping people from all walks of life reshape their personal vision of what's possible. His powerful messages of possibility, opportunity and action have created powerful change in thousands of organizations and millions of individuals worldwide.

He is a sought-after keynote speaker, bestselling author and marketing maven. Mark's credentials include a lifetime of entrepreneurial success and an extensive academic background. He is a prolific writer with many bestselling books, such as *The One Minute Millionaire, The Power of Focus, The Aladdin Factor* and *Dare to Win,* in addition to the *Chicken Soup for the Soul* series. Mark has made a profound influence through his library of audios, videos and articles in the areas of big thinking, sales achievement, wealth building, publishing success, and personal and professional development.

Mark is the founder of the MEGA Seminar Series. MEGA Book Marketing University and Building Your MEGA Speaking Empire are annual conferences where Mark coaches and teaches new and aspiring authors, speakers and experts on building lucrative publishing and speaking careers. Other MEGA events include MEGA Marketing Magic and My MEGA Life.

He has appeared on television (*Oprah,* CNN and *The Today Show*), in print (*Time, U.S. News & World Report, USA Today, New York Times* and *Entrepreneur*) and on countless radio interviews, assuring our planet's people that, "You can easily create the life you deserve."

As a philanthropist and humanitarian, Mark works tirelessly for organizations such as Habitat for Humanity, American Red Cross, March of Dimes, Childhelp USA and many others. He is the recipient of numerous awards that honor his entrepreneurial spirit, philanthropic heart and business acumen. He is a lifetime member of the Horatio Alger Association of Distinguished Americans, an organization that honored Mark with the prestigious Horatio Alger Award for his extraordinary life achievements.

Mark Victor Hansen is an enthusiastic crusader of what's possible and is driven to make the world a better place.

Mark Victor Hansen & Associates, Inc.
P.O. Box 7665
Newport Beach, CA 92658
phone: 949-764-2640
fax: 949-722-6912
Visit Mark online at: *www.markvictorhansen.com*

Who Is Heather McNamara?

What began for Heather as a part-time freelancing job in 1995 turned into a full-time job as editorial director for Chicken Soup for the Soul Enterprises in 1996. She coauthored *Chicken Soup for the Unsinkable Soul* and *Chicken Soup for the Sister's Soul*.

"I feel so fortunate to have a job that brings joy to so many people," Heather says. Her love of literature grew from her third-grade teacher Mrs. Lutsinger, who read to the children every day after lunch.

Today Heather owns her own home in a rural outpost of the San Fernando Valley, where she enjoys the panoramic view of the valley, her garden and her four dogs—all adopted strays. Her oldest dog, an abandoned "junkyard" dog, continues to patrol her yard, despite the fact that "he is blind in one eye and doesn't hear so well. But he still has a good sniffer," Heather proclaims.

Heather and her husband Rick are expecting their first child in July 2005.

You can reach Heather at:

Self-Esteem Seminars
P.O. Box 30880
Santa Barbara, CA 93130
phone: 818-833-1954

Who Is Marci Shimoff?

Marci Shimoff is coauthor of the *New York Times* bestsellers *Chicken Soup for the Woman's Soul, Chicken Soup for the Mother's Soul I* and *II, A Second Chicken Soup for the Woman's Soul,* and *Chicken Soup for the Single's Soul.* She is a top-rated professional speaker who, for the last eighteen years, has inspired thousands of people with her message of personal and professional growth. Since 1994 she has specialized in delivering *Chicken Soup for the Soul* keynote speeches to audiences around the world.

Marci is cofounder and president of The Esteem Group, a company specializing in self-esteem and inspirational programs for women. She has been a featured speaker for numerous professional organizations, universities, women's associations, health-care organizations and Fortune 500 companies. Her clients have included AT&T, American Airlines, Sears, Junior League, the Pampered Chef, Jazzercise and Bristol-Myers Squibb. Her audiences appreciate her lively humor, her dynamic delivery and her ability to open hearts and uplift spirits.

Marci combines her energetic and engaging style with a strong knowledge base. She earned her MBA from UCLA; she also studied in the United States and Europe to earn an advanced certificate as a stress-management consultant.

In 1983, Marci coauthored a highly acclaimed study of the fifty top businesswomen in America. Since that time, she has specialized in addressing women's audiences, focusing on helping women discover the extraordinary within themselves.

Creating *Chicken Soup for the Soul* books and sharing their message of love, hope and laughter in keynote speeches has been especially fulfilling for Marci. Currently at work on a book about living with an open heart, she feels blessed to bring inspiration to millions of people throughout the world.

To schedule Marci for a *Chicken Soup for the Soul* keynote address or seminar, you can reach her at:

The Esteem Group
57 Bayview Drive
San Rafael, CA 94901
phone: 415-789-1300 • fax: 415-789-1309
Web site: *www.marcishimoff.com*

Contributors

A few of the stories in this book were taken from previously published sources, such as books, magazines and newspapers. These sources are acknowledged in the permissions section. If you would like to contact any of the contributors for information about their writing or would like to invite them to speak in your community, look for their contact information included in their biographies.

The remainder of the stories were submitted by readers of our previous *Chicken Soup for the Soul* books who responded to our requests for stories. We have also included information about them.

Carolyn Armistead, mother of two daughters, lives and writes in a rural suburb of Boston. Her writing has appeared in several magazines and the books *365 Ways to Connect with Your Kids* (2000) and *Shape Your Life* (2003). She is currently pursuing her MFA at the University of Southern Maine.

Rita Billbe is a retired high school principal. She and her husband own a resort, Angels Retreat, on the White River in northern Arkansas. She has been published in *Chicken Soup for the Sister's Soul* and *Journal of American Donkey and Mule Society*. She is currently working on a devotional book, *Prayer by Principal.*

Mary Kay Blakely is the author of the critically acclaimed memoirs *Wake Me When It's Over: A Journey to the Edge and Back* and *American Mom: Motherhood, Politics, and Humble Pie*. She writes regularly for national magazines and newspapers. She currently teaches magazine writing at the Missouri School of Journalism and is writing a book on political depression "for otherwise healthy people who feel traumatized by the news."

Arthur Bowler, a U.S./Swiss citizen and graduate of Harvard Divinity School, is a writer and speaker in English and German. His work has appeared in several bestselling anthologies and in a bestseller in Switzerland. Look for his book *A Prayer and a Swear* and visit his Web site: *www.arthurbowler.ch.*

Jean Brody received her B.S. degree in journalism from Washington University and graduate degree in education. This is her eighth story in a *Chicken Soup for the Soul* publication. Scholastic publications recently bought one of her stories for their nonfiction *From the Inside Out.* Another of her stories will appear in *If Life Is a Game, These Are the Stories,* published by Andrew McMeel. Other books by Jean Brody are *Braille Me* and two books for children on minority pride. Jean lives with her husband Gene and Miss Aggie cat on their thoroughbred horse farm in Kentucky.

LindaCarol Cherken is a lifelong Philadelphian. Her writing has taken her from an interview with the Beatles for her school paper to weekly food and health columns for the *Philadelphia Daily News* to a syndicated advice column. Today she writes features for newspapers and magazines, including essays for several of the *Chicken Soup* books.

Anne S. Cook lives in New Jersey with her husband and three children. She is the author of the novel *Sounds of the Sea* and a collection of holiday short stories, *Christmas Promises*. Readers can contact her at *Booksbycook.com*.

Bonnie Davidson, M.Ed., is a full-time real estate agent and college instructor, living in a coastal community in Massachusetts. Bonnie is the mother of three. Her passions include breast cancer advocacy and husband, Paul. Please e-mail her at *bonnie17d@aol.com*.

Karen Driscoll lives with her husband and their four children in Connecticut. Her work has been published in *Woman's World; Brain, Child; Chicken Soup for the Soul; Chocolate for a Woman's Soul; Angels on Earth; Mothering Magazine;* and the anthology, *Toddler*. She can be reached at *kmhbdriscoll@hotmail.com*.

Gerrie Edwards' prime interest in life is clarifying the stereotyped Indian. As Eagle Clan's "Grandmother Two Bears," she delights children with classroom presentations and storytelling. Her work appears monthly on the Internet at *www.healinghandsoflight.com*, and she has written a book, *The Story Teller, Native American History and Stories*.

Linda Ellerbee is an outspoken journalist, award-winning television producer, bestselling author, one of the most sought-after speakers in America, a breast cancer survivor and a mom. Her book, *Take Big Bites: Adventures Around the World and Across the Table*, was released in May 2005.

Debbie Farmer is the author of the nationally syndicated column "Family Daze." Her essays have appeared in *Family Fun Magazine, Family Circle,* the *Washington Post, Reader's Digest,* several *Chicken Soup* anthologies and hundreds of regional parenting publications around the world. For more information, or to sign up for a free monthly "Family Daze" e-column, visit her Web site at *www.familydaze.com*.

J. T. Fenn is a longtime entrepreneur and aspiring screenwriter who has written for several animated television series that still air on Nickelodeon. Someday he may venture to publish some of the other children's stories that are gathering dust in his file cabinet. Feel free to e-mail J.T. at *jtfenn@hotmail.com*.

Bonnie Feuer had her own column ("Wisdom and Warmth") in several newspapers and was published in *Better Health Magazine*. She won *Better Health*'s Writer of the Year with her story, "Silver Linings." Employed by the board of education, she is currently writing an interactive book for children.

Rusty Fischer is a freelance writer who lives with his beautiful wife, Martha, in Orlando, Florida. This is his third story to be published in a *Chicken Soup* book.

Dorothy Gilchrest is married and the mother of two. She holds a B.S. in occupational education and is presently self-employed as a radiographer in occupational medicine. Her inspirational writing has produced journal articles as well as nostalgic lifetime stories and poetry offering spiritual balance between work and family.

Marian Gormley is a freelance writer and photographer whose work has appeared in regional and national publications. She has a background in software engineering, public relations and marketing. She enjoys writing about issues related to parenting and family life, education, and health. Marian resides in northern Virginia with her husband and twin children.

Jennifer Graham lives in the Chicago suburbs where she teaches writing and communications at both Benedictine University and Robert Morris College. She is grateful to her husband, son and, especially, her daughter for allowing her to publish such a personal story. Contact her at *jenny.cambridge@att.net.*

Mimi Greenwood Knight is a freelance writer and artist in residence. She lives in Folsom, Louisiana, with her husband, David, four children, Haley, Molly, Hewson and Jonah, and far too many dogs and cats. She enjoys gardening, photography, Bible study and the lost art of letter writing.

Cynthia M. Hamond has been published numerous times in both the *Chicken Soup for the Soul* series and Multnomah's *Stories for the Heart.* Her stories have been printed in major publications and magazines. She has received two writing recognitions and her short story "Goodwill" has become a TV favorite. Contact her via e-mail at: *Candbh@aol.com.*

Sue Thomas Hegyvary is a professor and dean emeritus at the University of Washington School of Nursing in Seattle. From her roots in Kentucky, she has traveled in more than fifty countries and now conducts research on global health. She enjoys bicycle touring, skiing, gardening, creative cooking and hiking at her family's cabin in the Cascade Mountains.

Melissa Hill is a wife and a mother of two daughters. She works as a preschool teacher and is very involved in her church. She enjoys reading, writing and spending time with her family.

Amy Hirshberg Lederman is a syndicated columnist, public speaker, Jewish educator and attorney. Her first book, *To Life! Jewish Reflections on Everyday Living* is available in 2005. She lives with her husband and two teenage children in Tucson, Arizona. Amy welcomes you to contact her at *amyleder@aol.com.*

Mary Ann Horenstein received a B.A. degree from Smith College and a master's and doctorate from Rutgers University. She taught English, then headed an experiential learning program in a New Jersey school before retiring. She has published two books and many articles. She can be reached at *madon@surfglobal.net.*

Ina Hughs is a full-time columnist for *The Knoxville News Sentinel* in Knoxville, Tennessee. She is the author of three books: *A Prayer for Children,* published by William Morrow and Simon & Schuster; *A Sense of Human,* published by

Scripps Howard Company; and *Storylines,* an audio book, published by Night Owl Productions. She has won numerous non-fiction and poetry awards. She lives in Louisville, Tennessee. She can be reached at *IJH@charter.net.*

In a former life, **Peggy Jaeger** was a registered nurse who always yearned to write. After the birth of her daughter, she became a full-time wife, mother and author. She's had numerous fiction short stories and nursing articles published and is currently working on a mystery-suspense novel.

Patricia Jones lived in New York City with her daughter. Her work has appeared in *Ms., Essence, Family Circle, Woman's Day* and the *New York Times.* Patricia wrote three novels *Passing, Red on a Rose* and her third and final novel, *The Color of Family* due out later this year.

Cheryl Kirking is the author of *Crayons in the Dryer: Misadventures and Unexpected Blessings of Motherhood.* She is a women's conference speaker who tickles the funny bones and tugs at the heartstrings of audiences nationwide. She has written five books, including *Ripples of Joy* and *Teacher, You're an A+,* and is the mother of teenage triplets! For booking information visit *www.cheryl kirking.com.*

Susan Krushenick earned her bachelor of arts degree, with concentrations in both sociology and creative writing, from Vermont College in June 2004. Susan writes the library column for her local newspaper, the *Valley Reporter,* and also worked as a regular contributing writer for *The Philosophical Mother.* She can be reached at *skrushenick@hotmail.com.*

Charlotte Lanham is a retired teacher and columnist. She is a frequent contributor to *Chicken Soup,* but also enjoys writing poetry and children's books. She and her husband, Ray, are cofounders of a nonprofit organization called Abbi's Room Foundation which provides beds and bedding for children of Habitat for Humanity families. E-mail her at *CharlotteLanham@sbcglobal.net.*

Ruth Lehrer calls herself the Grandma Moses of the personal essay. She was an elementary school teacher who published her first essay after her retirement—at age sixty-two. Now, fourteen years later, Ruth has written almost one hundred stories. "Personal writing is my best form of therapy," she says. Contact her via e-mail at *ruthlehrer@aol.com.*

Jaye Lewis is an award-winning writer who lives and writes in the Appalachian Mountains of Virginia. Jaye is writing her first book, *Entertaining Angels,* and one of her stories will also appear in *Chicken Soup for the Recovering Soul.* E-mail Jaye at *jayelewis@entertainingangels.org* or visit her Web site at *www.entertainingangels.org.*

Jacklyn Lee Lindstrom, retired, at last has the time to concentrate on oil painting and writing. She just completed a novel about a teenage girl growing up in the 1950s, a time when life seemed so simple (on the surface, anyway.) Jacklyn lives at 314 Windsor Court, Spearfish, South Dakota.

Vicki Marsh Kabat received her bachelor of arts in journalism from the University of Missouri at Columbia. She is editor of *Baylor Magazine* for Baylor University in Waco, Texas. She wrote a newspaper humor column for ten years which was distributed nationally. Her work appeared in *Chicken Soup for the Golden Soul*. She and her husband, Bruce, have three grown sons: Michael, Jeffrey and Brian. Please e-mail her at *Vicki_Marsh-Kabat@baylor.edu.*

Linda Masters is the proud wife, mother of three, and grandmother of four. She and her husband Les, are restoring their 170 year old home located alongside western New York's Eric Canal. Despite her battle with multiple sclerosis, Linda is currently enjoying her career in obstetrics and gynecology, after having been a professional mom and volunteer for ten years. Linda's son, Josh, a Lance Corporal in the Special Securities Division of the Marine Corps was awaiting deployment to Saudi Arabia when he was killed by a drunken driver.

Renee Mayhew teaches prekindergarten in North Carolina where she writes children's books and paints in her spare time. Her husband and children are her greatest inspiration.

Paula McDonald has sold over a million copies of her books on relationships and gone on to win numerous awards worldwide as a columnist, inspirational feature writer and photojournalist. Paula McDonald lives on the beach in Rosarito, Mexico, and writes to the sound of the waves. She can be contacted in the United States by writing to Paula McDonald, PMB 724, 416 W. San Ysidro Blvd., Ste. L, San Ysidro, CA 92173 or by e-mailing *eieiho@msn.com.* Or visit her Web site at *www.paulamcdonald.com.*

Kim McLarin is the author of the critically acclaimed novels *Taming It Down* and *Meeting of the Waters*. She is a former journalist for the *New York Times* and the *Philadelphia Inquirer* and is currently writer-in-residence at Emerson College.

Walker W. Meade began to write stories at the age of fourteen. When he was twenty, *Collier's* magazine published his first short story. He wrote short fiction for the *Saturday Evening Post, Good Housekeeping, Gentleman's Quarterly* and *The Texas Quarterly* among others. He also wrote nonfiction for many magazines. He began his publishing career as articles editor of *Cosmopolitan*, became the managing editor of that magazine and then managing editor of *Reader's Digest* Condensed Book Club. His last position in publishing was as president and editor in chief of Avon Books where he published such writers as Jorge Amado, Bob Woodward, Carl Bernstein, Gabriel Garcia Marquez, Richard Adams, Colleen McCullough, Margaret Atwood and Eric Segal. Upstart Press published his first novel, *Unspeakable Acts* in August 2001. *Adam Rising* is his second novel.

Bonnie Michael lives in Winston-Salem, North Carolina. Her work has won state and national awards and has appeared in twelve anthologies including *When I Am an Old Woman I Shall Wear Purple*. She wrote for public radio and has been published in *Good Housekeeping* and literary magazines.

Jann Mitchell is an American writer living in Stockholm, Sweden. She and her Swedish husband travel widely. She sponsors a preschool and AIDS orphans in East Africa. A frequent *Chicken Soup* contributor, she is the author of "Home Sweeter Home" and "Love Sweeter Love." Contact Jann at *jannmmitchell@aol.com.*

Susan Clarkson Moorhead is a children's librarian and writer in Westchester County, New York. She is currently working on writing a mystery series and a children's book. She loves anything to do with books, words, and writing, and although her family might find it hard to believe—she loves her three kids and husband even more than the printed page! You can e-mail her at *JoyMoor@aol.com.*

J. Eva Nagel, Ph.D., is the proud mother of four, grandmother of two and wife of one in upstate New York. She is a Waldorf teacher and a psychotherapist. She co-founded Side By Side, a Youth Leadership program that uses the arts to teach diversity and leadership. When not growing people she nurtures flowers and vegetables in her ever-expanding garden. She can be reached at *jevan424@aol.com.*

Sally Nalbor earned a B.A. and law degree from Creighton University and an M.F.A. in creative writing from Columbia College, Chicago. Her writing has appeared in a variety of publications, and she received Midwest Writers 2003 Manny Award in nonfiction. She recently completed a collection of short stories, *Missing Children.*

Betsey Neary attended Drezel University and she is a housewife and mother of two wonderful adult children. Betsey enjoys being with her children, traveling with her husband Tom, quilting and reading. She resides in Omaha, Nebraska. Betsey can be reached at *bneary@tconl.com.*

James A. Nelson holds a B.A. in economics from Eastern Washington University. Divorced with several grandchildren and four children, he has self-published a book entitled *The Way IT Was* and *The Way It IS—Fifty Nostalgic Short Stories.* He has been published over sixty times locally, nationally and internationally, including a story in *Chicken Soup for the Expectant Mother's Soul.*

Peggy Newland-Goetz was awarded New Hampshire's Art Council fiction fellowship for 2005. She has published in *Chelsea, Mississippi Review, Northern New England Review,* and *Grit,* and her essays have appeared in Breakaway Books anthology *Bike Love.* Her memoir, *The Adventure of Two Lifetimes* has been optioned for film. She has recently completed her first novel.

Phyllis Nutkis taught preschool and kindergarten for fifteen years. She now works as a grantwriter for a nonprofit social service agency. She published her first book, a children's picture book, in 2004. She and her husband have three children and are also the grandparents of two delightful little boys. You may contact her at *Norman8631@aol.com.*

Erica Orloff is a novelist who lives in Florida and is the author of *Spanish Disco* (declared "hilarious" by *Cosmopolitan* magazine), *The Roofer, Diary of a Blues Goddess,* bestselling *Urban Legend* and others. She lives with her family and their menagerie of pets, and she may be reached at her Web site: *www.ericaorloff.com.*

Jaie Ouens writes plays and short stories and lives in Townsville, Northern Australia. In this tropical city, Jaie also paints pictures and acts in professional theatre. Various of the plays have been created with young people, and Jaie also works frequently on arts and cultural development projects involving women.

Mark Parisi's "Off the Mark" comic panel has been syndicated since 1987 and is distributed by United Media. Mark's humor also graces greeting cards, T-shirts, calendars, magazines, newsletters and books. Lynn is his wife/business partner, and their daughter, Jenny, contributes with inspiration (as do three cats).

Victoria Patterson is the mother of two boys, Cole and Ry Patterson, ages six and four, and lives in South Pasadena, California. She is currently at work on her second novel. She earns money as a waitress at a fine dining establishment. She is known to tip well. She lives in South Pasadena, California, with her family: Chris, Cole and Ry Patterson.

Saritha Prabhu is originally from India and has been living in the United States for twelve years. A freelance writer and newspaper columnist, she also enjoys cooking, reading and traveling. She lives in Tennessee with her husband and two sons. E-mail her at *sprabhu@charter.net.*

Carol McAdoo Rehme, one of *Chicken Soup's* most prolific contributors, recognizes motherhood as her most important calling—it keeps her humble and hopping. She is "Mom" to four plus two sons-in-love. Carol directs a nonprofit, Vintage Voices, Inc., which brings interactive programming to the vulnerable elderly. Contact her at *carol@rehme.com; www.rehme.com.*

Carla Riehl is a national speaker and author. Her motivational seminars have been attended by thousands in churches, universities and Fortune 500 classrooms. Carla won an Emmy for singing TV commercials and has recorded four Christian pop albums. She loves to teach creative writing and enjoys helping people put their experiences down on paper. Her stories have appeared in *Chicken Soup for the Christian Woman's Soul, Recovering Soul, Bride's Soul* and others.

Phyllis Edgerly Ring writes on issues of family, culture, health and spirituality from her New Hampshire home. Her articles and essays have appeared in *Christian Science Monitor, Hope, Mamm* and *Yankee.* A former nurse, she lived and worked in China, where she taught English to kindergartners. More information about her current book projects is available at *www.phyllisring.com.*

Dan Rosandich lives in Michigan and has spent twenty-six years as a full-time cartoonist. He operates his online cartoon catalog, *www.danscartoons.com* and licenses his cartoons for use in presentations, calendars, newsletters, books and Web sites, etc. Dan can be reached any time at *dan@danscartoons.com* or at his Web site to access information.

Reverend Kathi Rose lives in Wisconsin with her husband Steve and daughter Sarah. She speaks at women's retreats/conferences on the biblical perspective of wholeness and healing. She also authored the book, *I Climbed a Mountain: A Mother's Diary of Tragedy, Grief and Triumph.* You can contact Reverend Rose at *skrose@mindspring.com.*

Kristy Ross is a teacher at Grace School in Houston, Texas. Her work has appeared in educational magazines, the *Houston Chronicle,* and other *Chicken Soup for the Soul* books. Her beautiful mother, Hazel Abernathy Hamm, is a continuing inspiration for living life with dignity, integrity and grace.

Joan Sedita has been an educator for twenty-five years. She currently is a reading consultant and teacher trainer. She lives with her husband and two children in Massachusetts. Her e-mail is *joanjoe@comcast.net.*

Vikrum Seth and **Deeptee Seth** became soul mates in 2002 in New Delhi, India. Blessed with their inspirational daughter Chinmya, the real creditor for this short story. Vikrum is successfully managing his hospitality business. Deeptee looks upon grooming Chinmya relatively well, expecting the least from what future has to offer. E-mail at: *vikrumseth@yahoo.com.*

Beth Crum Sherrow graduated from Lafayette High School in Lexington, Kentucky, and attended Midway College. After living in Versailles, Kentucky for eighteen years she relocated this year to Ocala, Florida to work for a major thoroughbred horse farm. Beth has three boys, Seth, twenty-four, Jared, eighteen and Gus who is twelve. Beth loves reading, writing, traveling and spending time with her husband, Mike.

Deborah Shouse is a Kansas City-area speaker, editor and writer who believes in celebrating the extraordinary in everyday life. Her latest book is *Making Your Message Memorable: Communicating Through Stories* (Crisp Publications). Her work has appeared in *Reader's Digest, Newsweek, Family Circle* and *Ms.* Visit Deborah's Web site at *www.thecreativityconnection.com.*

Jen Singer is the author of *14 Hours 'Til Bedtime: A Stay-at-Home Mom's Life in 27 Funny Little Stories,* and the creator of *www.MommaSaid.net,* a Web site for at-home moms.

Alice Steinbach received the Pulitzer Prize for Feature Writing while working at the *Baltimore Sun.* Currently a Woodrow Wilson Visiting Fellow, she has taught journalism at Princeton and Washington & Lee Universities and is the author of two books: *Educationg Alice: Adventures of a Curious Woman* and *Without Reservations.*

Joan Sutula has previously been published in *Chicken Soup for the Cat & Dog Lover's Soul.* She has poetry appearing in numerous anthologies, including ten *Lyrical Iowa Poetry* books. She lives with her husband, a cat and a dog. She loves writing, hiking, and her children and grandchildren. Contact her at *twig-penlady@mchsi.com.*

Georgette Symonds works as a nurse on Long Island. She coauthored *Thoughts On Life from My Desk Chair*. Georgette enjoys traveling and spending time with her family and friends. She is currently editing her novel about an Irish family and plans on having it published next year. Contact her at *georjetsymonds@optonline.net*.

Mother Teresa gave her life in service to the poorest of poor. Inspired by God, she opened hospices, orphanages and homes for lepers, founding the Missionaries of Charity in the process before her death in 1997. She has received universal acclaim, including the Nobel Peace Prize.

Karen Trevor is a freelance writer and lives with her husband and three children in a suburb of Chicago.

Sophia Valles Bligh received her bachelor of arts in journalism from San Diego State University. She is a freelance writer who enjoys writing about health and women's issues. Sophia enjoys yoga, reading, sewing, the beach, and spending time with her family and friends.

Lynda Van Wyk has roots deep in the Northwest soil. Married for twenty-seven years, she and Doug raised their two kids five miles from the land homesteaded by her great grandparents. She writes poetry and family stories and owns Speckled Hen Country Store in Snohomish, Washington.

Karen Waldman, Ph.D., loves working as a psychologist. She also enjoys writing, dancing, music, acting, playing in nature, traveling with her husband Ken, and spending time with their wonderful families, friends, children and grandchildren (Lisa, Tom, Lana, Greta, Alyson, Brian, Eric, Maryann, David and Laura). Her e-mail is: *krobens@aol.com*.

Luan Warner was born in Logansport, Indiana, on July 28, 1950, to Arnold and Virginia Foust, the oldest of their six children. Her mother was a housewife and her father a carpenter, out of work in the winters and trying to catch up financially the remainder of the year. Luanna received an associate's degree in photography and worked for an audio-visual production company. In 1983, her lifelong interest in writing became a career in advertising as a copywriter. She is still an active freelance copywriter and a beginning novelist. Luanna has one daughter, Carey, who has become a wife, mother and remarkable woman. Her daughter, her son-in-law, John, and grandchildren, Coltan (14), Sarah (13) and Alex (4 months) live about an hour away, but she makes it a point to see them often.

Nancy West has received numerous awards as a Colorado author. She graduated from the University of Colorado and pursued a career as editor of *Where to Live*, a magazine devoted to real estate. Her published works include children's books and stories.

Maggie Wolff Peterson became a freelance writer upon the birth of her son eleven years ago. Previously she was a newspaper reporter and worked as a staff writer for an international health organization.